# Applying Elliott Wave Theory Profitably

### John Wiley & Sons

Founded in 1807, John Wiley & Sons is the oldest independent publishing company in the United States. With offices in North America, Europe, Australia, and Asia, Wiley is globally committed to developing and marketing print and electronic products and services for our customers' professional and personal knowledge and understanding.

The Wiley Trading series features books by traders who have survived the market's ever-changing temperament and have prospered—some by reinventing systems, others by getting back to basics. Whether a novice trader, professional, or somewhere in-between, these books will provide the advice and strategies needed to prosper today and well into the future.

For a list of available titles, please visit our Web site at www.WileyFinance.com.

# Applying Elliot Wave Theory Profitably

STEVEN W. POSER

WILEY

John Wiley & Sons, Inc.

Published by John Wiley & Sons, Inc., Hoboken, New Jersey.
Published simultaneously in Canada.

For general information on our other products and services, or technical support, please contact our Customer Care Department within the United States at 800-762-2974, outside the United States at 317-572-3993 or fax 317-572-4002.

Wiley also publishes its books in a variety of electronic formats. Some content that appears in print may not be available in electronic books.

For more information about Wiley products, visit our web site at www.wiley.com.

*Library of Congress Cataloging-in-Publication Data:*

Poser, Steven W.
  Applying Elliott Wave theory profitably / Steven W. Poser.
    p.  cm.
  ISBN 0-471-42007-7  (CLOTH)
  1. Speculation.  2. Stocks.  I. Title.
  HG6041.P677 2003
332.63'2042–dc21

2003002418

Printed in the United States of America.

10  9  8  7  6  5  4  3  2  1

For my best friend and wife Lisa,
and our two gifts from G-d, Alana and Kenny.
Without you, there would be no impulse waves.

# Acknowledgments

I began my life as a technical analyst in the late 1980s. After graduating college as a computer programmer, I found that I liked working with people much more than I enjoyed working with computers. I was rescued from my programming duties by Deutsche Bank's U.S. securities division, and started work there by developing the international fixed-income research database. More importantly, I got to learn all about the bond markets.

The person in charge of fixed-income research at the time, Hung Q. Tran, was an economist by trade. However, unlike most economists, he had a penchant for drawing trend lines on all of his currency and yield charts. After I spent some time acting as a rocket scientist, providing quantitative analysis research, Mr. Tran and I decided that technical analysis was a missing part of Deutsche Bank's research puzzle. I borrowed his copy of John Murphy's *Technical Analysis of the Futures Markets* (New York Institute of Finance, 1986) and was on my way.

After having been a computer programmer for so long, I found that old habits do not die very easily, and had the bank write a check for a copy of Compu-Trac, the old technical study system. I wrote all sorts of trading systems that were quite successful in correctly forecasting the direction of U.S. and foreign bond and currency markets. Unfortunately, when it came time to write about my research, it was more than a little difficult keeping to "The model is long," or "The model is short." Quite accidentally, I came upon Prechter and Frost's early compilation of R.N. Elliott's works, known as *The Major Works of R.N. Elliott.* (New Classics Library, 1980 and 1990). I immediately began seeing three-wave and five-wave patterns everywhere and shifted my technical focus to Elliott by 1990.

I thought that as my Fibonacci 13th year approached of using Elliott Wave Theory as my principal technical forecasting tool, it was time to give something back and write a book that showed how to use Elliott profitably. I've always enjoyed teaching, and this was a way to get the message out quickly and efficiently. I always knew that writing a book was a major undertaking, but I never realized that major should have been written in bold, and in something like a 50-point size (italics would also help). Such a project cannot be completed without having many to thank. I apologize ahead of time for leaving out those that helped, but whom my memory has caused me to miss.

First, I would like to thank Pamela van Giessen, the chief editor for John Wiley and Sons on this project. She encouraged me to write a book on Elliott even though I wanted to author yet another general technical analysis book. Lara Murphy from Wiley also deserves kudos, especially since it mostly fell upon her to ensure that I was getting the work in. The book never would have been completed without the blood, sweat, and tears of Joanna Pomeranz and her miracle graphics team at PV&M Publishing Solutions.

This book also never would have gotten done if it had not been for the Market Technicians Association, the professional society of market technical analysts in the United States. The countless people whom I've met over the years, many of whom encouraged me to take on this project, have been invaluable. *Applying Elliott Wave Theory Profitably* never would have made it to the presses without the likes of Bruce Kamich, Michael N. Kahn, John Bollinger, Jim Stanton, or Fred Hillier. These gentlemen provided me with ideas, data, and even computer programs that aided me in my research. I even got to test some of the charts for this book on Mr. Kamich's technical analysis class at Baruch College of the City University of New York. Richard Swannell of Elliott Wave Research in Australia was kind enough to show me some of his groundbreaking work in computer generated Elliott Wave counts.

Of course, if it wasn't for the many fine books written by Robert Prechter Jr., I probably never would have even heard about Elliott. Although I have a slightly different way of using Elliott's ideas, there is probably not a single technical analyst using the Elliott Wave Theory who doesn't have Mr. Prechter to thank.

I also want to thank Tony Plummer of Rhombus Research Ltd. Not only did he write a wonderful foreword to this book, but his tome *Forecasting Financial Markets* (John Wiley & Sons, 1991), in my opinion, is the best book ever written on technical analysis. Some of the ideas he proposed in that book provided the inspiration for the content of Chapter 4 of this effort.

The most important thanks go to my family. My wife Lisa, who had to watch me sit at the computer all hours of the day and night, while she entertained our very active five-year-old son Kenny, along with his older sister Alana, should be nominated for Wife of the Century, even though the century is just a few years old. Nobody has ever believed in my ability to write this book, or to forecast the markets, more than she has. Thanks also go to Alana and Kenny, who didn't always have use of the computers, or their father, when they really wanted one or the other.

# Contents

# Foreword

Human behaviour is determined essentially by deeply embedded subconscious beliefs about the world. Of course, these beliefs change over time, but mostly the changes are of a gradual nature, requiring very little overt consideration on our part. However, sometimes we are confronted by the realization that something no longer "works"—that our beliefs are, in some fundamental way, no longer appropriate. Then there is a crisis, and a new paradigm—a new way of looking at the world—emerges. Because they are born of a crisis, such shifts are extremely uncomfortable. Nevertheless, they are Nature's way of overcoming our natural resistance to change.

It seems to me that the academic world of economics and finance is on the cusp of such a paradigm shift. Traditional models of economic behaviour, which assume independent behaviour by rational human beings, are no longer applicable to a global economy that is laced with excesses and disequilibria. The models no longer help us either to understand what is going on or to apply countervailing policy measures with any degree of confidence. The unspoken doubt in academia is that the models no longer work.

One of the solutions is very simple—even if there is no clear way of immediately incorporating that solution into existing theoretical frameworks. This is to recognize that all of us have a psychological imperative to do things together—that is, we are all preprogrammed to commit part of our energy to broader social groupings, whether these groupings be sports clubs, religious communities, nation-states, or a particular concept of civilization. Of course, a distinctly individual dimension—an impulse to reach beyond the given—still remains. Nevertheless, our tendency to integrate into groups always will modulate our tendency to be self-assertive; therefore, potentially random individual behaviour partly actualizes as nonrandom group behaviour.

It is the power of the group that ensures that we are all sufficiently suffused with a common mood to participate together in activities such as buying houses, selling stocks, or wearing particular styles of clothing, that enables the great oscillations in economic and financial behaviour, and that creates the recurring patterns within those oscillations. This is why technical analysis (which focuses directly on patterns and energy in markets) can be so effective; it is also why economic analysis can be so impotent. Technical analysis explicitly analyses group behaviour; economic analysis implicitly denies that such behaviour exists in the first place.

Therefore, any system that provides insights into the patterned oscillations of group behaviour is worthy of our interest. This is why the work of Ralph Nelson Elliott deserves both deeper analysis and wider attention. His wave principle is a powerful method of interpreting and forecasting financial markets. Unfortunately, his original insights were couched in sufficiently arcane terms that they were treated either as completely unscientific by sceptics or as inviolable truths by adherents. In fact, both responses are mistaken. Elliott's original research was painstaking and thorough, and there is no known wave pattern that falls outside of his schema. Nevertheless, his theoretical justifications for that schema lacked depth and are open to development.

It is, therefore, a matter of some importance when an analyst who has many years of experience working with Elliott's wave principle offers some of his findings to the wider investment community. Steven Poser's careful presentation of Elliott's wave patterns, and trading guidelines for using them, brings a directly practical dimension to the wave principle. It also helps to make Elliott's work more accessible to those who want a coherent intellectual framework within which to conduct their trading and investment. Crucially, however, it also arrives at a time when our need to understand market behaviour has probably never been more pressing.

TONY PLUMMER
Director, Rhombus Research Ltd.
London, England

Author of *Forecasting Financial Markets*

# Introduction

The alarm went off at 3:00 A.M. on a wintry New York morning. It was bad enough getting into Manhattan from the New York City suburbs by 6:00 A.M. to prepare for the daily onslaught of questions from the firm's traders, salespeople, and clients. I woke up early for a preliminary telephone interview with a large investment bank in London. The job sounded great and I figured I should be wide awake (as much as one can be at that time of the night), so I made sure to set the alarm for an hour before the interview to give me time to prepare. Preparation included reviewing the charts of the U.S. bond market and several currency markets and, more importantly, drinking copious amounts of coffee. The executive search firm was very excited because they felt I was easily the most qualified person available for the position, and I was ready for a move at the time.

The interview seemed to go very well. I hit it off with the interviewer, who would have been my boss if I got the job. I went off to work that morning thinking about the long weekend I would take in London visiting some friends I had there when I went for my next interview (happily imagining them putting me on the Concorde to get me there as quickly as possible). Then, I got the phone call from the search firm: The bank was not interested. They were very impressed with all of my writing samples, as well as my record in forecasting the financial markets. However, they had no interest in hiring somebody that specialized in the Elliott Wave Principle.

Technical analysts are used to rejection from their brethren in the investment community. The uninformed masses that live and die by the largely discredited random walk theory remain in charge of most research departments on Wall Street and in the City of London, where much of the world's money transacts. Those of us who look at charts and indicators for a living are used to suffering slings and arrows from economists and fundamental research analysts. They ask, "How can you ignore the earnings potential or management of a company in pronouncing it a buy or a sell?" Our answer, as technicians, is that price patterns tell us if we should believe in management and earnings. All the while, the fundamental analysts ignore the fact that nearly every trader and money manager uses some amount of technical analysis in his or her trading and investment decisions.

My interview rejection did not come from a Wall Street economist or academician comparing technical analysis to "reading chicken entrails." The negative response came from another technical analyst. This person did not understand the Elliott Wave Principle or felt it too complex for the bank's customers. It was at that time that I realized that the available books on using Elliott were not doing their job. There was a lack of accessible and practical information on how to apply Elliott to the real world. Most books went to one extreme or the other: They either made Elliott more complicated than it needed to be, or in an effort to overcome the perceived complexity of analysis using Elliott, the books oversimplified the process.

Learning how to profitably apply the Elliot Wave Principle to your trading and investing decisions need not be a daunting task. Although spending years of your life learning the Holy Grail of the markets might be a worthy endeavor, few people have the necessary cash flow to accomplish the task. Furthermore, if there is a Holy Grail out there, the Elliott Wave Principle is not it. However, a little knowledge can go a long way. My aim in this book is to show you how to apply Elliott to improve your investing and trading decisions. It took me many years, as a professional Elliottician (one who spends way too much time in front of stock ticker screens) to feel knowledgeable enough in the field to attempt this book. The lack of a great source in the subject spurred me on to write this book so maybe the next time, the interviewer will be the Elliott Wave analyst or trader.

## WHAT'S DIFFERENT ABOUT THIS BOOK

There are several books on the market that explain Elliott Wave Theory. The true story, direct from the author's life, is why I am writing this book. The tomes currently available on the market do a fine job of explaining what the Elliott Wave Theory is. You can even purchase most of R.N. Elliott's original writings. Unfortunately, none of the books explain *how to profitably apply Elliott Wave Theory in a clear and concise manner*. Most of the negative arguments I have heard over the years regarding Elliott come from the subjective nature of counting waves. There is no doubt that different human beings will perceive the patterns created by investors and traders in different ways. With proper study, and a good trading plan, you will know very quickly how correct your wave count is, and be able to adjust your position to maximize your trading rewards.

This book shows the reader, in a step-by-step fashion, how to analyze a market in terms of market psychology. The Elliott Wave Theory is founded firmly in market behavior and psychology. Each wave cycle can be related directly to a market mood; each move has a characteristic look and feel to it. If the market does not act as your assumed wave pattern says it should, you either have the wrong wave count, or you are looking at the wrong time frame.

One of the keys to trading is discipline. Whether you are using Elliott, candlesticks, Gann, or trading systems, you must employ your rules consistently. You cannot cherrypick when to listen to your system and when not to. You do not know when your system is going to be right and when it is going to be wrong. Your system is written to make money over a period of time with a certain probability of success. Until somebody discovers the Holy Grail, and is then kind enough to share it with you, there will be no system that can predict the markets with 100 percent accuracy. If you develop a system or methodology that is correct 60 percent of the time and has a profit-to-loss ratio of 1.5:1 or 2.0:1, you will make money in the long run. However, if you try to choose which trades are going to make money ahead of time, you will be defeating the purpose of your system.

A quick story might give you a good example of why picking and choosing your trades ahead of time will not work for you. I worked for many years as the chief technical analyst, supporting the sales and trading effort for Deutsche Bank's U.S. government bond operation in New York. Among my many duties, besides talking to the bank's clients, was to write a daily report which forecast short-term direction in several fixed-income and currency markets. I made daily trade recommendations: long bonds, short two-year notes, long Eurodollar futures, short the U.S. dollar versus the yen, for example. I tracked my trading recommendations, and started my profit-and-loss statement over every January. One year, I got out of the starting gate with a great big thud, managing to be incorrect on my first nine ideas. Needless to say, my colleagues were afraid to sit near me for fear of catching my bad luck streak.

As soon as my title of trading floor pariah was officially bestowed upon me, I embarked on one of the most amazing streaks of my life, providing the firm and its clients with 80 percent accuracy for the next two months. Unfortunately, after my less than auspicious start to the year, nobody even read what I had to say for almost a month, and by the time everybody was clamoring around my desk for my recommendations, I was ripe for another losing streak.

In *Applying Elliott Wave Theory Profitably*, I take you through all the steps of how to make money using Elliott, review how and why technical analysis works, and show you where Elliott fits into that picture. The book reviews each of the basic and advanced patterns that the market might trace out and discusses what kinds of market conditions typically produce these patterns. From there, the book shows how you can use this knowledge to build a trading plan and then how to continuously update the plan in real time as the market provides you with further information in the way of a constant stream of prices, volume, and even news.

This book takes you step-by-step through the process of understanding how and why the Elliott Wave Theory works and shows you how to combine it with other technical analysis concepts, as well as how to read the markets' reactions to news items to improve your trading accuracy. Reviewing the market from multiple time frames is discussed, so you know what degree of price retracements to expect, as well as what your risks and rewards may be. I also attempt to show you when and where you are most likely to be able to profitably apply Elliott Wave Theory to improve your trading. Although the theory works at all times, you may find certain trading behaviors that do not lend themselves well to your style, or to how you read the waves. You do not need to be in the market all the time, and this book helps you to recognize when you should be in and when you should be out.

*Applying Elliott Wave Theory Profitably* is organized into four sections:

1. The first three chapters cover how to read the waves. I have attempted to focus on real-world examples and to always discuss how one might look at each pattern from a trading or investing perspective. My aim in these chapters is to provide you with a series of practical lessons on how to use Elliott Wave Theory in your trading.

2. Chapter 4 covers some theoretical special issues regarding using Elliott Wave in markets other than equities. It discusses my view that although Elliott was correct in his characterization of five-wave and three-wave patterns in stocks, this is not necessarily correct in other markets, and for that matter, may not hold even in the stock market across all time periods. I have found that when the underlying fundamentals shift, five-wave patterns develop in the direction of the new fundamentals. For example, since disinflation, deflation, and budget cuts became fashionable, yields have fallen in five-wave patterns. If inflation returns, that should shift. However, due to the change in underlying fundamentals, there ought not be a requirement that the five-wave and three-wave patterns link, although intrawave relationships should hold, and retracement levels will also likely continue to attract attention.

3. The next three chapters guide you through the steps of analyzing the markets and actually defining a trading or investing strategy.

   Chapter 5 details the steps in creating an Elliott Wave–based trading plan. It discusses how to analyze the market and reviews setups, combining news and sentiment, as well as other technical indicators, into your action plan.

Chapter 6 is actually a set of sample trading plans. Time frames from short-term day trading to investing and asset allocation are covered. I discuss differences in attitudes and strategies depending on whether you are concentrating on trading or investing, and are leveraged or unleveraged. The differences in stops and projections are reviewed, depending on whether you are in options, cash products, mutual funds, or futures. Each product might have different expectations, risks, and rewards. Although Elliott can be used for each product, your strategies may need to be a bit different. Also discussed is how different patterns may develop in different markets—the difference between trading secular trending markets versus cycle-based assets that likely trade in wide ranges over generations (e.g., stocks versus bonds or currencies).

By the time you reach Chapter 7, you will know how to apply the Elliott Wave Theory profitably. However, as Tony Plummer noted in the foreword, trading and investing are wholly human endeavors and the markets trade accordingly. This chapter ties together the underlying principles that allow technical analysis in general, and the Elliott Wave Theory* specifically, to work.

4. Chapter 8 provides a road map for the next several years, with a forecast for U.S. and Japanese stock and the U.S. dollar.

Unlike many technical analysis–oriented books, I have no desire to tell you that fundamental analysis does not work. I have the fullest faith that it does. In my opinion, the market psychology that ultimately draws the charts that you analyze is formed in the minds of traders and investors based, at least partially, on the underlying economy, as well as, in the case of stocks, the quality of the corporation, its management, and its business plan. I leave the technical-versus-fundamental battle to the academics and those who wish to spend their time duking it out with their colleagues. This book shows you how to make money by keeping an open mind to all flavors of financial research while focusing most heavily on what I believe to be one of the most powerful tools available to anybody who wishes to work hard to make their money in the markets.

---

*R.N. Elliott named his methodology the Elliott Wave Principle. A principle means that the ideas are proven—a basic truth. Many authors have continued to apply this nomenclature. Others have chosen to use theory instead of principle, most likely because Elliott Wave has not been rigorously scientifically tested. The terms can be used interchangeably. For consistency's sake, this book uses "Elliott Wave Theory."

# CHAPTER 1

# Surfing Basics

In his 1938 monograph, "The Wave Principle," R.N. Elliott wrote: "Very extensive research in connection with practically all human activities indicates that social-economic processes follow a law that causes them to repeat themselves in similar and constantly recurring serials of waves or impulses of definite number and pattern. It is likewise indicated that in their intensity, these waves or impulses bear a consistent relation to one another and to the passage of time."[1] Although this sounds rather lofty, it is little different in meaning from the definition of technical analysis as maintained by the Market Technicians Association[2] in their constitution: ". . . the study of data generated by the action of markets and by the behavior and psychology of market participants and observers. Such study is usually applied to estimating probabilities for the future course of prices for a market, investment or speculation by interpreting the data in the context of precedent."

Elliott is somewhat more specific than the Market Technicians Association is. Both refer to the underlying concept that crowd theory, or human interaction, is a key explanatory factor in how prices are determined in a free market. Elliott opined that the price patterns develop in a specific set of waves that, through study, can be learned and used to forecast future price direction. The Elliott Wave Theory (EWT) is just one of many tools that a technical analyst or technically based trader or investor can employ in pursuing his or her craft.

## THE BASIC PATTERN

Each cycle in the direction of the current trend develops in five waves. Counter trend moves usually trace out a three-wave pattern. Every wave has a set of typical characteristics. Third waves are typically the most powerful move in a five-wave cycle. Identifying a third wave should be fairly easy. Classical technical momentum and volume indicators are one aid. More importantly, at least in the case of a third wave of large enough degree, market sentiment should strongly confirm the price action. Many analysts, investors, and traders incorrectly assume that the public can never be right on the market. This is patently incorrect—the period of time where prices move most forcefully in the direction of the trend is exactly when the public becomes aware of a shift and climbs on board.

Degree, in EWT parlance, refers to time and price. Any given impulse move, and its correction, represents a move of the same degree. Subwaves of a five-wave cycle are of a lesser degree. For example, as is discussed when reviewing the fractal nature of market price activity, each move with the trend in a five-wave rally is divisible into five smaller waves. These five smaller waves are of one lesser degree than the larger uptrend.

## INVESTOR PSYCHOLOGY AND SENTIMENT

The Elliott Wave analyst might not even need to look at price indicators, price charts, or volume statistics. He or she should be able to pick up the business pages and find the news talking about a powerful third-wave move. Even the fundamental news, as highlighted in Figure 1.1, which might trail the price action, will confirm price at this juncture. The market

**FIGURE 1.1**   Cisco Systems, weekly

sentiment characteristics on their own may be enough to identify the third wave. Wave-specific characteristics are covered in greater detail later.

The key to understanding EWT, and profitably implementing it into your trading or investing, is to understand how and why the waves develop and then to learn to recognize the characteristics in real time as they develop. For long-term investors, this will come from weekly and monthly charts, longer-term fundamental research and the reaction to these reports, and the general press. The single most important task you will have is to determine whether the developing price pattern matches the outside information. If they are not in sync, you might need to go back to the drawing board.

Day traders can also use EWT in their activity. However, as is always the case in day trading, you must be much faster in your decision making. Furthermore, you still need to keep aware of the longer-term patterns, because trading against a major daily trend, even if there is clearly need for a correction, requires much tighter scrutiny. There also is a good deal less ancillary information available for the day trader. A countertrend correction within a powerful third wave could wipe out a highly leveraged day trader on the wrong side of the move. Day trading and leverage require you to follow the chart patterns much more closely, and always be prepared to quickly exit a trade that does not develop according to your wave forecast.

## PSYCHOLOGICAL BASIS FOR TECHNICAL ANALYSIS AND THE ELLIOTT WAVE THEORY

Any form of technical analysis is best applied via an understanding of crowd behavior. In EWT, each wave, especially those of larger degree, is easily labeled by an overall depiction of investor sentiment: Hope, greed, and despair can all be seen in the wave counts.

This is not groundbreaking news. The Dow Theory also enumerates investor sentiment ideals in its explanation of market cycles. R.N. Elliott developed his theories when Dow Theory was already in practice, and many authors have compared EWT with Dow. Although there is little comparison vis-à-vis actual application and forecasting, both methodologies directly trace their roots to investor psychology.

Current research into market gyrations has begun to shift away from the myriad of confusing indicators and equations used by today's modern technicians. Paradoxically, analysts are moving back to the roots of technical analysis: crowd behavior. The "new new thing" in market research is Behavioral Finance. Academicians study group investing behaviors with psychological tools. Essentially, technical analysis then becomes the application of the theory. The Market Technicians Association, the U.S. organization of professional market technicians, of which the author is a member, is involved actively with many universities in promoting research and education in both technical analysis and Behavioral Finance.

A brief warning is warranted here. Individual equities do not always lend themselves well to EWT. A free, open, and liquid market is required for EWT to work well. Certainly, the most liquid stocks should be tradable with these methods. Compare the wave patterns in Figure 1.2 between 1-800-Attorney, a company with a market capitalization of barely over $1 million, and that of Circuit City Stores, the giant electronics retailer. Shares of companies that "trade by appointment" should be avoided. It is highly questionable whether or not technical analysis can be properly applied to less liquid issues. There must be a "crowd" for technical analysis to work properly, and if there is not a crowd, then the analysis might not be accurate. Before blindly using Elliott, or any other form of technical or fundamental research, investors or traders should do their homework first and make sure that the tools they wish to employ have relevance to the security they are investigating.

## THE RIGHT CHARTS

Technical analysts employ four basic types of charts: bar charts, Japanese candlestick charts, point-and-figure charts, and line charts.[3] The only chart that is 100 percent accurate for the purposes of EWT would be a line chart that shows every single tick. Even in this day and age of powerful and inexpensive computers and technical analysis charting packages, using a line chart is impractical. Counting waves based on every tick will lead to you focus on minute waves that are virtually untradable. The cost of execution (commissions, slippage, human error, etc.) will easily consume any possible profits. Furthermore, the mere act of a stock trading at the bid and then the ask price would give the appearance of a series of wavelets that cannot truly be counted.

You are also subject to a great amount of noise, or what I call, "the bathroom trade," when trading based on each and every tick. Consider the day trader in a highly leveraged futures position. Many day traders take on extreme risks. Futures brokers often permit day traders to take positions well beyond exchange-regulated margin limits intraday, since these limits are not applied until the close of trading. The highly leveraged positions can easily go awry at the drop of a hat. Leaving your terminal for even a few moments can be costly. It is better to close the position than to return from a "rest" with a huge losing position simply because you were not around to take what the market had briefly offered you while you were away!

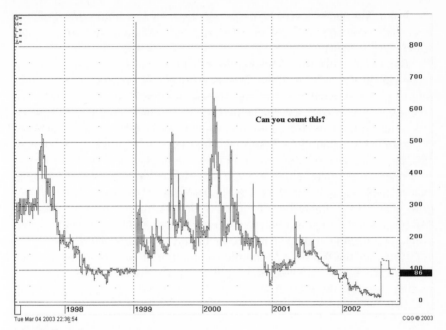

**FIGURE 1.2***a*   1-800-Attorney, weekly

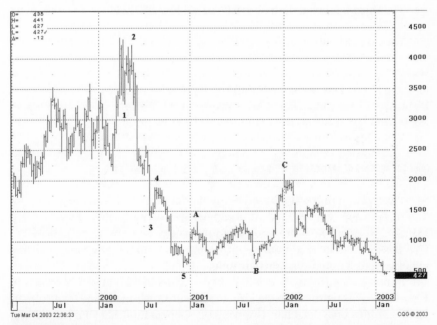

**FIGURE 1.2***b*   Circuit City stores, weekly; note how much clearer the count is for the more liquid Circuit City.

Point-and-figure charts, by definition, ignore price action that does not exceed their box size. This eliminates using point-and-figure charts for your Elliott Wave analysis.

Bar charts, and their cousins, Japanese candlesticks, provide much more information. Although they are not perfect, they do provide a high, low, and close price (candlestick charts always show the open price, and most modern bar charts do as well). Unfortunately, for the Elliottician, it may be important to know which came first: the high price or the low price. Without tick data, you can never be sure. You may be able to get some fairly recent tick data from the exchanges, or from some vendors, which would allow you to properly label your charts. Without that, the best you can do is to assume that if the close is above the open, the low came first. You can then label your charts accordingly. Of course, as trading unfolds in front of you, you can always note on your charts which came first, the high or the low, but when looking at historical charts, you can only estimate what occurred.

Consider the following example to understand why a bar chart does not provide enough information to allow you to properly label your wave counts. Assume the market has completed a down leg and is now rising and that:

- The first bar has a low of $10.00 and a high of $12.00.
- The second bar has a high of $13.00 and a low of $8.00.
- The third bar has a high of $15.00 and a low of $12.50.

You do not know where wave 1 ended. Was it at $12.00 or $13.00? Which came first: $8.00 or $13.00? If $13.00 came first, wave 1 ends at $13.00 and wave 2 ends at $8.00. Now consider wave 3. Did it end at $13.00, or did it end at $15.00? Did wave 4 overlap the high of wave 1 or has wave 4 even begun yet? Using bar charts, we have no way of knowing unless we also know which came first, the high price or the low price.

## THE BASIC FORMATIONS—IMPULSE WAVES

The EWT posits that all market action can be broken down into five-wave and three-wave structures. Five-wave structures (excluding corrective triangles) are called *impulse waves* and three-wave cycles are called *corrective waves*.[4] There is a great deal of confusion among novices regarding exactly what a five-wave move means.

Impulse moves are always five waves. The classic pattern is shown in Figure 1.3. This pattern can develop in virtually any time frame, from a matter of minutes on a tick chart to several years on a monthly chart. In theory, an impulse wave should be easily identifiable. Volume should be higher during the three waves with the trend, and lower during the two counter

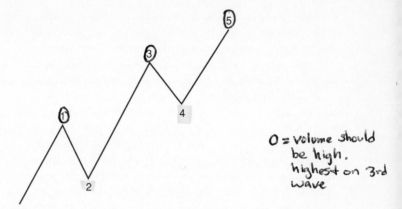

O = volume should
be high.
highest on 3rd
wave

**FIGURE 1.3** Classic five-wave pattern

trend moves, with the highest volume typically occurring during wave 3. However, remember this is a generality and may not hold for some very short-term intraday patterns. For example, as shown in Figure 1.4, volume in the fifth wave up for Intel was stronger than during wave 3. Wave 5 took place at the opening bell, and turnover is typically highest during the first half-hour and last half-hour of trading. Other factors that may wreak havoc with volume comparisons include pre-holiday shortened trading days,

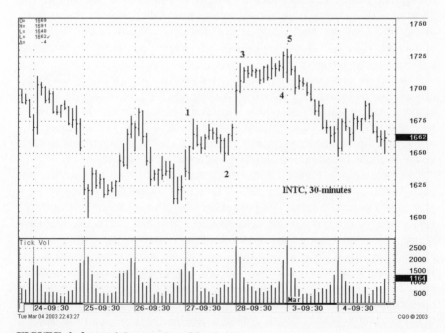

**FIGURE 1.4** Intel Corporation, 30 minute

circuit breakers, and seasonal patterns. For example, trading volume typically dries up in August and December. Any attempt to compare turnover between December and October would therefore be highly suspect. The analyst must be cognizant of such exogenous factors before jumping to a conclusion based just on a wave-to-wave volume comparison.

As mentioned above, all impulse waves are five-wave affairs. Wave 3 in any impulse move can never be the shortest wave, and is usually the largest leg of a five-wave cycle. In addition, with one special exception, wave 1 and wave 4 should never overlap. This means in an advance, the low price achieved in wave 4 cannot move below the top of wave 1. In a five-wave fall, the high price of a corrective wave 4 must not be greater than the low price seen in wave 1. Some analysts will accept a very small overlap between wave 1 and wave 4 in the case of derivative securities, such as futures and options on cash assets and liabilities. Others suggest that an overlap is okay in very short time frames. In general, allowing overlaps is a dangerous precedent. I cannot remember a single time when I gave in to permitting an overlap, and was not sorry later on that I made that decision. I would not suggest attempting to apply wave counts on tick charts, however, because the mere movement around the bid-ask spread leads to overlaps on a regular basis.

Within a five-wave impulse cycle, subwave 1, subwave 3, and subwave 5 are also impulse waves, whereas subwave 2 and subwave 4 are corrective waves. A subwave is a wave of lesser degree in time and price. All waves, except the tiniest actions (such as would be found on a one-minute bar chart or a tick chart), break down into even smaller waves. This is commonly referred to as the *fractal*[5] nature of stock price movement. Some scientists have found evidence of fractals in market prices as well, relating the patterns to chaos theory.

One of the most common errors I have seen made in applying EWT is to assume that five-wave cycles are bull markets and three-wave actions are bear markets. As you will soon see, three-wave and five-wave moves can occur both with and against the major trend in both bull markets and bear markets. The key is that three-wave cycles correct five-wave cycles. If the current trend is down, action in the direction of the trend develops in five waves.

For example, in Figure 1.5, the dollar sank in five waves versus the yen from August 1998 until January 1999. A second five-wave drop traversed from May until December 1999. The period between those two five-wave drops had a pair of three-wave corrective rallies. In other words, all five-wave impulse cycles develop in the direction of the current trend. Two five-wave cycles joined by a three-wave move may correct a five-wave action of the same or one larger degree. Proper labeling requires a thorough understanding of how and why waves develop. Just because you see a five-wave structure does not mean that the recently completed trend has ended. It just implies that a correction of the current or next larger degree trend is now active.

**FIGURE 1.5**   U.S. Dollar versus Japanese Yen, weekly

Note the use of the term *correction* here in reference to a gain in the dollar. This is because the dollar's gains, at the time, were against the larger trend to a weaker American currency. I discuss some of the issues involved with nomenclature, especially with reference to the foreign exchange and fixed-income market, when we develop our trade plans in Chapters 5 and 6.

## THE BASIC FORMATIONS—CORRECTION WAVES

Understanding that corrections, in Elliott Wave parlance, are movements against the larger trend is very important. Many analysts unfamiliar with EWT use the equity market–based idea of corrections as being represented by falling prices, which leads to a great deal of confusion in counting waves. Corrections are merely activity against a larger trend, and are always either comprised of three waves, triangles, or combinations of the two, as covered below. A correction is merely a wave cycle against a larger impulse wave. For example, using the classic equity market basis, during a bear market the corrective waves are toward higher prices.

The fractal nature of market price movements can make the task of identifying and trading countertrend moves extremely challenging. If the primary trend is up, the countertrend move would be lower. That trading action should develop in three waves. However, unless the correction occurs as a triangle, at least one of the subwaves will develop as a five-wave (impulse) move. This is probably the single most daunting part of applying EWT in real time: understanding how to properly count and recognize trading action of varying degrees, and making your entry, exit, and stop decisions accordingly.

All three-wave corrections are labeled with an A wave, B wave and C wave. Wave A is the first leg and corrects the current larger trend. Wave B moves with the larger trend, essentially correcting the correction. Wave C is always five waves and again moves in the direction of the correction and against the larger trend. Note that the exact labeling (uppercase or lowercase, underlined, circled, etc., depends on the degree of the pattern and is covered later in this chapter). There are three basic types of corrective moves (see Figure 1.6):

1. *Zigzag:* This is the most easily recognized correction and the most severe. Zigzags are always three-wave countertrend moves formed by two five-wave impulse moves against the larger trend (wave A and wave C), separated by a three-wave move that moves in the direction of the larger trend (and against the correction's price action). The intermediate move is labeled as wave B. Zigzags are also often referred to as *5–3–5 corrections.* The name comes from the number of subwaves in each leg of a zigzag correction.

2. *Flat and irregular:* In these reactions, wave A develops in three waves, with wave B retracing nearly all of wave A (flat), or in the case of an irregular correction, moving past the starting point of the correction. This is one of the hardest parts of counting waves, since such a move gives the initial appearance of a breakout. Wave B should also be three waves. Wave C always develops in five waves and usually ends at a price near where wave A terminated. Flats and irregulars are sometimes referred to as *3–3–5 corrections.*

3. *Triangles:* This type of correction develops in five waves with each leg subdividing into three waves. These patterns relate directly to the classical technical analysis triangle patterns. However, EWT provides for much more robust breakout targets. Also, by applying your knowledge of EWT, you should be able to more accurately forecast the direction prices should move on breaking out of the triangle. There should no longer be any doubt as to the direction in which a symmetric triangle should resolve. I have even found that EWT has correctly forecast failures in what appeared to be developing ascending and descending triangles. That is, an ascending triangle is not always bullish and a descending triangle is not always bearish.

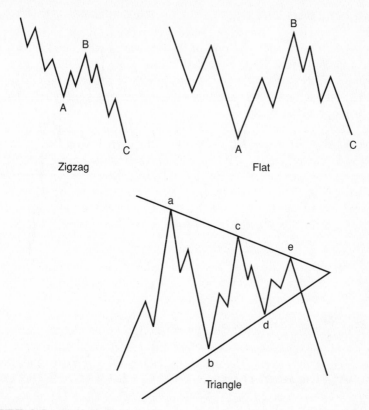

**FIGURE 1.6** Corrections

In the examples shown in Fig. 1.6, the zigzag and the flat/irregular moves are corrections of uptrends, whereas the triangle is a correction of a downtrend.

One insight into trading corrections may be useful here. I have found over the years that exactly counting the waves of a correction can be very difficult. At times, corrective waves can be nearly unfathomable, especially in shorter time frames, such as intraday out to several weeks (see Figure 1.7). That does not mean the Elliott Wave–based trader cannot act during such times. However, slightly wider stops and longer time frames are advisable. If you normally trade on 15-minute charts, consider decreasing your trade size, widening your stops, and using 30- or 60-minute charts instead. The best advice, however, is to wait for an impulse move in the direction of the main trend to develop. Using that strategy should raise your percentage of profitable trades and decrease the probability of getting caught in whipsaws.

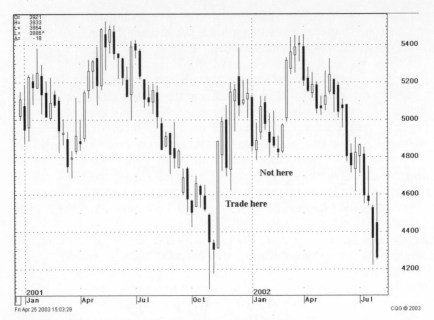

**FIGURE 1.7**   U.S. 10-Year Treasury note yield, weekly

## THE BASIC FORMATIONS—WAVE CHARACTERISTICS

In the Investor Psychology and Sentiment section of this chapter, I discussed much of the theoretical underpinning of the Elliott Wave Theory. By combining investor psychology with Elliott Wave and classical technical analysis, you will learn to trade profitably.

If there is one piece of advice that I can give you, it is that impulse waves should be easily recognizable. If you have to stand on your head, borrow your third grader's prism, and use a Dick Tracy Decoder Ring to find a five-wave count, then there is a pretty good chance that you are not in an impulse wave. Over the years, I found that the simple maxim, "If you can't count it, it is a correction," works quite well.

Telling you that you should be able to recognize a five-wave move probably is not particularly helpful on its own. Some key points are:

1. Activity usually increases during impulse moves. The one exception might be following a capitulation at the end of a major bear market or after a blowoff top signaling the end of a bull market.

2. Corrections against the new trend should see lower volume than the turnover witnessed during the impulsive legs.

3. Most non-Elliott-Wave-based analysts—even technical analysts—will probably think the preceding trend is still in place during the first leg of a reversal five-wave impulse move.

In the case of the end of a major bear market, even following a clear "V" bottom, most analysts will be bearish and the press will almost certainly specialize in end-of-the-world scenarios. At the market bottom following the Long Term Capital Management debacle in October 1998, virtually all technical and fundamental market strategists were bearish until the Fed (Federal Reserve Bank) came in and surprised with a rate cut. This was despite a nearly textbook "V" bottom. One of the keys to technical analysis in general, and EWT in particular, is to permit the trader to avoid the pitfalls of emotions and blindly following the crowd. Unfortunately, these are also the most difficult times to fade the market.

Investors do not like going it alone. They find comfort in numbers, and prefer to jump on the bandwagon as the financial media spout the virtues of the stock they own, or are considering purchasing. Unfortunately, by the time everybody knows about it, the smart money is probably already in the market, and while you still might make a profit by following the crowd, perfect timing will become more essential than if you were an early adopter. In a study produced by financial services consultancy firm Dalbar, Inc.,[6] the company found that despite the S&P 500 averaging returns of 16.3 percent per annum during the 1984–2000 period, the typical mutual fund investor only managed to take home a bit more than one-third of that total. This is because investors tend to wait until most of the trend is over to jump, and then wait too long to sell. Understanding the sentiment, Elliott, and other technical signposts will allow you to take a much larger fraction of most trends.

## THE CONTRARY OPINION TRAP

Traders and technical analysts often are better at going against the flow. I remember speaking to an owner of a day-trading shop in the late 1990s. He told me his traders made the most money on down days. This was during the height of the Internet frenzy, when the market was racking up impressive gains on a nearly daily basis. The traders could not stand to hold positions that needed public acceptance to be profitable. They also wanted to get the best price, and tend to look for minor reversals that allow them to set very tight stops. I would not be surprised to hear that since late 2000 or so this same group of traders, if any were left standing and profitable, found themselves trading from the long side more often than not, as the massive bear market unfolded.

Unfortunately, trading against the whole world often can lead to gargantuan losses. Although the Internet sector was a house of cards, shorting net stocks in 1999 and early 2000 was as sure a road to ruin as ever existed. During a mania, as the stock market and especially the technology and Internet sectors were in at that time, there is absolutely no reason to fight the trend, no matter how ridiculous you find the action. Just make sure you are capable of taking profits when the signals tell you it is time to get out! Contrary opinion is almost never enough of a reason to establish a position against the trend.

## SENTIMENT AND TECHNICAL CHARACTERISTICS OF WAVES

In the paragraphs that follow, I will outline the technical and sentiment evidence you will often see during various waves. This most closely applies to longer-term time frames (articles about the end of investing are not published during 1 percent corrections of bull markets). However, many of the short-term sentiment indices and technical indicators will be valid across multiple time frames and Elliott Wave degrees. For the purposes of this discussion, I will use the normal stock market–based nomenclature: a bear market is a major trend to lower prices and is a correction of a bull market.

### Wave 1

First waves rarely are recognized at their inception. When a first wave starts, the news is just about universally bad. The previous trend is seen as still being strongly in force. Analysts are revising their estimates for the markets lower, and it is not proper in polite company to discuss such investments. Those who were short may stand aside at social events, with knowing smiles, as they are now accumulating long positions following the end of the just completed final leg of the bear market. Sentiment polls are typically at historically bearish extremes. Technically, there is much greater interest in put options than there is in call options, and implied volatility is also typically quite high as investors and traders desperately seek insurance for their investments. Volume might pick up a bit as prices rise, but not by enough to alert very many analysts. The investment community warns that this is merely a "bear market correction," and that the downtrend will resume shortly.

As an Elliott Wave expert, you will recognize that the bear trend has been completed. You will also note the five-wave advance, easily recognizable even at this early stage. Volume should pick up, unless the bear trend ended with a capitulation move, and preferably is not very high. If it is, then the rally is more likely part of a bear market correction, with rampant short covering going on. A slow and steady price increase fits more closely to the start of a new bull market.

If you are tracking futures markets, it is not uncommon to see open interest slip initially following the market's turn even though the contract is now moving counter to the old trend. By the time the latter stages of wave 1 take hold, open interest should confirm the new bull trend. Volatility usually eases in the options markets as prices reverse higher (this may not be the case in the foreign exchange markets, where it is a bull market for one currency and a bear market for the other).

## Wave 2

This leg will lead all the brilliant analysts to boldly announce that they "told you so." Victory is at hand for the bears as the trend lower resumes. Unfortunately, defeat shall be snatched from the jaws of victory as prices never take out the previous lows. The drop should be in three waves (remember that if we get an a–b–c zigzag down, wave a would still develop in five waves, but the retrace amount of wave 1 should be rather small by the time wave a completes). Volume should be lower than it was during wave 1. Prices typically retrace 38 percent to 62 percent of the losses, and will often convince the crowds that the previous down trend is alive and well. If we are fighting off a major, entrenched bear market, or alternatively, are working on a very short time frame, the retrace can easily exceed 62 percent. Wave 2 can never retrace more than 100 percent of wave 1. There are no exceptions to this rule; in general, if prices retrace more than 62 percent, there is high risk that your count is incorrect and that the bear market is actually still active.

## Wave 3

The third wave is the wave that Elliotticians dream about. Prices rise rapidly and anybody waiting for a pullback to enter will be sorry, because pullbacks will be short-lived and shallow. Volume is usually extremely high. Wave 3 is where much of the public will realize that the bear is over. It is at this juncture that the Elliott Wave analyst must be careful and remember that it is okay to be on the same side as the crowd some of the time. Wave 3 is usually at least 1.618 times as large as wave 1 in price terms, although since it is very powerful, it will probably take less than 1.618 times as long to complete. As is always the case, wave 3 should develop in five clear impulsive waves, three up and two down. Momentum almost always confirms the price highs.

## Wave 4

All the books say that wave 4 retraces 38 percent of wave 3, and sometimes it does. However, very often it does not. Fourth waves are almost always clearly corrective. Price losses are shallow and volume is much lower than in wave 3. Volatility probably will not pick up very much during a fourth wave, even though prices are dropping.[7] Wave 4 can take a long time to develop, but should not take longer than previous impulse waves. However, if that is the only inconsistency in a fourth wave count, I should forewarn you that I have seen fourth waves take as long to complete as the first three waves to date took to complete in total. Possibly the single most distinguishing feature of fourth-wave corrections is that they are difficult to count. It is the first time that some analysts may start warning that prices have gone too far, and the most antsy investors and traders may take profits on their longs here. Unfortunately, they will later tend to rush back in once wave 5 exceeds the fourth-wave high, leaving them little room for error on their late longs.

## Wave 5

The fifth and final wave in an impulse move often ends with momentum divergences, just as one would expect from classical technical analysis. Volume is usually lower in this leg than it was in wave 3, although it might be as high, or higher, than it was in wave 4. Remember, wave 5 is still an impulse wave and should traverse through a full five-leg advance. It is in wave 5 that everybody is bullish, all the data suggest that the good times can never end, and bears are scorned and ridiculed. Think back to late 1999 and early 2000 when the naysayers warned of impending doom in the Nasdaq. Note that at the end of some major five-leg advances, such as we had at the end of the Nasdaq mania/bubble, final tops might end with high volume as a blowoff. The initial reversal will be heralded as a "once in a lifetime buying opportunity." Imagine buying that Internet stock at $50 per share when it was $128 just three months ago. Roll forward to 2002, and find it trading at $1.19 and you will realize how wrong such thinking can be!

## Wave A

Corrections are almost always more difficult to count than impulse waves. One of the biggest problems is that they are three-wave moves. Many technicians and strategists look for breakouts from interim corrections. In a three-wave cycle, that breakout often is false and ends up being the tail end of the recovery. The exception to this, of course, is when A–B–C is of a much larger degree, as in a bear market. For example, the decline since 2000 in the global equity markets might actually be part of an enormous fourth wave. Certainly, this bear does not fit into the characteristics of a fourth wave that were described earlier. The degree of this fourth wave involves the correction of a decades-long bull run. One must always remain cognizant of the price move implied by the position in the trend when applying general wave behaviors. Wave A typically is seen as a correction of the then-current trend, when it is actually the first leg of a reversal, or larger correction. It may traverse five waves, but can also complete in three waves (as part of a flat, irregular, or triangle). One sign that a larger corrective trend is under way would be that open interest in related futures markets had been falling in the previous up wave, and is now rising as prices fall. Also, volume actually might pick up in wave A and volatility will also rise, albeit not nearly enough by its end to imply a bottom.

## Wave B

B waves are almost universally the most difficult animal to track. They are always either three waves or triangles. In a flat, they should retrace nearly all of wave A, and at least 62 percent of it, and by definition retrace more than 100 percent of wave A in an irregular. If wave A was five legs, the retrace is usually less than 62 percent. Zigzags have far more bearish overall implications than flats and irregulars do. Wave B usually is completed on low volume.

## Wave C

The C wave is often very impulsive. It is always a five-wave affair and is a close relative of third waves. In zigzags, the C wave usually exceeds wave A in time and size. Volume may also be higher in wave C than in wave A. Some studies suggest that a C wave should not continue beyond 1.618 times wave A, although I have seen other research suggesting that assumption is incorrect. My experience also has found many C waves that extended beyond the so-called 1.618 limit. If wave C completes a flat, its length is usually similar to that of wave A.

## DOW THEORY AND ELLIOTT WAVE THEORY

One often sees commentators point out the similarities between the Elliott Wave Theory and the Dow Theory. These similarities are largely illusory and mostly rooted in their similar nomenclature and the fact that Elliott himself almost certainly studied Dow Theory and built on it in his work. Probably the single most outstanding connection between Elliott and Dow is that both typically are described in terms of investor sentiment and crowd behavior. Recall that both Elliott and Dow developed their ideas long before computers were available, so there was little available in the

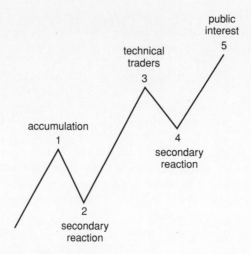

**FIGURE 1.8**  Primary bull market

way of charts or easily computed technical indicators. The easiest way to describe any theory of stock market behavior would have been to draw on the psychology of the investors and traders who made up the market.

The other major comparison between the Dow and Elliott Wave Theories is that both speak of waves. The Dow Theory refers to an accumulation phase, the period when "technical traders" enter the market, and the final phase of a run-up, when the "public" enters a bull market. These may roughly coincide with the upward legs of a five-wave impulse move. However, note that there are also three downwardly biased legs in a bear market as depicted in the Dow Theory, but there are only two such cycles in Elliott. Furthermore, the Dow Theory merely relates to the overall business and index cycle, whereas Elliott's framework is applicable to any freely traded asset, liability, or commodity. Finally, the Dow Theory's signals are dependent on confirmation from specific indices (the Transports must confirm the Industrials). Confirmation of trends in Elliott comes from the price and volume action directly (see Figure 1.8).

The Dow Theory does have one other point in common with Elliott: Dow Theory discusses primary, secondary, and minor trends in the market. This is a manifestation of the fractal nature of the markets in which larger trends subdivide into smaller actions and reactions. Secondary trends are comparable to corrections in Elliott Wave parlance, and the Dow Theory even suggests that secondary trends are constructed of three minor subwaves. The Elliott Wave Theory is built upon this sturdy foundation.

## THE FRACTAL NATURE OF PRICE MOVEMENTS

A fractal, as defined by Benoit Mandelbrot, the famous mathematician and chaotician, in his article "A Multifractal Walk Down Wall Street,"[8] is *"a geometric shape that can be separated into parts, each of which is a reduced-scale version of the whole."* Although the term *fractal* was coined by Dr. Mandelbrot in 1975, the actual activity that it describes was clearly identified by R.N. Elliott, in both the financial markets and in nature itself, long before Mandelbrot "discovered" it.[9] Of course, Elliott never proved his theory mathematically, and computers are only now approaching the computing power to permit us to retrieve and examine enough market data to validate his work, but that does not diminish Elliott's findings a half-century prior to Mandelbrot's seminal works.

The fractal nature of market prices is easily seen when you look at a detailed chart of any price series of a freely traded stock, bond, currency, or commodity. The stylized graphic shown in Figure 1.9 depicts the fractal underpinnings of Elliott as well. All impulse waves break down into smaller impulse waves. A first wave is made up of five smaller waves, and each of the five small waves subdivide into fractionally smaller five- and three-leg cycles.

The fact that a market is fractal is not important unless you understand that the market can be forecast. Although Elliott certainly did not have the wherewithal, or the mathematical background, to compute Mandelbrot's chaos generators, he clearly found a reasonably accurate approximation via his theory. The beauty of EWT is that it provides a framework for discovering periods when Modern Portfolio Theory (MPT) may break down. A portfolio based on MPT's efficient frontier will very efficiently accrue losses

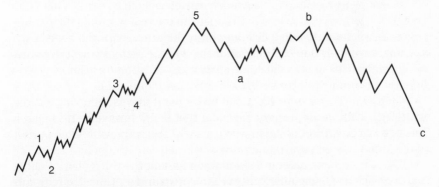

**FIGURE 1.9**  Fractal waves

at such times. That is, by a complete understanding of the wave theory, one can accurately forecast 6 sigma and 10 sigma[10] events, such as those which helped sink the Long Term Capital Management (LTCM) hedge fund. Price and time projections had forecast a major turn lower in the stock market just as it topped in the summer of 1998, and a high in bond prices perfectly coincided with the capitulation phase that resulted from the Russian debt crisis and LTCM debacle.

## IMPULSE VERSUS CORRECTION AND THE TIME FACTOR

Some practitioners make the choice of applying technical analysis, fundamental research, and specific methodologies (such as EWT) into a nearly religious decision. They act as if technical analysis in general, and EWT in particular, were completely determinate—the Holy Grail. If EWT is, this author admits that he has not figured out how to interpret the waves in a 100 percent foolproof matter. However, understanding the characteristics of waves, and how one cycle and degree relates to another, can allow you to forecast the markets more accurately than most think possible.

I cannot over emphasize how important it is to understand the difference between an impulse wave and a corrective wave. Furthermore, you must realize that corrective cycles may be comprised of small impulse waves of their own. This is probably the single most challenging part of forecasting price movements with Elliott—as soon as you think the market is correcting a trend, a five-wave pattern appears against the trend. Practitioners without a firm grounding in EWT consistently misread five-wave moves that are parts of corrections and revise their counts to reflect incorrectly labeled impulsive reversals.

Consider, for example, previously mentioned Figure 1.9. This is, of course, a stylized version of what happens in the real world. In the picture, some fairly complex subdivisions within the wave patterns are shown. Look at wave b. The initial rally after the wave a bottom was a five-wave cycle higher. This might lead some analysts to question their initial wave a five-wave count lower. However, five-wave price moves never occur alone as an initial price segment (they can be terminal moves following a three-wave leg). This would be your first hint that the five-wave rally is merely part of a larger correction. Also, wave a itself only retraced a small portion of the larger five-wave advance shown.

The Elliott Wave analyst need not just look at the price chart. Volume and open interest, indicators, and even the press and sentiment surveys can all help you to pinpoint your chart patterns with greater accuracy. Classical technical patterns, such as head and shoulders and triangles, also have a

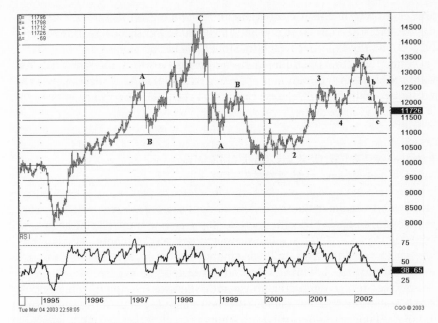

**FIGURE 1.10**   USD-JPY, weekly

place in EWT. Momentum divergences often appear at the end of fifth waves, but usually confirm the price action at the end of wave 3. If wave 3 appears complete and momentum does not confirm the action, it probably means either that the wave cycle is a c wave, that is, the end of a correction, or the end of a first wave of a larger third wave. Your momentum indicator could also fail to confirm price action because it is measuring a longer or shorter time period than the wave count covers. You wouldn't use a 21-day momentum calculation as confirmation of a 5-day long trend.

Figure 1.10 highlights these tendencies. Note that at the top of wave C in the middle of 1998, weekly relative strength (RSI, 14-week) diverged. That is, RSI was not as high at the price peak as it stood at the previous lower swing high. The analyst may also have been inclined to assume that the dollar's collapse following the wave C peak, which ended at JPY114.40 (the number of Japanese yen you need to buy one U.S. dollar) in October 1998, was the end of the correction. However, this would mean that a three-year rally was corrected in three months. For that reason, the analyst, though cautious, ought to have looked for a five-wave fall off the highs, a three-wave correction of that move, and then another five-wave drop. The dollar did move higher, in three waves with a fourth subwave, into November

1998 and then declined, completing a five-wave drop in January 1999 at
JPY108.24. A second five-wave decline concluded the correction of the
1995–1998 rally by late November 1999 at JPY101.27.

Since that time, the dollar rallied in five waves through early 2002. At
that time, Japan's economy was seen as a basket case, and several analysts
had extended their USDJPY forecasts to levels north of JPY150 and even to
JPY200. In 1999, when the dollar was trading near JPY101.27, forecasts were
revised for sub-JPY100, with many calling for new record USD lows. Most
Elliotticians recognized the technical failure near JPY135.00, and forecast a
drop below JPY120. Note the momentum divergence as the dollar made its
high. Ultimately, a move north of JPY150 is likely, but not before late 2003.

Another example comes from the headlines of September 2001. Understanding how to determine the likely amount of time a wave cycle will take
to complete can help you increase your forecast and trading accuracy. Consider Figure 1.11. Note how the stock market surged higher shortly after
achieving an emotional low following the September 11, 2001 terrorist attacks
on the United States. While the buy and hold and bull market cheerleaders
incorrectly tried to suggest that the bear market was over, many followers of
Elliott suggested that the highs achieved in January 2002 represented the
end of the bear market correction higher.

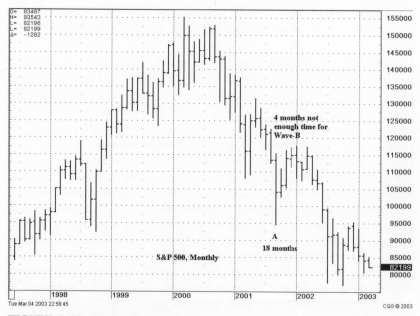

**FIGURE 1.11**   S&P 500, weekly

It is highly unlikely that a bear move that took from March 2000 until September 2001, a period of 18 months, could completely correct in less than four months and retrace such a small percentage of the losses. The continued sideways price action following the new lows set in July and October 2002 meant that the wave B idea was most likely incorrect and that a fourth wave was developing instead. A detailed forecast is presented in Chapter 8.

## PRACTICAL PATTERN RECOGNITION

In the 1989 movie "Field of Dreams," Kevin Costner's character is told, "If you build it, he will come." When it comes to Elliott Wave, I like to say, "if you can't count it, it isn't an impulse wave." It really is as simple as that. Impulse moves should be recognizable. Volume should be strong. The terminus of wave 1 and wave 4 should not overlap (except in one special case). Prices should not retrace in an impulsive manner, wave 3 can never be the shortest wave, and volume should be lower during the retrace periods.

Some of the points I noted in the above paragraph, and elsewhere in this chapter, deserve a bit more attention:

1. "Volume should be strong." Volume is not always measurable. Many futures markets do not report intraday turnover, and the foreign exchange markets are over the counter with no volume reported at all. Even in the stock market, intraday volume is a dicey game. There is typically very high turnover near the open and the close. It is entirely possible that a correction might see higher volume than an impulse move if the correction is an intraday action and mostly takes place near the open or the close. Analysts must take care to understand the specific vagaries of the market they are working on.

2. "Impulse waves should be easily recognizable." Well, almost always. The caveats here include remembering that when wave 1 begins, most of the world still believes the trend is in the other direction. It takes a very strong will to jump on the first wave's bandwagon. To a degree, the trader or analyst must anticipate the action early on. By the time you can recognize the pattern as impulsive, the wave cycle is probably nearly complete! Adding to the complexity factor is something known as a diagonal (or terminal) triangle. This encompasses the situation where the first and fourth waves overlap. Although diagonal triangles complete in a five-wave structure, each subwave breaks down into three waves instead of the normal five waves. Diagonal triangles usually appear in wave C or wave 5. They should never develop as a third wave since diagonals typically are a sign of a weakening trend. They rarely occur in the

first-wave position in cases where the market psyche is totally unac-
cepting of a reversal of fortunes, leading to a subpar first-wave reversal.

3. The word "correction." As you will find in later chapters, Elliott consistently used little forethought in his nomenclature. The term *correction* should more correctly be called *non impulse* or *consolidation*.
Corrections sometimes end at levels above the high of an upward-sloping
impulse move or below the low of a downward-sloping impulsion. In
addition, one of the most common Elliott patterns is the misnamed
*irregular correction*. In this pattern, the b wave moves past the fur-
thest extent of the previous impulse move. Irregular corrections are
about as common as regular corrections. There is also a running correction. The ending point of a running correction is actually beyond the
prior impulse wave's terminal. In an upward move, it is above the prior
impulse wave's high. When prices are falling, the running correction
ends at a price level beneath the previous impulse wave's low.

4. "Corrections are three-wave moves." Except when they are triangles.
Then they complete in five waves. Also, the individual legs of a correction might be five waves. In a zigzag, both legs are five waves. In a flat
or irregular, the c wave is five waves. In a triangle, none of the waves
traverse in five waves (though as you drill down to lower degrees, you
will find that individual legs of each three-leg pattern are usually five-
wave zigzags).

5. "Corrections almost always are more difficult to count than impulse
waves." Zigzags are pretty easy to count. They are comprised of two
five-wave impulse moves. However, large patterns may appear (and
often are) very impulsive, and do not fit into some of the characteristics
I noted earlier in this chapter. The bear market in stocks that began in
early 2000 might very well be part of a fourth-wave correction. Corrections get difficult to count when they continue for long periods. Then,
we start to see multiple patterns strung together by what many analysts
who do not understand EWT call the Elliottician's fudge factor, the "X"
wave. Also, irregular corrections and running corrections can be very
hard to identify *a priori* unless you understand where and why they are
most likely to appear.

The real key to the kingdom here is to keep things as simple as possible. There are steps you must take to ensure that you understand the current market process, develop a reasonable wave count, determine what
that wave count means going forward, identify where that wave count is
proven wrong, and what to look for that will allow you to exit any positions
taken, possibly with a gain, even if your analysis is wrong.

This process is iterative. You constantly must review your assumptions
and update them as more information comes in. Entering a trade and doing

your homework before the trade is not even half the battle. You must monitor price and volume action, and even the news, in your investment, and in related assets as well, to make sure your trade idea and wave count still stand up to scrutiny. If they do not, you must revise your projections. You might need to alter your targets and/or stops, and you might even need to exit the position.

## MULTIPLE TIME-FRAME ANALYSIS

I have been writing a daily newsletter which covers global stock, bond, currency, and commodity markets since the early 1990s. Elliott Wave Theory has provided the backbone of nearly all my forecasts during that time. One reason I decided to write this book is so I can provide an easy-to-read and understandable reference on how to use Elliott to my subscribers. Writing about the markets using Elliott can be quite a challenge. Because the markets are fractal, the corrections have corrections! This means the author must take extreme care in word choice, consistently referring to price cycles in the same way, based on the expected size of move, in both time and price.

### Elliott Wave Time Frames

One must be consistent from day to day as well. For example, if a market has rallied for two weeks, and the larger trend is negative, I might call the rally a correction. This will cause problems for some since the standard non-Elliott definition of a correction usually describes a period of falling prices. As you can see from Figure 1.12, that rally was merely wave A of a

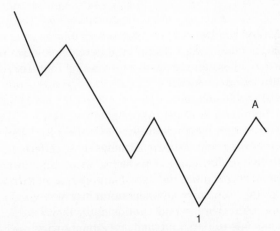

**FIGURE 1.12** Labeling difficulty: corrections versus trends

larger correction *to higher prices.* Wave B will then correct wave A, or correct a correction. However, using the term *correction* for both wave A and wave B would be very confusing.

Elliott did provide for at least some amelioration to this problem by defining a nomenclature that describes the different degrees of the various wave cycles. Prechter and Frost later expanded these naming conventions in their book *Elliott Wave Principle: Key to Stock Market Profits.*[11] As you can tell from the title of the book, the wave-labeling schema suggested by Frost and Prechter is still based on the equity markets' bias to higher prices, and would be rather limiting for markets that trade more cyclically, such as foreign currencies, many commodities, and fixed-income securities.

## Wave Labels

I am a proponent of the "KIS" method (Keep It Simple)—I dropped the last "S" to avoid discriminating against the intelligence challenged. Unless you are attempting to chart many years of data and plan on including levels of extreme detail, it is unlikely that you would ever need anything more than three levels of impulse and correction labels. Since most charting packages do not have the ability to put circles around the labels, I use the following, from smallest to largest degree:

- For impulse moves:
  - i, ii, iii, iv, v
  - 1, 2, 3, 4, 5
  - I, II, III, IV, V
- For corrective moves:
  - (a), (b), (c)
  - a, b, c
  - A, B, C

You can always add additional levels of detail, as long as you are consistent. With more advanced software that permits greater control of fonts, you might choose to bold or italicize labels or use script fonts for some degrees, as well parenthesizing the labels.

Frost and Prechter extended Elliott's label names by adding a very short-term cycle to the Elliott list. Although my work uses intraday labels, I rarely follow Elliott's nomenclature (see Chapter 8). I have not seen a good definition of what any of the time frames these different cycle degrees represent, and each Elliottician seems to use them differently. The lack of standard definitions precludes the use of any real naming standards. Frost and Prechter made a similar recommendation in their book, though in their work, they quite correctly and consistently apply their own schema.

I have seen some traders and analysts attempt to apply Elliott to tick charts.[12] The level of noise in the markets, coupled with the simple fact that the bid-ask spread in most instruments could easily lead to poor wave counts, leaves this author convinced that applying wave counts to tick charts is not a skill worth developing. Day traders do need to shorten their scale, and for very liquid stocks, exchange rates, and futures contracts, one-minute or five-minute charts are certainly viable alternatives to tick charts as a basis for your analysis. However, remember that the shorter the trading time frame, the more commissions and bid-ask spreads become a factor in your profitability. Also, recall that random noise becomes a proportionally larger factor as you shorten your trading time frame.

Whether you use classical technical analysis or Elliott Wave to help you make your trading and investing decisions, you must look at multiple time frames. Day traders should review 5-minute, 30-minute, and even daily and weekly charts. A short-term swing trader ought to use 30-minute or hourly charts, on out to weekly as well. Investors and medium-term players should study daily, weekly, and monthly (or longer) time-frames.

When analyzing using Elliott, knowledge of time frames and larger-degree wave patterns is absolutely critical. Look at Figure 1.13. Prices fell in a clear three-wave pattern from the highs on the five-minute chart for the July 2003 soybean futures. Without knowing the counts prior to that period, you could not possibly forecast the size of the next move. To suggest a mere retrace/correction without knowing if another three-wave or five-wave

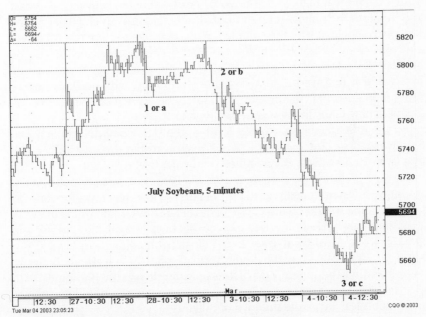

**FIGURE 1.13** July 2003 soybean futures, 5-minute bars

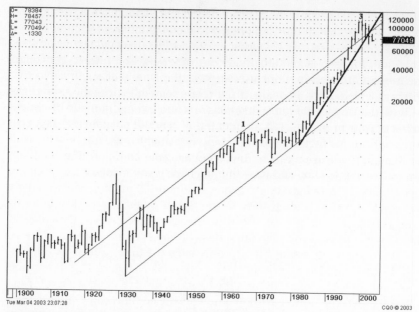

**FIGURE 1.14**  Dow Jones Industrial Average, annual

move preceded the price action is not possible. If it is a three-wave leg lower from a local high, you still would not be able to accurately forecast more than the very short-term outlook. For example, if the high set on the chart also coincided with the completion of a daily degree five-wave pattern, one could assume that the three-wave pattern completed may merely be the first three legs of a large five-wave impulse move to lower prices. However, if it followed a relatively short-term rally, with no daily degree completion apparent, the drop might merely be wave a of a small correction, with new highs likely within two days.

At the time this book is being written, the U.S. stock market is mired in its worst drawdown since the stock market tested the post-1929 crash lows from 1937 to 1942. Some indices show net losses going back to 1997. As shown in Figure 1.14, even the venerable Dow is off substantially. There are many different views regarding the current long-term wave count for the Dow. Some well-known analysts believe the Dow could tumble to 1,000. Others are less bearish, but still expect this bear market to continue and take the Dow down to at least come close to matching the lows set in October 1998, following the Long Term Capital Management debacle. Understanding the magnitude of the possible losses in 1999 and 2000, because of the apparent end of a very long-term cycle, would have meant saving countless investors millions of dollars.

This highlights why Elliott is useful, not only to traders, but to investors. Understanding that the stock market was likely to fall at least 20 percent, if not more, in the next several years, as of early 2000, would have permitted wave-savvy investors to shift funds out of stocks and into fixed-income securities. Although my forecasts suggest the Dow will reach new highs within the next 10 to 20 years, if the more bearish prognosticators prove correct, the Dow might not see 12,000 for several generations! With that as a risk, one ought to think twice about the Wall Street wisdom that says that stocks go up in the long run. The long run might take you beyond your retirement. If you are trying to fund a college education, owning stocks, in general, might no longer be the right place for your savings.

## SUMMARY

With these very basic patterns defined, you should be able to begin to recognize some big-picture wave cycles. Before you go on to the next chapter, I suggest you review the sample figures from this chapter. Then, if you have access to the Internet, go to a web site that shows stock, futures, or currency charts, look at some daily, weekly, and monthly graphs, and see if you can start to make out some wave counts. Look at several different time frames so you can compare waves of different degrees.

In the next chapter, more complex correction and impulse patterns are introduced. These include terminal triangles, and doubles and triples. In the following chapter I will also detail how to compute retrace levels, and time and price targets. Once you have completed reading and studying the next two chapters, you will be ready to learn how to take this theoretical knowledge and turn it into a trading plan. You will even learn how to make money when your wave counts are incorrect!

# CHAPTER 2

# Advanced Concepts

In the first chapter, I spent a good deal of time showing you the basic Elliott Wave patterns. We discovered that when an impulse move appears, it should be easily identifiable. We also spent some time discussing ways of recognizing corrections. However, I gave corrections the short end of the stick in the first chapter, largely because it was important to understand the characteristics of each kind of wave, and because corrections can be incredibly difficult to count.

In Chapter 1, I defined zigzag, flat, irregular, and triangle corrections. However, corrections are often formed by compounding multiple formations: two or three zigzags run together, or a flat followed by a zigzag, or any other of the many possible combinations of these various formations. These types of corrections are covered in this chapter.

This chapter is not just about corrections. It also covers the one type of impulse wave where wave 1 and wave 4 can overlap. Elliott called this a *diagonal triangle*. Others have renamed it a *terminal triangle*. I will use diagonal in this book. We also cover channeling and alternation,[1] Fibonacci numbers and retraces, and price and time targets in Chapter 3.

The most frequent complaint I hear regarding Elliott Wave Theory is that the patterns are easily seen after the fact, but not while they develop. This is just not true. Corrections are very difficult to count, but we will develop the tools in this chapter to help you identify and forecast likely trading patterns. As I have said before, EWT is not the Holy Grail. There is a great deal of subjectivity in wave count determination, and the correct count, *a priori*, is never 100 percent known; however, with experience, you can get it right often enough to be very profitable in your trading or investing.

Traders and analysts often jump to the conclusion that a three-wave move has completed a correction. They do not bother to think that their a–b–c might be a larger wave A of a flat or irregular, or that it could also be part of a far more complex corrective pattern. Understanding where a complex or simple pattern might develop, as well as a complete knowledge of time-versus-price relationships and likely retrace targets, will help you avoid these common pitfalls. The next several sections give examples of complex corrections.

## COMPLEX CORRECTIONS

The aim of this section is to lend a harsh dose of reality after everything seemed so nice and friendly in the first chapter. You will now find that all those A–B–C corrections can turn into some pretty hard-to-handle trading patterns in the real world. The wave formations discussed here merely compound the simple triangles, zigzags, and flats discussed in Chapter 1. There are several guidelines and tips I can offer you that will help you to determine the proper wave count with a greater level of accuracy.

You will achieve this greater precision by adding new tools to your Elliott Wave arsenal. I will take the abstract discussion regarding time and price to much greater detail. The section covers how deep a corrective wave should retrace and how long it should take to complete, and looks at other technical indicators you can use to help confirm your wave-based forecasts. With these tools in hand, you will be able to go to the next level, and start building trading plans! First, let's look at some of the different types of complex corrections.

### Double Threes and Triple Threes

All corrections (except for triangles) are comprised of three-wave moves. The simplest of these are zigzags, flats, and irregulars. A zigzag contains two impulse (five-wave) legs, separated by a three-wave leg that moves with the direction of the larger trend (and thus against the direction of the correction). That is, it corrects the correction. A flat is formed by two three-wave legs, the first against the trend and the second with the trend, followed by a five-wave impulse move that corrects the larger trend. Sometimes, zigzags are called 5–3–5's and flats and irregulars are called 3–3–5's.

One of the great challenges in EWT is for the analyst to avoid jumping the gun. All too often, following a beautiful three-wave correction, the halls of Elliottdom reverberate with pronouncements that the trend shall now resume, and sometimes it does. Often, unfortunately, it does not. Take a look at Figure 2.1. Do you think the nice three-wave fall completes the correction? For those who are jumping out of your seats, waving your hands, going, "Ooh ooh ooh, pick me Mr. Poser. The answer is no," you're wrong. The answer is that you really do not know, but if you answered, "Probably not," you are correct.

Consider the pattern under review. Prices rose in five waves, so a correction is due. The rally took 55 days to complete. Prices then fell in three

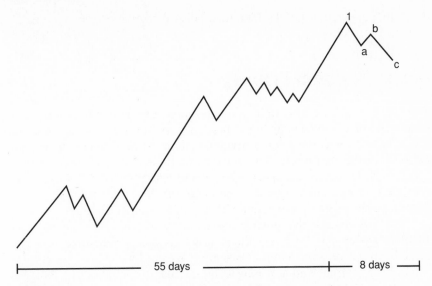

**FIGURE 2.1** Correction is too shallow and short to be complete.

waves over a period of eight days. The losses were pretty small as well, and did not even reach the start of the last major leg higher. Although it would be far from impossible for the drop to represent the whole correction, such a shallow and short-term move would be an unlikely candidate following a large 55-day impulse. If the wave 1 labeled was actually part of a larger third wave, there might be a chance that prices would trace out a very shallow and short-term correction, but I would still venture that the action I illustrated would most likely only be the first part of a larger period of consolidation or correction.

Note that Elliott does not directly use the term *consolidation* in describing the waves. However, common usage relates a consolidation to a period of range trading, whereas corrections typically refer to larger moves against the trend. In Elliott parlance, triangles and flats describe consolidations, whereas zigzags fit better with the typical definition of a correction. However, zigzags, flats, and compound patterns are all called corrections under the auspices of EWT.

Double-threes and triple-threes are formed by triangles, zigzags, or flats or irregulars lining up consecutively. They are separated by a three-wave move against the direction of the correction. These wave structures are called *X waves*. It takes a great deal of time and study to understand where and how to apply an X wave. Many technical analysts that are not familiar with EWT believe that the X wave is the Elliottician's fudge factor. They believe that Elliott Wave–based analysts use it when they missed a

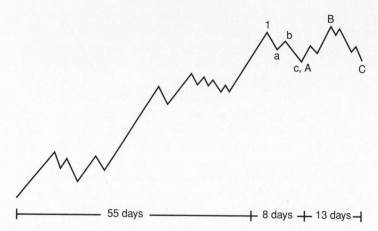

**FIGURE 2.2**  Though shallow, enough time has elapsed for completion.

count and do not know how to fit it into a nice neat scheme. This is completely untrue. As I will discuss below, there are many situations in which an X wave would be expected, given the already observed price action. An X wave can be any corrective pattern—a zigzag, flat, or triangle, or a complex correction as well.

Back to analyzing our sample price chart: The rest of the wave might play out in a myriad of ways. First of all, since the drop was merely a three-wave affair, this might simply be the first leg of a 3–3–5 correction, as depicted in Figure 2.2. Do not be fooled by a three-wave rally that takes prices to a new high, past the top of wave 1. That would almost certainly represent the end of wave B, and suggest that an irregular was forming. Only a very impulsive third wave higher that makes a new high on increasing volume and momentum, and which exceeds the first wave up by a factor of at least 1.618:1.0 would move the idea that the correction is over to favored status. However, the question as to whether a full correction of the 55-day rally is over is not really answered as yet.

Let's consider the facts and alternatives:

1. If the correction is over, then prices should start to rally in an impulsive manner. That means volume ought to increase as prices move higher.

2. If the correction has not completed, turnover will likely remain fairly low.

3. The A–B–C is a classic irregular. An irregular correction would mean that the underlying trend that it is consolidating is very strong. This would allow for a shallow and short-term correction. This move was very shallow, and at 21 days, fairly short in time. If we go with this interpretation, one would expect a very clear rally to start immediately.

4. Beware that a five-wave rally would not be enough to signal the correction ended. If the total distance of the move is relatively small, and especially if turnover does not increase, I would assume that the five-wave move was wave a of a larger a–b–c X wave, or part of a leg of a triangle.

There are many hints the Elliottician can look to in an attempt to determine what comes next. I did not really give you enough information to fully determine what kind of pattern should develop going forward. For example, if the five-wave move shown was actually the fifth wave of a larger five-wave trend, then it is clear that the three-wave irregular would not nearly meet the requirements for a correction of a trend of that magnitude. Second-wave corrections also tend to be fairly deep, so the likelihood of further losses, if this A–B–C was in the second-wave position, would be relatively high.

Traders need not just use Elliott in their attempts to determine the current trend's direction. Figure 2.3 depicts one possible final outcome for this theoretical correction. All Elliott Wave patterns have parallels in classical technical analysis. For example, the high at wave B would be the top in a head-and-shoulders pattern, with wave 1 and wave X representing the two shoulders. The neckline would be drawn connecting waves c, A and C. However, Elliott gives much more precise price targets than the classic explanation of equality between the peak and neckline added to the neckline breakout point. Instead, you would look for price relationships among the various waves, allowing you to compute more exact targets. Retrace levels relating to the previous impulse wave higher would allow you to further sharpen your price target focus.

There are many other indicators that you can use to help you determine if a move is at or near an end. Momentum, trend lines, ADX[2] and oscillators

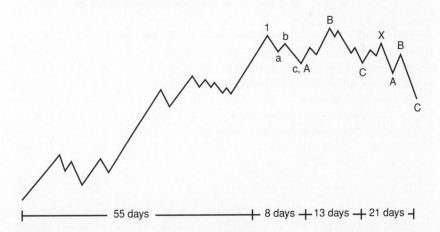

**FIGURE 2.3** Possible outcome—a double three

all have a place in your analysis. For example, third waves usually see Welles Wilder's Relative Strength Index (RSI) and other momentum indicators confirm price action. One of the most common mistakes analysts make is to look for a major reversal when RSI is very high in an uptrend. In a third wave, RSI can remain overbought for a very long period. Although an RSI of 75 (14-day) might herald an upcoming period of range trading (a fourth wave), it is highly unlikely that a final top would be in at that point. An example of this comes from research I performed in the late 1990s on the U.S. Treasury bond futures. I found that even though high 14-day RSI's (above 78) typically warned of impending corrections, they almost never signalled a major top *if this was the first time RSI reached that high level* in that active market cycle. You would want to combine price target tools with momentum and retrace levels to help you pinpoint where to start looking for the consolidation to begin.

Momentum indicators classically diverge at the end of moves. This is quite common at the end of a fifth wave or a C wave. Of course, a mere divergence is not enough to signal the end of a trend. The beauty of EWT is that there are so many tools to help you pinpoint where the trend might end. Adding the comfort of confirmation from a indicator or two is an added bonus.

Elliott Wave analysts excel at trading against the majority. Although countless technicians and fundamental analysts might be screaming buy or sell, just because a moving average broke or momentum failed to confirm a move, the Elliottician can calmly look at his wave counts and retrace and target measures to determine whether the crowd is correct or not. The crowd is not always wrong. When the market is in a third wave or in a major C wave, you should be trading or investing with the crowd. Knowing where you are in a wave cycle allows you to overcome your natural desire, whether you tend to always fade or always succumb to the markets.

**Sample Analysis: International Business Machines.**   International Business Machines Corporation (IBM) peaked in July 1999, well before the broad stock market hit its high in early 2000. As you can see in Figure 2.4, I show a complete five-wave cycle counted out as of the high in 1999. I can fathom arguments favoring a mere three waves complete since 1972. One argument favoring that count would be the very short period allocated to wave IV. That momentum confirmed the highs in 1999 would argue for wave III still being active. However, price projections, which I will discuss in Chapter 3, lead me to favor a completed five-wave count. Volume (not shown) was also somewhat lower at the peak than it was at other swing highs.

There are other reasons as well. The Elliottician should consider evidence gleaned from more than one source if a wave count is not totally

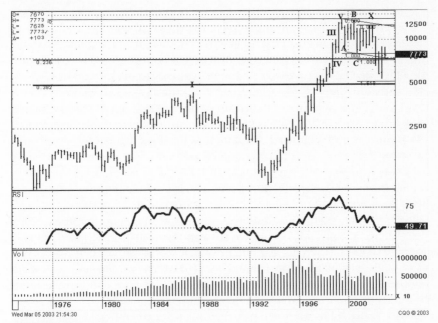

**FIGURE 2.4** IBM, quarterly

clear. In the case of IBM, understanding the deep risk for the overall equity
markets adds force to the preferred count. Expectations for a return to levels not seen since the October 1998 lows in the overall market imply lower
prices to come for IBM and the market in general. Given that price already
fell below the most recent price leg low and that the current retrace is
greater than 50 percent of the leg higher that began in 1993, it is very difficult to avoid counting the pattern as anything but a five-wave run complete
as of 1999's high.

Additionally, the current drop, since the X wave peak, does not yet look
complete. That is, at least one more leg lower looks likely, although prices
are probably near at least a short-term turning point. A final argument
favoring the idea of the correction lower still being active is that momentum confirmed the lows on the monthly and quarterly charts.

As you can see, there are many factors you must consider when attempting to nail down a wave count. Wave patterns are absolutely paramount.
You can never have a fourth-wave overlap, except in the case of a diagonal
triangle (see the next section). You must also consider the timing of the
moves—that is, how long it takes for each leg to complete. Elliott Waves
tend to equality, or to complete in time and price ratios related to the Fibonacci number series. Although the time ratios were not good fits, the price
ratios had excellent matches for the IBM chart.

One also must consider other factors and probabilities when developing a wave count. Beyond simple technical analysis, you must be aware of the overall sentiment picture. Remember, EWT is firmly planted in crowd and behavioral theory. In the case of IBM, that the stock could not make a new high during the technology led bubble is a strong hint that the correction currently underway is something more than a fourth wave.

I am also a very strong advocate of intermarket analysis. That means looking at charts of companies and markets related to the company or asset class you are reviewing. In the case of IBM, the bear market forecasts point to lower levels to come, making it very difficult to count the current drop as a fourth wave. Although the stock might very well outperform other technology stocks, there is little chance that IBM has seen a bottom as of June 2002.

Remember, corrections can play out in very complex patterns. IBM's price was in an uptrend, a five-wave advance, from 1972 until 1999. That is 27 years. To believe that a 27-year bull run can possibly correct in three years is most likely wishful thinking. I can fathom IBM moving sideways to lower for another seven years or longer. If that is what develops, then this pattern will become much more complex. As of the time this was written, the stock was working on a double three, and may have been due for a b wave higher within the second three-wave move. This b wave could turn into a triangle, a flat, or a zigzag. Given timing concerns, I would expect yet another X wave and a final three-wave or triangle lower that may take us to 2009 or later!

Just because a price pattern is complete does not mean the whole move is done. An a–b–c correction may tell you that countertrend action is due. It does not tell you that the correction ended. The correction of a 100 percent 10-year rally will not likely end with a 10 percent six-month correction, even if it is a perfect a–b–c zigzag that conforms to every EWT rule ever discovered. The savvy analyst will realize that and understand that any rallies at that point are setups for further shorts. Although those with a short-term time frame, such as traders holding put options, where time decay is an issue, probably need to cover short trades and possibly consider action from the long side, investors either need to use the rally to add to shorts or find another issue to trade from the long side.

In the next chapter, we develop more tools to help you determine price and time targets. First, we need to complete the review of a few more pattern types and their typical characteristics.

## Diagonal Triangles

Now that you are an expert in identifying corrective phases, as well as impulse moves, it is time to throw you a couple of curve balls. The first is a pattern that I referred to several times already: the diagonal triangle. A diagonal triangle is one of the most difficult patterns to count properly. It is

**FIGURE 2.5** Diagonal triangle

an impulse wave, since there are five legs in the direction of the trend. Unfortunately, unlike most other impulse moves, the individual legs, both with and against the trend, develop in three-wave patterns. This makes proper identification very difficult because you are likely to improperly identify the price action as part of a larger correction.

Diagonal triangles (as in Figure 2.5) should look quite familiar to technicians that specialize in chart patterns. Classical technical analysts would call this pattern a *wedge*. A wedge pattern foretells a sharp reversal, but until the lower trend-line support is breached, it is best categorized as a continuation pattern since higher prices are expected.

From a psychological perspective, the wedge pattern is a sign of a weakening trend. A strong trend would be bounded by a channel line, but in a wedge (diagonal triangle), prices are not able to reach that far, falling short and touching a line instead that ultimately meets the underlying trend line. Each leg higher in a bullish wedge, or lower in a bearish wedge, is shorter than the previous leg. From an Elliott perspective, this weakening of the trend is implied by an impulse move formed of three-wave rather than five-wave cycles, where wave 3 is not the largest wave and where the extreme of wave 4 overlaps the terminus of wave 1. Momentum divergences are fairly common at the end of fifth waves, and are virtually universal if wave 5 is a diagonal triangle.

Some Elliott Wave analysts call diagonal triangles *terminal triangles*. This is because they usually appear in the fifth-wave position or as wave C in an Elliott Wave cycle. Unfortunately, these patterns periodically show up in the first wave, or as an a wave or b wave. For this reason, I have chosen to employ Elliott's nomenclature.

Remember, a diagonal is an impulse move. Just because the market shows signs of a weakening trend does not mean that you should anticipate a price turn. It is not uncommon for the fifth wave of the diagonal to exceed the top of the resistance line. As long as wave 3 is not your shortest leg, you should assume that prices are in an impulse move and that the trend is still active.

A diagonal is a sign of a weakening trend. That means that when the support line breaks (if the diagonal is at the end of an uptrend), you should expect a pretty large move lower. The rule of thumb is to look for a correction at least back to the start of the pattern. However, if a large five-wave move just completed, I would expect a deeper correction than that. It is supposed to represent a weaker than normal situation, so a drop below the start of the diagonal (which is, of course, the extreme of wave 4) would be a reasonable expectation.

A word of caution here: Do not start looking under every rock for diagonals. They are not all that common. They rarely show up in first waves. I also would not look for them in the fifth wave of wave 1. In addition, I would never expect to see a diagonal as wave v of a larger wave 3. Although there is no rule against such activity, a diagonal is supposed to represent a weakening of the active trend, and a third wave is usually the most impulsive move in a five-wave cycle. Remember, wave characteristics are very important, and a diagonal in the fifth position of a third wave does not fit well into that characteristic.

Look at Figure 2.6. Prices made a new high, but only on a three-wave move. The subsequent drop then fell below the start of the first leg up off

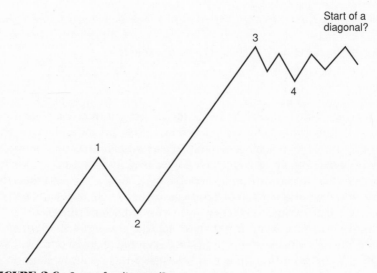

**FIGURE 2.6**  Start of a diagonal?

**FIGURE 2.7** AUDUSD, monthly, probably not a diagonal

labeled wave 4. Do you think that is a good assumption? The answer to the question is: probably not. I warned earlier not to look under every rock for a diagonal triangle. Consider the facts in your analysis of Figure 2.6:

- Wave 2 was steep and regular.
- Wave 4 as labeled barely retraced wave 3.
- The rule of alternation would suggest that wave 4 should be irregular, or if not irregular at least complex.

The most likely result here is that wave 4 is still not complete. As I implied above, you should expect wave 4 to retrace more than was shown, and probably take more time to finish than what is depicted in the figure. More likely than not, the new high is wave b of wave 4 with wave c of wave 4 active. Another possibility is that wave 4 is developing a five-wave triangle. Then, the ultimate low for wave 4 would already be in, and any overbought situation would be alleviated by a longer period of price consolidation.

Another common error in labeling usually involves the belief that prices overlapped a first-wave extreme, leading the analyst to incorrectly label the price action as a diagonal. Consider Figure 2.7. It is very tempting to assume that the rally from 1998 to 1999 overlapped the low of a first wave down in the Australian dollar's cross with the U.S. dollar. However, the drop in what would be the third wave looks more like five waves than three waves. If the drop was five waves, then the third leg down, if it is part of a diagonal, cannot yet be complete, so overlap with wave 1 would not be an issue here. However, if you count wave 3 here as five waves, then it is mighty strong to be part of a diagonal. A diagonal triangle is supposed to represent a weakening trend! That means that the wave counts need adjustment. I would assume that wave 1 actually terminated in 1989 and not in 1993. That would make the 1993 low an irregular b wave in wave 2 and would mean that wave 4 as labeled is probably correct and does not overlap the low of wave 1.

**Proper Identification of Diagonal Triangles.**  The point I have been trying to make in this chapter is that you should understand where to look for the patterns discussed in these pages. The diagonal triangle is usually at the end of a trend, typically in wave 5 of an impulse cycle. Although it does periodically appear in first waves, that is a relatively rare occurrence. Similarly, as a terminal move, it does not typically show up in wave A, but might in wave C.

We discussed wave characteristics in Chapter 1. I cannot overemphasize understanding the normal characteristics of wave formations. This provides a direct link to market sentiment and behavior. A diagonal triangle still represents a continuing trend, but compared to a typical fifth wave, this pattern is relatively weaker. Each leg only traces out three waves instead of the normal five waves. Furthermore, prices do not even come close to forming a price channel. The market appears to be in a correction or consolidation. As in most fifth waves, momentum divergences are the norm. Volume should typically be lower on each succeeding price swing higher, and when price finally clearly breaks below trend-line support, we expect turnover to increase.

Remember, a diagonal triangle is a wedge formation in the classical technical analysis sense. Although it is called a *continuation pattern*, by the time a non-Elliottician recognizes it, price probably is well on its way to reaching the end of the road. The ability to tie a wedge to a proper Elliott location will add to your confidence in the pattern itself.

Without the benefit of sentiment and Elliott Wave, the classical technician will often identify a wedge pattern only to ultimately have to retract that forecast as prices break out and enter into a channel, thus confirming the trend. Or, price might reverse immediately, signaling a trend reversal. The Elliottician understands that the first cycle of a new trend is unlikely to unfold as a diagonal. If there is a contracting pattern early in a trend, there is a good chance it will break out or reverse. If the price action with the

**FIGURE 2.8**  U.S. 30-year yield, 5-minute bars

apparent new trend is in five waves, look for a break out; if it is in three waves, the risk is that the previous trend is still active.

The possible contracting pattern shown in Figure 2.8, the 30-year U.S. Treasury bond yield five-minute chart, does not fit into a normal wave pattern. It is at a trend reversal point, and to that juncture, the price action could just as easily be the first three waves of a five-wave move. That is exactly what happened. Yields continued to fall substantially. The classical technician might have been looking for the wedge to break higher to continue the prior minor trend to higher yields. EWT would have suggested caution at that time. Some classically oriented technical analysts would argue that wedges are not intraday price patterns, but all long-term patterns appear at intraday time frames as well.

## Channels and Trend Lines

A rising or falling market within a well-defined channel can be a thing of beauty (see Figure 2.9). Elliott opined that the wave patterns usually rose within channels. However, markets do not always move within channels and to be honest, as a practical matter, by the time you have found the proper

**FIGURE 2.9** Micron Technology, daily

channel to follow, the pattern is so well defined that the channel itself only adds a small amount of information. I will go into greater detail regarding how to use channels for measuring price targets in the next chapter.

That does not mean that channels are of no use. Quite the contrary. Failure for a channel line to hold during an impulse move is often a sign that what you thought was an impulse move is merely a correction. For example, if you draw a line connecting the start of a five-wave move with the bottom of wave 2, prices should not breach that trend line, as occurred in Sears (Figure 2.10). In this case, prices did briefly accelerate above the channel resistance, but quickly dropped below it. Prices then overlapped the top of what would have been wave 1, which also would have invalidated the wave counts. However, one could have held out some hope for an extended third-wave rally (with the drop from the high acting as wave ii within the larger wave 3). Unfortunately, once price fell below the trend line connecting the start of the five-wave rally and the end of wave 2 (the 0–2 trend line), the probability of that likelihood decreased substantially.

Conversely, any price movement past channel-line resistance may very well suggest that prices are accelerating in the direction of the trend and you should look for a price extension. One example of this phenomenon is shown in Figure 2.11. In that chart, cocoa futures rose past channel

**FIGURE 2.10** Sears, daily

**FIGURE 2.11** Cocoa Futures, weekly

resistance, setting the stage for an irregular fourth-wave correction and further spike higher during wave 5.

## ELLIOTT WAVE AND CLASSICAL TECHNICAL ANALYSIS

An Elliott Wave analyst is a technical analyst. Elliotticians combine price, time, volume, and other information drawn from the markets to help them determine the likely direction of future price action. Followers of EWT track market sentiment more closely than most technicians. This is because the definition of all wave patterns is so closely married to crowd (market) behavior. A bull market cannot start if everybody already has positive market expectations. A third-wave explosion cannot begin without the crowd enthusiastically jumping on the bandwagon; that is, it is highly unlikely that prices can ever maintain an explosive surge at a trend reversal point. That does not eliminate a "V" top or bottom, but it clearly legitimizes the classic technical analysis testing phase. A "V" top or bottom could easily occur at the end of an extended fifth wave, for example. It may also take place at the end of a correction of a major trend, such as the 1997 and 1998 event-driven stock market drops and the post-attack low in September 2001 in equities. These represented major but temporary market reversals.

The one reversal behavior I have always found difficult to tie in to a clean Elliott Wave count is the rounded bottom or top (also known as a *saucer* or *cup and handle*). The volume patterns fit with typical Elliott progressions, but the wave patterns are quite sloppy. The sentiment characteristics of a rounded bottom are a good match for a first wave. That does not mean they are incorrect. In fact, at times you can find small five-wave rallies after the bottom has been reached. The eventual explosion higher does fit with Elliott (wave 3 or wave iii of wave 1), and the constant backfilling could be what is called *nesting*. Nesting occurs when a market produces a series of five-wave impulse moves in the direction of the trend, but the waves clearly overlap. This certainly fails to comply with normal Elliott Wave requirements. However, instead of considering the action a failure or part of another correction, the proper count would be a series of 1–2–1–2's. Eventually, a powerful third wave develops, and then a group of finishing 4–5's are traced out to match the 1-2's and thus complete the five-wave swing.

I have discussed most other common technical patterns and how they fit into the world of Elliott: head and shoulders, wedges, and channels in Chapter 2 and triangles in Chapter 1. Also discussed were matching indicator signals with Elliott pattern recognition. Elliott Wave Theory permits you to consistently determine whether a technical pattern under development will complete, and then provides value added by aiding you in computing time and price targets.

## FAILED FIFTH WAVES

A failed fifth wave occurs when the fifth leg in an impulse move does not move past the extreme point of the preceding third wave. In a bullish run, this means that the high of wave 5 does not exceed the high price attained at the end of wave 3. In a falling market, this means that the low price reached in wave 5 is above the low price achieved by the falling third wave.

Some Elliott Wave analysts believe there is no such thing as a failed fifth wave. Although they are extremely rare—I can only think of one or two cases of them in all the years I have been using EWT in my work—they do seem to exist. More often than not, however, the initial belief that a failed fifth wave occurred is incorrect and in the end proves to be part of an irregular fourth-wave correction instead. A stylized example is shown below in Figure 2.12. Some general rules and admonitions are worth noting here to help you recognize possible failed fifths and to avoid mislabeling other price patterns:

1. A fifth wave need not exceed the extreme price level posted during an irregular fourth wave. For example, in a bull market, an irregular fourth would result in a new price high beyond the top of wave 3. Wave 5's peak, though normally expected to exceed the irregular top of wave 4, need only surpass the wave 3 high to properly complete a five-wave impulse move higher.

2. A failed fifth wave should still show a five-wave structure. A three-wave advance followed by a sharp drop with an overlap of the first leg in wave 5 is most likely not a failed fifth (unless the fifth wave is part of a diagonal triangle, but then all the legs of wave 5 should be in three waves and not in five waves).

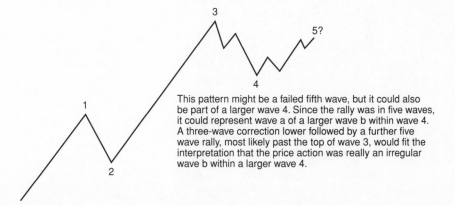

This pattern might be a failed fifth wave, but it could also be part of a larger wave 4. Since the rally was in five waves, it could represent wave a of a larger wave b within wave 4. A three-wave correction lower followed by a further five wave rally, most likely past the top of wave 3, would fit the interpretation that the price action was really an irregular wave b within a larger wave 4.

**FIGURE 2.12**   Failed fifth wave?

3. One would never expect to see a failed fifth wave except at the very end of a move. It should not show up as the fifth wave of wave 1 or the fifth wave of wave 3. A failed fifth is a sign of an end of the trend, and first and third waves are found in the earlier parts of the trend.

4. Watch your day counts. If all of the previous three waves took at least two weeks to complete and your three-wave fourth-wave drop took three days, there is a good chance that you are still in wave 4. Also, if wave 2 was a zigzag, there is a good chance, via the rule of alternation, that wave 4 will be complex and probably irregular. Do not be so quick to call a pattern a failed fifth. Try everything else first.

That does not mean there are no failed fifth waves. However, almost every time I have given in and labeled something as a failed fifth wave, I was eventually sorry. One decent example of what is almost certainly a failed fifth wave can be found in the foreign exchange market. The U.S. dollar had been rallying from early 1995 into late 2000 versus the Swiss franc. A deep correction ensued followed by another rally that did not result in a new high, as shown in Figure 2.13.

Note that I did not place wave 4 at the end of the first down leg from the late-2000 peak. At this point, this might prove to be incorrect. However, placing wave 4 at the initial bottom is probably not a great idea. Here's why:

**FIGURE 2.13**  U.S. Dollar versus Swiss Franc, monthly

1. Wave 4 is very short in time. Wave 2 is very short as well, and by alternation, I would expect a more drawn out fourth-wave correction.

2. Although you cannot see it from this chart, the leg lower was very impulsive and shows a fairly clear five-wave pattern. That means a zigzag was active so one would expect a lower low before wave 4 completed.

My biggest concern is not whether there was a failed fifth—I am absolutely convinced of that. However, the rally off the initial drop looked more like a fifth wave than the rally following the labeled wave-4 low. Final determination of which spot to place wave 5 will require further price developments.

## SUMMARY

In this chapter, we covered many of the more advanced and complex price patterns that develop in the markets. We covered diagonal triangles, channeling, and trend lines as well as X waves and their related patterns, the double three and triple three. We also studied the failed fifth wave, and discussed how to avoid falling into the trap of calling for these relatively rare patterns when there are more common explanations instead. Finally, we showed how classical technical analysis patterns relate to Elliott Wave–based analysis to help the non-Elliott-oriented technicians get a head start in adding Elliott to their technical tool box.

In the next chapter, I will take things up a notch. Understanding the patterns is not enough. We have already discovered the importance of both time and price. Chapter 3 covers in detail how to compute price and time projections and how you can couple that information with classical technical tools and other Elliott Wave analytics already discussed to greatly increase your probability of correctly determining the future direction of prices.

Remember, our aim here is to help you to increase the returns on your investment and/or trading accounts. Although you should never have an ego over a position, there is no rationale for taking a position unless you expect it to end up profitable. With the methods presented in this book, you will be able to better estimate the future direction of prices in your liquid investments, and also learn how to recognize when your analysis is either wrong or at least needs revision.

There is no Holy Grail, and you must continuously update your expectations based on the information the market provides you. However, with these tools, along with the trade plans I will unveil in Chapters 5 and 6, you will have the tools to increase your investment and trading profits.

# CHAPTER 3

# Tsunami or Wavelet— Measurement Techniques

I am sure you have been anxiously waiting for me to get to the Fibonacci series. No Elliott Wave analyst worth his or her weight in salt can possibly do the job without a thorough understanding of the Fibonacci number sequence and how to apply it to the Elliott Wave Theory. I will dispense with the historical oratory regarding the mathematician, Leonardo of Pisa (a.k.a. Fibonacci). Suffice it to say that Fibonacci, born in the city of Pisa around 1175 A.D., was considered by many to be the greatest mathematician of the Middle Ages. In addition to introducing the "/" for describing fractions, in his great book *Liber Abacci* (the book of calculation) he posed the following problem:

*A certain man put a pair of rabbits in a place surrounded by a wall. How many pairs of rabbits can be produced from the pair in a year if it is supposed that every month each pair begets a new pair which from the second month on becomes productive?*[1]

The French mathematician Edouard Lucas named the number series that gives the answer to the above problem *the Fibonacci sequence*. The sequence is defined such that the current number is the sum of the previous two numbers in the sequence $f_n = f_{n-1} + f_{n-2}$ and where $f_1 = 1$ and $f_0 = 0$.

R.N. Elliott took Fibonacci's number sequence and applied it to the financial markets. His research, coupled with older work discussing the *golden ratio*, led him to determine that there was a natural order in the markets and that this natural order was defined by the Fibonacci number sequence.

## THE GOLDEN RATIO

The golden ratio is the resultant ratio of a number in the Fibonacci sequence when it is divided by the prior number in the series. As the sequence approaches infinity, the ratio approaches 1.618034 . . . (it is an irrational number). The term *phi* ($\phi$) is the portion of the number following the decimal place, and is also the inverse of the golden ratio. $\phi$ has many fascinating properties, including the following mathematical oddity: $1 - \phi = \phi^2$.

The golden ratio has been found throughout nature as well as in the layouts of ancient Egyptian temples, which, of course, predated Fibonacci by thousands of years. While this certainly lends credence to some of Elliott's rather grandiose assumptions regarding a natural order to the stock markets, I personally have attempted to refrain from making the study and application of EWT into a religion or cult, but have chosen a more practical course, and use EWT simply as the superior analytical tool that it is. However, one must certainly give credit to Elliott and to his use of the Fibonacci sequence, which so clearly has a large effect on crowd behavior and thus the development of price patterns themselves.

In the following sections I show you how to apply Fibonacci numbers and ratios to determine price and time projections as well as likely support and resistance levels. The Fibonacci number sequence is used throughout EWT. Starting with the mere fact that many wave cycles are composed of a Fibonacci number of waves or legs, on to price projections, ratios, retracements, and day counts, you will see that the Elliottician cannot possibly achieve competency without understanding the applications of Fibonacci numbers. Consider a large five wave pattern. We typically have 34 waves in each move: Waves 1, 3, and 5 are composed of 5 subwaves each, and the corrections would be three waves each, totaling 34. Of course, flats and irregulars do not total to a Fibonacci number ($3 + 3 + 5 = 11$), but zigzags ($5 + 3 + 5 = 13$) do.

## RETRACEMENTS

The Elliott Wave analyst or trader often looks to Fibonacci-based ratios for key retracement levels. Markets often will find support or resistance at these prices. The most common ratios are the 38.2 percent and 61.8 percent levels. Recall that 61.8 percent, or 0.618, is commonly known as the golden ratio, or $\phi$. It represents the number, as $n$ approaches infinity, of the ratio of the $n$th number divided by the $(n + 1)^{st}$ number in the Fibonacci sequence. The 38.2 percent level (which is $1 - 0.618$ and $0.618^2$), is the result of the $n$th number in the sequence divided by the $(n + 2)^{nd}$. Many observers have found that prices will often retrace 50 percent of a move. Although that is not a Fibonacci ratio, it is the ratio of the second and third numbers in the sequence: 1 and 2. Other levels occasionally sought by prices include the 23.6 percent retracement level ($n/n+3$) and 76.4 percent, which is 1 minus that level. Note that 76.4 percent is not a Fibonacci ratio on its own. Some

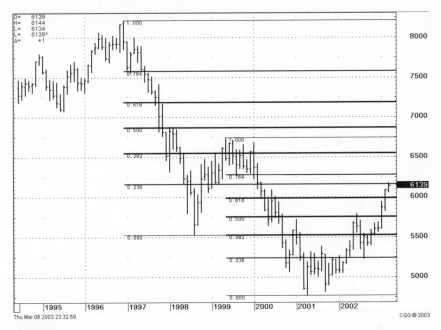

**FIGURE 3.1** AUDUSD, monthly

analysts have noted a tendency for the markets to approach a retracement level of 78.6 percent. This is the square root of $\phi$ (0.618). I usually stick to 76.4 percent, and in general, except from a very long-term perspective, there is usually little difference between the two levels anyway.

Figure 3.1 shows the monthly chart for AUDUSD (the Australian dollar versus the U.S. dollar) starting with late 1994 and continuing to the middle of 2002. Notice how the 38.2 percent retracement level of the late 1996 to mid-1998 fall initially rebuffed the Australian currency's recovery? Although the retracement level did not prove to be a final top in the AUD's bear market correction, it did offer initial resistance. On the other hand, the rally off the 2001 low halted very close to the 50.0 percent retracement. I will cover trading tactics around support and resistance levels in this chapter and throughout the book when we discuss trading plans.

A word of warning with regard to retracement levels: Just as you can keep drawing trend lines and find an infinite number of moving averages to show how a methodology works in finding reversal prices, cycle times, or horizontal support and resistance levels, you can also compute a never-ending list of retracement ratios. Look at Figure 3.2, which shows a daily chart of Newmont Mining from the first half of 2002. Almost every retracement line shown on the chart was touched, or nearly touched. But if you consider that the whole price range shown was just over 14 points and that

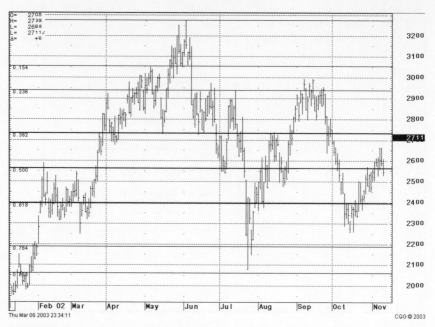

**FIGURE 3.2**   Newmont Mining, daily

there was a retracement line every 2 points, you can see that the probability of a brief turn *not* being near a retracement level is prohibitively low.

I only use 23.6 percent, 38.2 percent, 50.0 percent, 61.8 percent, and 76.4 percent, mostly focusing on the middle three. I have seen analysts use other levels, but if you have a retracement every 5 percent or 10 percent by definition, prices will reverse at or very near one of those levels. Unless you are trading every tick, the proper method is to study how prices react at or near key computed price levels (as well as at channels, trend lines, and previous low or high prices) to help you determine whether your preferred wave count should still be favored. Computation of a retracement level is very easy:

1. Find where a wave began (B) and ended (E). Note that this is not always the high or low prices in the sequence.

2. Compute the absolute value of the difference between the two: $D = |B - E|$.

3. Multiply that by the retracement percentage you wish to use: $N = \text{ratio} \times D$

4. Add N to B if you are computing a retracement of a down move, or subtract N from E if you are computing a retracement of an up move.

Here is an example: Compute the 23.6 percent, 38.2 percent, 50.0 percent, 61.8 percent, and 76.4 percent retracements of the drop in the FTSE-

100 (the *Financial Times* index of London Stock Exchange issues) from 5,411.2 in December 2001 to its July 2002 low of 3,625.9 (see Figure 3.3).

1. $|B - E| = |5,411.2 - 3,625.9| = 1,785.3$
2. 23.6% retrace change $= 0.236 \times 1,785.3 = 421.3$
3. 38.2% retrace change $= 0.382 \times 1,785.3 = 682.0.$
4. 50.0% retrace change $= 0.500 \times 1,785.3 = 892.7$
5. 61.8% retrace change $= 0.618 \times 1,785.3 = 1,103.3$
6. 76.4% retrace change $= 0.764 \times 1,785.3 = 1,364.0$
7. 23.6% retrace level $= 3,625.9 + 421.3 = 4,047.2$
8. 38.2% retrace level $= 3,625.9 + 682.0 = 4,307.9$
9. 50.0% retrace level $= 3,625.9 + 892.7 = 4,518.6$
10. 61.8% retrace level $= 3,625.9 + 1,103.3 = 4,729.2$
11. 76.4% retrace level $= 3,625.9 + 1,364.0 = 4,989.9$

Note that you do not need to compute the 61.8 percent and 76.4 percent retrace changes as shown in steps 5 and 6. Instead, you could just take the 38.2 percent and 23.6 percent amounts determined in steps 3 and 2 and subtract those amounts from the starting price instead to achieve the same results.

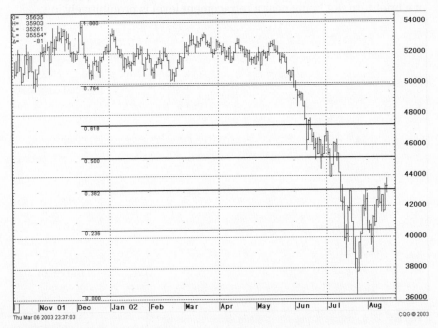

**FIGURE 3.3**  FTSE-100, daily

## Fibonacci Retracements Work Best When You Least Expect It

How well do these retracements work? The 38.2 percent retracement worked quite well for the FTSE-100 in the above example. Often I have found that Fibonacci retracements work best during periods of high volatility. When price gyrations are substantial, there is often little for traders to hang their hats on. Trend lines are either too steep to be meaningful, or very far away. Also, moving averages typically will trail price action by too substantial an amount to be useful. However, retracement levels may attract more attention. Stops will often sit at or near these price marks.

This observation is not intuitively obvious. One would expect key price levels to fall more easily during periods of high emotion. Why should prices stop on a dime during such times? However, as I noted above, there is often little else to go on outside of these levels, and the markets seem to succumb to Fibonacci retracements and projections to a greater degree during such periods. In fact, support and resistance levels in general, be they moving averages, channel and trend lines, or past highs and lows, seem to act as better barriers during periods of increased volatility. Look at the chart of the Hong Kong Hang Seng Index (Figure 3.4). Notice how the market turned almost exactly at the 62 percent retracement back to zero as global

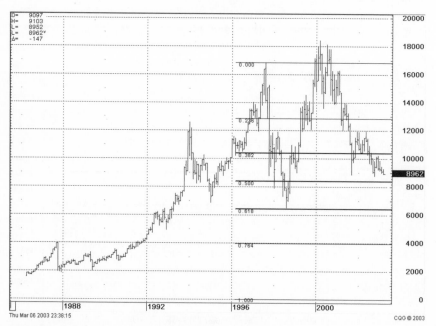

**FIGURE 3.4**   Hong Kong Hang Seng Index, monthly

equity markets tumbled in response to the Russian debt crisis and the Long Term Capital Management debacle in the summer of 1998.

The advantage that Fibonacci levels have, when compared to a simple trend line or moving average, is that these levels have a reason to hold. That is, based on the current wave and its characteristics, you might have a good reason to expect that price point to act as a potential reversal point in a trend. A trend line might break, and so might a moving average. You can determine, with some degree of accuracy, the probability of a Fibonacci-based retracement halting a trend. Unless the trend line or moving average is very near a key level based on the Elliott Wave picture, you would have very little reason to believe that the trend line or moving average level will hold under attack during a period of high volatility.

I am not saying that Fibonacci retracement levels will automatically hold, nor am I suggesting that trend lines have little or no value. Certain levels tend to act as support or resistance within wave cycles. This assumes that you have the proper wave count. Also, beware that any price target, be it a retracement level or a projection, which we will cover later in this chapter, will have a higher probability of holding if there is more than one reason for that price to hold. By this I mean that if there is a retracement from two different degree waves (62 percent of a minor subwave and 38 percent of the next larger-degree wave), you should feel more comfortable that level might hold. However, you might find that a wave c equals wave a projection coupled with a retracement would also be a better bet to hold than just a simple retracement. Other ideal places to look for confirmation of the importance of a price level might be the congruence of old price highs or lows, an Elliott Wave channel or price line projection, or even a moving average coupled with a retracement level.

One place where many novices make errors is in determining the beginning (B) and end (E) points from which you compute your retracements. Notice that I used the words "begin" and "end," rather than "high" and "low." This is because you will not necessarily be using local high and low prices when computing the retracement levels. You must use the beginning and end points of the waves you are retracing, which might not necessarily be the local high and low points.

Consider the drawing shown in Figure 3.5. As you can see, wave 4 was an irregular. That is, the high of wave 4 exceeded the best price achieved in wave 3. Clearly, as wave 3 terminated, you would look to compute third-wave retracements from the start and end points of wave 3, which in Figure 3.5 are labeled as points 2 and 3, respectively. However, once a new high is made, those who do not use EWT, or those who do not apply the rules correctly, might decide to compute their retracements between point 2 and point b. Some also might decide that a full five-wave advance completed at wave b and look for retracements between point 0 and point b. The correct

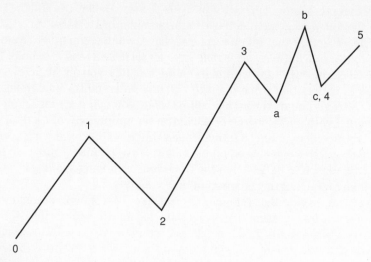

**FIGURE 3.5**   Use point 0 and point 5 for retrace.

points to use for determining retracement levels of the whole five-wave pattern would be bounded by point 0 and point 5.

You can avoid incorrectly using wave b by recalling that wave b is neither part of impulse wave 3 nor of impulse wave 5. There is no reason to use wave b as a place for price retracements of either of those waves. Although it might be tempting to use wave b as the end of the five-wave advance, remember that wave b is nonimpulsive, so it cannot be five waves. Wave 5, even if it is a failed fifth (does not exceed the top of wave 3), or a diagonal, still traverses five waves. Wave b is always a three-wave move, unless it is a corrective triangle (not a diagonal), which would complete in five three-wave cycles.

An additional point of order is worth noting here with regard to Figure 3.5. As I drew the chart, the peak of wave 5 is below the peak of wave b. Although the likelihood of such an occurrence is relatively low,[2] this pattern is not an example of a failed fifth wave. The only requirement for wave 5, to avoid calling it a failed fifth wave, is that the top of wave 5 surpass the top of wave 3. Of course in a downtrend, the criteria are reversed: Wave 5's low should be beneath wave 3's nadir even if it does not fall below the bottom print of wave b of an irregular wave 4.

## Typical Retracement Targets in the Waves

Now that you know how to compute your retracement levels, some guidance regarding what to expect when a wave cycle completes would be useful.

In Chapter 1, I spent a lot of time discussing wave character. Wave character is quite important in determining what to expect in the way of price retracements as well.

We discussed many of these factors in Chapter 1, but with the additional grounding you now have from a more detailed understanding of Fibonacci ratios, coupled with our coverage of complex patterns and advanced concepts in Chapter 2, you should be far better prepared to both absorb and apply proper retracement targeting at this juncture. The following situations will be considered in greater detail:

1. Wave 2, which retraces wave 1
2. Wave b, which retraces wave a
3. Wave 4 which retraces wave 3
4. Retracement by flats and irregulars as compared to retracements by zigzags
5. Retracements within legs of a triangle (corrective or diagonal)

## Wave 2 Retracements

It is rare that a second wave occurs at a point when the market under consideration believes that the currently active trend is properly characterized as being in the direction of the just completed first wave. Remember from Dow Theory that the early parts of a bull market or a bear market are precipitated by early adopters. I hesitate to use the term *smart money* as these same people may not be smart enough to exit on time when the trend finally reverses. That means that when wave 1 runs out of fuel, the second wave drop is often deep and powerful. Most analysts, along with the investing public, will gleefully remind you how smart they are by adhering to the market trend prior to wave 1. This is especially true of long, drawn-out bear markets. The typical bottom in such a bear market would result in multiple rallies and failures before a strong enough base exists from which to catapult the market higher and into wave 3. This means that wave 2 rarely retraces less than 38.2 percent of wave 1 and often achieves 61.8 percent. The one exception to this tendency is that the second subwave of wave 3 is often very shallow.

I have seen many examples of deeper retracements. Do not forget, however, that wave 2 can never retrace more than 100 percent of wave 1. That is, the end point of wave 2 should never move past the beginning point of wave 1. If what you thought was wave 2 traverses beyond the start of wave 1, wave 1 was most likely part of a correction of the previous trend rather than the beginning of a new trend in the opposite direction.

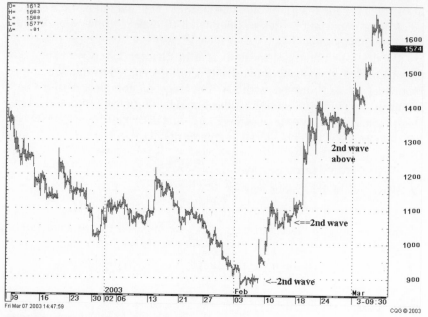

**FIGURE 3.6**   Imclone's second waves

There are no hard-and-fast rules for second waves. Although they are often fast and furious, it really depends on where prices are in the overall wave cycle. Remember that in a zigzag correction, each leg is a five-wave impulse move. That means there is a second wave in each five-wave impulse move within a corrective zigzag. Additionally, if a wave b within an impulse subdivides, there will always be a wave 2 within subwave c of wave b. Remember, all C waves are always impulse moves. A second wave that is part of a corrective wave is not likely to be as powerful as a wave 2 that is correcting the initial wave of a major reversal.

Consider Figure 3.6. I have indicated various second waves throughout the rally during January and February of 2003 for Imclone's 60-minute chart. As you can see, very few of these second waves can be considered anything more than consolidations or slow corrections. Few are particularly fast, and many only show minor retracements of the short-term trends.

## B Wave Retracements

Wave b, the second leg in an a–b–c correction of an impulse wave, is without a doubt the most difficult of the Elliott Wave patterns to forecast *a priori*. In a zigzag, wave b typically corrects 38 percent to 62 percent of wave a. In a flat, wave b corrects all or most of wave a, and, in an irregular, wave b's terminus is actually beyond wave a's starting point. Wave b itself can play out as a zigzag, flat, or triangle. The triangle is the most confusing since it is composed of five three-wave legs instead of the normal three-wave pattern.

All is not lost in attempting to determine how far wave b should retrace. First of all, you already know what wave-a was: Three waves means either a new impulse wave is due (i.e., wave b already took place during the just completed three-wave pattern) or we are in for a triangle, flat, or irregular. If wave a was five waves, then the a–b–c correction in progress is a zigzag. Here are the possibilities if wave a was three waves:

- Wave b must be three waves or a triangle.

–and–

- The whole correction will be a triangle. Then, wave b will probably retrace about 62 percent of wave a.

–or–

- The whole correction will be a flat, meaning that wave b will retrace all or most of wave a.

–or–

- The whole correction will be an irregular, meaning that wave b will retrace more than 100 percent of wave a.

–or–

- The correction is actually over and the three legs completed should have been labeled as a–b–c complete.

Proper wave labeling is all about recognizing wave characteristics and probabilities. For example, if wave a was just three waves, but achieved a deep retracement of the prior impulse wave, then probabilities favor a resumption of the prior trend. However, if wave a was also very fast, even if the retrace was deep, the odds would favor a period of range trading. This would imply a triangle, flat, or irregular, and possibly even a more complex correction, such as a double three.

Knowing that a triangle or flat is likely to develop gives you an advantage. You should feel very safe taking tactical range-trading positions, such as using oscillators to enter and exit your trades. You can use options to collect premiums while the market remains range-bound.

Of course, if there are only three waves completed, wave a might not even be done. Again, if the retracement is already quite deep, you can feel safe in favoring a completed wave a, or even a fully complete correction. If the correction has been shallow, however, you should probably look for a fourth and fifth wave to complete a five-wave wave a, as part of a still unfolding zigzag.

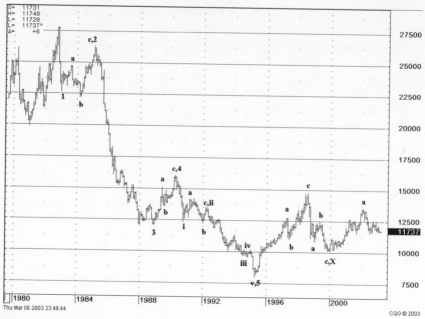

**FIGURE 3.7**   USDJPY, monthly

Figure 3.7 shows several wave b examples. Note that this is a monthly chart, so a great deal of detail is lost. However, you can see some irregular b waves as well as some b waves that lasted for several months. Some were fast and some stretched over substantial periods of time. The current wave count is actually quite interesting. I labeled the fall into 2000 as an X wave. It might also have been wave B in a larger A–B–C off the 1995 lows. I chose the X wave idea for several reasons: (1) The high in 1998 was a very small retracement of the drop from the 1980s and I would expect a higher peak correcting that drop; (2) the 1998 peak was done in three waves, and a flat correction would be unlikely to significantly exceed the 1998 high; (3) wave c of wave X was short, but the overall retracement was deeper than 62 percent, but not deep enough to expect a flat; and (4) the rally from the lows at JPY101.27 was in five waves, but did not exceed the 1998 peak. That most likely means we are due for at least one more five-wave rally once a new low is attained later in 2002 or early 2003.

## Wave 4 Retracements

In a lot of ways, wave 4 depends on wave 2. Most generalized Elliott Wave discussions imply that fourth waves tend to be shallow and stretched out. Although second-wave corrections often are said to reach 62 percent retracement levels, fourth waves often are described as retracing 38 percent. Generalities, unfortunately, can be dangerous to your health. I have seen fourth waves that retraced less than 23.6 percent of wave 3, and I've seen others cover more than 62 percent of wave 3.

## THE TENDENCY OF ALTERNATION

You may recall the "rule" of alternation, which I call the "tendency" of alternation. It states that wave 2 and wave 4 will not look similar. Some analysts take this to mean that if wave 2 is regular, wave 4 will likely be an irregular. My experience has shown this to be an incorrect application of this so-called rule. First of all, as implied by my revision to the word "tendency," rather than the word "rule," there is no hard-and-fast requirement that wave 2 and wave 4 look different at all. The only true rules in Elliott Wave are that wave 1 and wave 4 cannot overlap except in a diagonal triangle, that wave 2 can never retrace more than 100 percent of wave 1, and that wave 3 can never be the shortest wave in a five-leg impulse move. That said, the likelihood that wave 4 will stretch out for a long period of time in a very tight trading range, for example, is much higher (tends to be greater) when the wave 2 correction is fast and deep than when it is long and meandering.

The most important point to understand regarding the tendency of alternation is that wave 2 and wave 4 usually will not look alike. A fast and deep zigzag in wave 2 will not typically be followed by another fast and deep zigzag in wave 4. A flat or irregular would probably be expected in wave 4, and the time frame likely will be longer for wave 4 than for wave 2 in this example. The alternation idea is not limited to time frames or fast versus slow and zigzag versus flat or irregular. Other properties might also alternate. For example, one wave might be a simple zigzag or flat, whereas the other could be a triangle or a compound correction such as a double three or a triple three. Also, beware that there are many different factors that can alternate. It is not necessary, and is unlikely, that all will alternate. For example, the alternation might simply be zigzag versus flat, even though the amount of time spent correcting could be exactly the same, or you might get two zigzags, but with substantially different retracement amounts in wave b and with dissimilar time frames to complete.

Given the above information, why does the idea persist that fourth waves retrace less ground and take more time than second waves? The answer is actually quite simple. Take a look back at the discussion of second waves. Second waves tend to retrace a large portion of wave 1. They are often fast and furious. The tendency of alternation thus would imply that wave 4 will retrace less ground than wave 2 and will also take more time to do it. Consider for a moment what is happening during wave 2 as opposed to wave 4. During wave 2, the crowd still believes the prior trend is still active, so prices reverse wave 1 very easily. During wave 4, most market participants are aware of the current trend. They are hoping for a deep correction to allow them to get into the move at better levels. They are greedy for further gains as well. This can lead to a period of range trading and sloppy trading patterns before the active trend reasserts itself.

After years of working with Elliott, I can honestly say that I have not seen very many fourth waves that retraced 38 percent of the prior third wave, even though this is exactly what many analysts suggest is the norm. Fourth waves cover a multitude of different forms, and are not easily categorized. They are very much like B waves in this respect. I have even seen fourth-wave consolidations take periods exceeding the amount of time that the first three waves of a move took to complete. Look at the two fourth waves shown in Figure 3.8. The first one takes almost as long to complete as the first three waves combined. The second fourth wave shown looks much like what I normally would describe as the kind of action typical of a second wave. I have always felt that there is a need to balance both time and price. It would be highly unlikely to see a very shallow and very short-term fourth wave. This also applies to second-wave corrections and impulse moves—a market is not likely to author a move that is shorter than

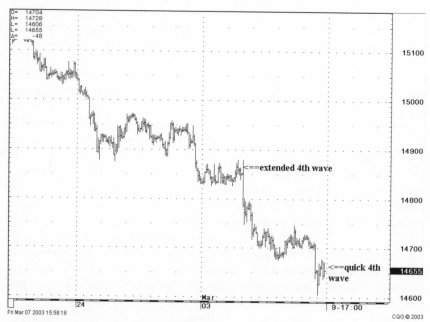

**FIGURE 3.8**   USDCAD, 80-minute bars

the norm in both size and time. Some semblance of balance between these two factors is required.

Fourth waves can produce any corrective pattern permissible by EWT. For this reason, generalized retracement tendencies and time frames are poor predictors of fourth-wave behavior. I always have suggested to my clients that if a wave count is unclear, then the market is in a correction. This goes double for fourth waves, which are often complex, even though the price action traversed is normally less than any of the other five legs of a five-wave progression. You will need to develop additional tools to accurately determine price targets for fourth waves. We will cover the necessary subject matter later in this chapter when price projections are explained.

## FLATS VERSUS ZIGZAGS

The two basic types of corrections that everybody is familiar with from all the stylized depictions of Elliott Wave patterns are flats and zigzags. Zigzags are the easiest to recognize, covering three legs with the first and third legs moving in the opposite direction of the main trend. They are impulse moves; that is, wave a and wave c of a larger zigzag are each five-wave actions that trend in the opposite direction of the larger trend that they are correcting. Wave b is either a triangle, a complex correction, or a three-leg pattern that moves with the larger current trend and opposite the direction of the correction. Zigzag corrections often move quickly and will retrace a large portion of the wave that they are correcting. For this reason, they are most commonly depicted as correcting second waves, but they can show up anywhere a corrective pattern can (including b waves). If a zigzag appears in a second-wave position but only retraces a small portion of wave 1, and also takes a very short time to complete, the probability would favor the zigzag either being the first leg of a larger complex correction such as a double three, or wave a of a triangle. It could also be part of a larger flat, as discussed below.

As I noted in Chapter 1, flat is a poor name choice. Flats represent a class of corrections in which the first two legs of the correction traverse three waves, while the third leg, the c wave, traces out a five-wave impulse pattern. The hardest part about identifying flats versus zigzags and other corrective wave cycles is that the first leg of a flat could represent a completed correction on its own, because it traverses three waves. Remember, wave a of an a–b–c flat is a three-wave affair, which could be a zigzag or a flat as well. The only way to determine whether this first three-wave move is a completed correction or the first part of something larger is to review and understand the probabilities you are faced with given the current larger patterns and behaviors within the market you are analyzing or trading.

You must use all of your skills derived so far to help you determine the likely pattern outcomes. For example, if the three-wave move was quick but only covered about 23 percent of a just-completed major first wave, I would assume that the move was going to develop into a larger and more complex correction, such as a double three. If the third leg was fairly large, I would closely track any corrective forces against the recent three-wave move. Do not eliminate the chance that the apparently completed three-wave move might become a clear five-wave cycle, meaning that it is the first leg in a larger zigzag correction.

If the three-wave move is too fast but provides for a reasonable retracement amount (about 50 percent in the case of a second wave, and probably less for a fourth wave, unless wave 2 was very shallow), I would assume that the completed three-wave move was the first leg of a triangle or a flat. Although it also could develop into a double three or triple three, this would be less likely if the completed three-wave action already had corrected enough in terms of price, but had not really offered enough time in consolidating.

I often suggest to my readers that they should not get caught up in the most minute patterns. Although Internet chat rooms are rife with people who try and analyze every single tick, more often than not you will not be able to see the big picture if you attempt to count every tick. Since you have to pay commissions and the bid-ask spread for almost every trade, spending precious time trying to analyze tiny intraday patterns does not offer enough reward for the efforts taken. The better way to look at such action is to find a time and price horizon where a correction is likely to target. You can start with typical retracements—38 percent for fourth waves and 50 percent or 62 percent for second waves—and use timing based on how long earlier waves took to complete. This will allow you to more easily see if your forecasts are panning out and whether or not you need to adjust your expectations.

I cannot overemphasize the importance of constantly asking yourself whether your assumptions regarding future price direction are valid *every step of the way*. Remember, the market does not care what you think. The market is a constantly changing and never-ending vortex of varying and opposing opinions. Consider that whoever stands on the other side of your trade thinks you are wrong at that exact moment in time, and that person also might be an Elliott Wave analyst. You can never build an ego around a position or forecast. If you do, you will ignore the signs of a change in market psyche that could permit you to profitably alter your expectations. Hoping that something happens, to help a clearly incorrect idea or losing trade, is not a step on the path to riches.

One of the great traps that I have seen many traders fall into is hoping that the market will get you out of a hole. Elliott Wave–based traders are particularly susceptible to this. Consider the fact that every five-wave move requires a retracement. Take the case of a three-wave rally. Your research might tell you that a new five-wave cycle lower is about to begin so you short the market late in that three-wave move. If you are open to new information and you see prices move lower in your favor, but on extremely low volume, you might update your thinking to suspect that the current move lower is merely a fourth wave in a larger five-wave cycle. This could permit you to exit the trade with a small profit even though your projection was patently incorrect.

The price reversal higher suggested in the previous paragraph might occur very quickly, which would not permit you to act fast enough to exit your short trade unless you placed a stop-loss order when you entered the position. However, if you are open to being wrong, you would probably cover your short as soon as a new short-term high price is achieved. Failing to do this would likely lead you to sit back and hope that after the fifth wave completes, the correction of that move will be deep enough to make you whole again. Unfortunately, there is no guarantee that the correction will get you anyplace near where you entered the market. Only unlimited funds and time could guarantee that you could ultimately make money on the trade if your expectation for an eventual turn lower is correct. The three panels of Figure 3.9 depict this situation.

One of the worst things that can happen to you, psychologically speaking, in such a situation is that the market saves you. Prices fall back below where you initially entered the trade and you successfully exit the position with a profit. This might embolden you to ignore things like stops because the market always comes back. Unfortunately, it does not always come back, and you still had a cost in lost opportunity. There was money to be made as prices moved above where you sold your stake, and even more money on the short side once the market reversed to move in the direction of your original forecast. Getting "saved" by the market could lead you to develop some very bad and expensive habits.

This is just one example of why you must understand the characteristics of every wave. Although it was reasonable to believe that the initial three-wave rally shown in Figure 3.9 was enough of a correction, the lack of downside momentum following those three waves should have been a clear warning that higher prices were due. The savvy trader who was open to the information the market was giving him or her could have reversed the short trade, possibly with a small profit, and accrued further gains as prices broke out to complete a five-wave rally off the lows. Applying your knowledge of how far and how long it should take for a corrective period to progress will help increase your profitability and decrease the odds of missing the clues the market offers you. It will also make it easier for you to avoid being fooled by short periods of noise that could otherwise take you out of your trading plan.

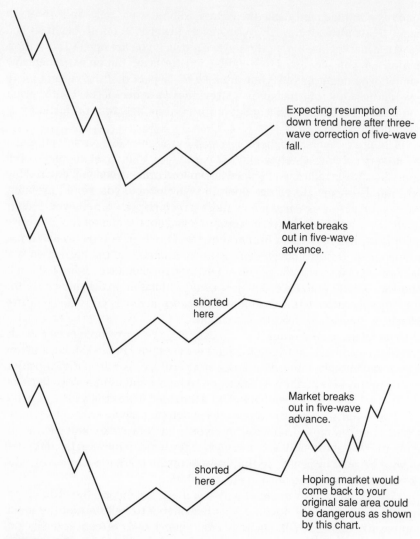

Expecting resumption of down trend here after three-wave correction of five-wave fall.

Market breaks out in five-wave advance.

shorted here

Market breaks out in five-wave advance.

shorted here

Hoping market would come back to your original sale area could be dangerous as shown by this chart.

**FIGURE 3.9**   Hoping for a retracement may not be a good idea.

## TRIANGLES

Classically based technical analysts should have no problem identifying triangles. They are the cornerstone of the consolidation and correction chapter of almost any introductory text on the subject. However, triangles in Elliott Wave Theory are a bit different:

1. An ascending triangle is not always bullish.
2. A descending triangle is not always bearish.
3. Triangles are always comprised of five legs.
4. Each leg of a triangle must be constructed of three subwaves.
5. The final leg in a triangle may overshoot or undershoot.
6. With the exception of diagonal triangles (which are wedges in classical technical analysis terms), all triangles are corrective; that is, the overall price action is opposite the current trend.

The guidelines discussed elsewhere in recognizing whether corrections are completed will aid you in determining whether a triangle is a possible outcome during a corrective or consolidative period. A three-wave move that takes a matter of days is unlikely to represent the end of a correction of a trend that had persisted for two months. However, if the correction had retraced a substantial portion of the previous impulse wave, the most likely outcomes would be, in this order: (1) flat or irregular correction, (2) triangle correction, (3) complex correction, or (4) resumption of trend. Given the timing assumed above, resumption of trend is unlikely. The complex correction idea, although possible, is not preferred since we already noted that the correction to date is already sufficient in price terms and a complex correction would likely lead to prices extending their correction. That leaves the first two choices as possibilities. Since a triangle takes longer to complete (five three-wave legs versus $3 + 3 + 5 = 11$ legs), if the first three-leg move was very fast, the probability of a triangle would be higher.

If you quickly identify a triangle under development in a short-term time frame, you may be able to take advantage of options strategies. In all likelihood, volatility will fall during the period, so sales of calls above the upper boundary of the range and sales of puts against the lower boundary of the range should be profitable. Expectations of a triangle once the first leg is complete could even allow you to sell options against the second three-wave leg at a level above the previous leg's low (if the triangle is correcting a downtrend, with the opposite being true if the triangle is correcting an uptrend).

The USDJPY exchange rate exhibited an excellent-looking triangle during the summer of 2002. As shown in Figure 3.10, the dollar completed a five-leg cycle lower at the end of June. That move began in early May and took 53 trading days to complete (two days short of 55, a Fibonacci number). The initial rally off the lows completed in 18 days. This could have represented the whole correction off the lows. Admittedly, the wave count labeled as wave a appears to have been a five-leg affair at first glance. However, the intraday counts showed too much noise for that to have been correct. With that in mind, I feel comfortable in using a three-leg count for

**FIGURE 3.10**   USDJPY, daily

wave a. The retracement of wave a was very deep. This would have further confirmed the idea that we should not be expecting a zigzag correction and certainly not a reversal to start a new USDJPY rally. The speed of the fall and the subsequent retracement clearly suggested that a more drawn-out—in time—consolidation was under way. The outcome was a 35-day triangle, which is, of course, one more than a 34-day Fibonacci count. This includes the U.S. Labor Day holiday, without which the time would have been 34 days (to be fair, if we removed holidays in wave 3, the day count moves to a less perfect 51 from 53).

Classical technical analysis would suggest that the fall after breaking below the triangle support should equal the height of the triangle. Elliott tells us it should be in a Fibonacci ratio in relation to wave 1 down. As a reminder, percentage retracements are preferred rather than actual point amounts.

Note that each retracement in the triangle was at least 61.8 percent of the prior leg and in several cases met or exceeded 76.4 percent. Consider how a triangle forms and you realize that a 61.8 percent retracement is essentially a minimum requirement for development of a triangle. More than 78.6 percent likely means a flat or irregular is in process.

The outcome of any pattern can never be 100 percent known *a priori*. The triangle discussed above, which looks virtually perfect, did not break lower. Although the dollar did initially fall upon running into resistance at the triangle's resistance line, the currency turned higher, pushing toward JPY120 within two days. Were there any hints that the triangle would fail? No pattern is perfect. The first leg higher did appear to be five legs, although I gave arguments for a three-wave count earlier. That first leg also ran for half the time it took for the whole pattern to develop. As you will learn in the following chapters, any trading decisions you make must always be updated as price patterns evolve. The inability of prices to continue lower meant that the dollar had an opportunity to break higher and target at least the low JPY120's in a zigzag correction higher. Anytime you take a position, you must have a plan:

1. What do you do if prices move the way you forecast?
2. What actions should you take if prices move in the right direction, but not in a pattern that agrees with your forecast?
3. Where are your stops? What are your targets?
4. Should you wait for your stops to get hit?
5. Should you reverse your trade if you realize you are wrong?

In the next chapter, all of these questions and more are covered in developing Elliott Wave–based trading and investing plans.

Before we move on to the trading plans, we need to cover one final type of retracement, diagonal triangles. We will also go into substantial detail on how to determine price and time projections in this chapter.

Diagonal triangles can be extremely difficult to identify unless you have a strong grasp of how the markets work, along with the timing and day count elements of EWT. Remember, unlike other triangles, a diagonal triangle is considered an impulse move—the price action develops in five waves, with the larger trend. In an uptrend, prices will develop with higher highs and higher lows. In a downtrend, prices will develop with lower highs and lower lows.

The difference between a diagonal triangle and a normal impulse move is that each wave in the diagonal is comprised of three legs apiece instead of the normal five legs. A normal impulse move progresses in a channel, or the channel might even expand. Support and resistance lines defining a diagonal eventually meet. A diagonal triangle is the one and only pattern where the extrema of wave 1 and wave 4 may overlap.

Diagonal triangles usually appear in wave 5 and may occasionally appear as wave C. That they appear at the end of a five-wave move is why some Elliotticians have named diagonal triangles *terminal triangles*. Note also that diagonals are essentially wedges using classical technical analysis terminology. They are a sign of overall weakness of the underlying trend. The minimum retracement target is to the start of the diagonal itself.

Diagonals typically do not result in failed fifth waves, even though they are a sign of weakness. As I've stated elsewhere in this book, I consider failed fifth waves to be relatively rare occurrences.

Diagonals are difficult to pick up early in their development because when the initial three-leg move with the trend takes place, the most likely forecast is for a complex correction developing rather than the resumption of the current trend. The only time an analyst might look for a diagonal would be after a very long and drawn-out fourth wave, since at that point it would be hard to fathom a further continuation of the consolidation.

It is very easy to visualize diagonals around every bend in market prices. Early in any five-wave sequence, there is likely to be a point at which prices retrace in a subwave that might give the appearance of a diagonal forming. However, I advise you to closely track the wave counts and you will often find that the first-wave cycle prior to the suspected substandard price action developed in five waves. Individual legs in a diagonal are always in three waves, which would eliminate the diagonal triangle as a possible wave count. The other likely outcome is that the period of non-impulsive price action may be part of an extended second-wave correction rather than part of a diagonal triangle.

## PRICE PROJECTIONS AND TARGETS

Elliott Wave Theory offers many tools besides retracements to help determine where a given wave sequence might terminate. Wave cycles typically relate to prior wave cycles via Fibonacci ratios. For example, wave 3 in an impulsive five-wave pattern usually at least exceeds the size of wave 1 by a ratio of 1.618:1.000. It may even reach 2.618 (1.618 × 1.618) or 4.236 (2.618 × 1.618) times the size of wave 1. Wave 5 often provides surprising symmetry to wave 1, approximating the same size as the first leg of a five-wave impulse move. Some other common relationships include:

- Wave 5, extending wave 1, reaches 1.618 times the size of wave 1.
- A weak wave 5 might only attain 61.8 percent of wave 1.
- If wave 1 and wave 3 are close in size, wave 5 will likely reach 1.618 or more times wave 1 (but wave 3 can never be the shortest wave).
- Wave C is often very close to wave A in size and usually does not exceed 1.618 times wave A during a zigzag.
- Weaker corrections may see wave C only reach 61.8 percent of wave A.
- In flats, wave C rarely exceeds a 1.000 ratio to wave A.
- The distance traveled by wave 5 usually reaches between 61.8 percent and 100.0 percent of the total price gain or loss covered by wave 1 through wave 3. A move greater than 100 percent likely means that the

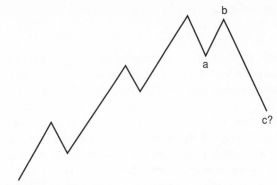

Unlikely that the second leg lower is wave c as it is too long. Look for a five-wave fall to develop as part of a larger correction.

**FIGURE 3.11** Wave c is probably too large.

current leg is actually a third wave of a very powerful third wave, rather than a fifth wave.

- Subsequent legs of a triangle will often reach 61.8 percent of the prior leg.

The above is a list of tendencies and is not meant to be exhaustive. It also is not a list of rules. However, when waves violate these tendencies, the analyst must further raise his or her antennae for signs of problems with his or her assumptions. When a C wave extends beyond 1.618 times the size of wave A, you should think twice about your idea that this is a C wave (see Figure 3.11). Instead, consider the possibility that the market is traversing a third wave within a larger A wave. If wave C fails to reach 62 percent of wave A, maybe the five-wave pattern just completed is just wave 1 of wave C, or maybe the prior leg was three waves and not five waves, and the market is tracing out a flat or a triangle.

I cannot overemphasize the importance of keeping your mind open to alternative interpretations. If prices develop in what seems to be an atypical manner, there is a good chance that your initial wave count assumptions are incorrect. You will need to adjust your timing and price projections. You might want to adjust the size of any trades you have made and alter your profit targets, as well as where you place your stops. I have a general rule of never widening a stop. Sometimes a revised wave count might imply a wider stop. However, if a wider stop is needed, you might wish to reverse your position when you see high risk of the market heading towards your stops. There really is no reason to ever wait for a stop to get hit as the market usually tells you that your expectation is wrong long before it reaches your stop level. The one exception to this is when there is news that causes an immediate price reversal and a gap to or through your stop.

## Price Targets: Percentage Moves versus Point Moves

I will go through several examples to show you how to compute price projections in later chapters. Except for very short-term price action, the preferred method is to use percent changes. That is, if wave 1 takes a stock from $10 per share to $15 per share and wave 4 ends with the stock at $20 per share, you should look for wave 5 to equal wave 1 in size, resulting in a 50 percent price increase to $30 per share, and not a mere $5 increase to $25 per share. It makes sense to compute the simple point gain, since many traders think in those terms rather than in percentage terms, and $25 would likely represent at least a brief top from which a subwave of wave 5 might terminate. Small percentage moves do not require you to do this extra work since the difference between the simple point change and the percentage changes will be minimal.

Note that most software programs that compute Fibonacci price targets use point values. Some, such as CQG, can compute percentage changes instead, which is the more correct manner. You might need to switch to a semilog scale to achieve this with some computer-based technical analysis packages.

It is always a good idea to determine price change targets as well. Even though this is not theoretically correct, remember that all forms of technical analysis are based on market psyche. There is not some hidden power that teaches investors and traders how to compute price targets correctly. Since it is easier to compute and look at simple price moves, many market participants look at equal-sized price moves despite the fact that they may vary substantially in percentage terms. If stock X rallies from $25 to $35 and then dips to $30, you can be pretty confident that there will be a whole crowd of investors, traders, and analysts looking for a $10 rally to $40 even though an equivalent percentage move would imply a rally to $42. You can compute that target quite easily: The rally to $35 from $25 was $10, which is $10/$25, or 40 percent. A 40 percent rally from $30 is computed as $30 × 1.4 or $42.

There is another reason why simple point changes might work well at times in computing price projections. Consider a typical investor who buys 100 shares of stock X. Regardless of what the price of the stock is, an increase of $10 per share is the same $1,000 gain. The investor probably does not think about the fact that as the price of the stock grows, each $10 increase means a smaller and smaller gain in percentage terms. He or she may consider percentages when looking at the value of his or her whole portfolio, but for that one stock, the dollars per share value is probably paramount.

Some markets do not typically exhibit large percentage price moves. Examples include money market futures, where the annual price range may be less than 2 percent. Other fixed-income futures may have wider annual ranges, but with daily trading ranges typically less than 1 percent of the total value of the liability, short-term projections on prices, rather than percentages, should not alter your targets by very much and are probably even preferable. Short-term variations in the foreign exchange markets also lend themselves to price or point-based targets rather than the more complex percentage change calculation. In these cases, given the psychological aspect of market price movements, I consider the point or price move as being the preferred method since it is not only easier to compute, but simply because for very short-term price action, the trader is unlikely to consider the more accurate percentage change methodology in determining targets. Since traders' minds are what help create the price patterns, that is what we need to focus on in determining price targets.

The arguments for percentage and price changes are both valid and should be presented here. I already noted that humans mostly will see things in terms of points when computing price changes; $10 is $10—if prices rose the first time by $10, they probably will look for a $10 swing the next time. That is a pretty strong argument for the price change calculation. Unfortunately, everybody does not think that way, and money managers are measured by their performance, which is computed in percentage terms. Since institutions make up the lion's share of trading in equities, there is certainly a strong incentive to use percentage change calculations when computing price targets.

There really is no 100 percent right answer here. A powerful argument favoring percentage moves comes from the examples I showed you before. In markets where prices can vacillate by several percentage points per day, the differences are so large between price and percentage targets as to make point calculations meaningless. Our wealth grows on a percentage basis, not on a point basis. To say that a drop from $20 per share to $15 per share is the same as a fall from $6 to $1 is ludicrous. Even though both moves represent a $5 per share change, in all likelihood the position size in the lower-priced shares would be larger, meaning that the $5 drop would lead to a much larger dollar loss.

There is one flaw in this argument. While the percentage change in my account value varies greatly when the price of my stock falls from $20 to $15 when compared with a tumble from $6 to $1, if my share holding remains steady, the actual number of dollars I make or lose remains steady. If I hold 100 shares of stock, I lose $500 either way. Therefore, one must determine what kind of price action and volume have been prevalent at various trading levels. If there is reason to believe that many positions were taken at the lower price level, then the percentage move is likely to produce better signals. The best way of telling this would be by comparing *dollar* volume at the various price levels.

Dollar volume means that you must weigh the price times shares traded, and not just the volume of shares. For example, if 1 million shares of Lucent changed hands at $20, that means the value of those shares was $20 million. If 10 million shares traded when the stock's price stood at $0.79, then the total value of those shares traded was only $7.9 million. That is 20 percent less value even though the number of shares traded rose 10-fold! This example is extreme. At $0.79, even though Lucent still has a large market cap, trading of the stock's shares is limited by many regulations. Those holding it since it traded over $60 have little more to lose, and a doubling of the company's value would be almost meaningless to them. All that really counts are relative changes for short-term swings for day traders, in this particular case. What I have highlighted here is how important it is to understand how and why prices might change, and what different price levels might mean as far as price changes go.

Remember that when you compute price targets, especially in a down-trend, prices cannot fall below zero. If the initial leg down was 50 percent and you expect equality, then the next leg down should also be 50 percent from the end of the next corrective rally. For example, if a stock falls from $20.00 to $10.00 and then rallies to $15.00, then you would look for a 50 per-cent fall to $7.50. If you expect the next leg to extend 1.618 times, then you would look for a fall of $\frac{1}{2}$ (1/1.618) to 30.9 percent of its previous value, or to $4.65 ($15.00 times 30.9 percent). Using this methodology, you will never get a projection to prices at or below zero.

Earlier in this chapter, we covered the importance of having more than one indication that a given price level should offer an opportunity for a trend change. This goes for price projections as much as it does for retrace-ments. When a price target comes very close to a retracement level, you know that will be an important price focus. Even if the market does not reverse there, you can take action based on how the market reacts to that key point. Past price extremes, trend lines, or moving averages converging near a projected price point also add to confidence that a projection will prove to act as a barrier, causing a retracement or trend change to start.

One of the best places to look for focal points in price targets comes from channels. Combining a Fibonacci ratio price target with channel resistance can offer some incredible trading opportunities. Figure 3.12 shows the French stock market index, the CAC-40, with monthly bars dat-ing back to 1994. Notice how prices have tumbled to channel support. Although it might be tempting to look to purchase the index right at the channel line, there is little other reason to enter into longs at that juncture. There are no other major support or resistance levels very near to the chan-nel line. Although not shown on the chart, the index had already slid well below the 76.4 percent retracement level back to the 1995 lows. However, there is some hope that losses could halt in the near future. In January 2003, the 1.618 extension, where wave 5 equals 1.618 times wave 1, hits the channel line. Based on that price action, it is possible to develop a plan of

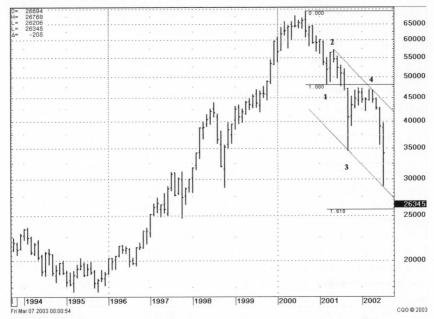

**FIGURE 3.12** CAC-40, monthly

action that likely would include expectations of a short-term rally or consolidation, to be followed by a drop toward the 2,583 target shown on the chart. Notice that we are using a 1.618 extension in wave 5 instead of wave 1. This is because wave 1 and wave 3 were almost equal.

## TIME CYCLES

I assume that anybody who has gotten this far into the book believes that it is possible to time the market. Usually, market timing refers to price targets, much as we discussed elsewhere in this chapter. Unfortunately, that is not enough information to make fully informed investment and trading decisions, especially when applying EWT profitably. It is always key to ensure that a pattern is developing characteristically, in terms of both time and price. This is one reason we draw channels, since channel breakouts, or turns before reaching channel boundaries, mean that there is something amiss with the time-versus-price continuum. Even if prices reach a Fibonacci price projection, if the time frame is too short, there is a very good chance that the current wave cycle is still active and a consolidation will begin. Although a temporary correction is possible, the end of the current wave likely would be forthcoming.

You might wonder why it is so important to have both time and price projections. As I noted above, the simple fact that prices reached a target does not mean that a wave cycle is over. We can compute multiple targets, and as I warned many times in earlier sections, one price target, without additional supporting evidence for the end of a wave, is usually not a good enough reason to look for a price turn. Remember, valuation changes need to change the crowd's behavior. This is measured not just by price, but by time. Of course, if prices change by a large amount and volume is also very large, then it is possible that the asset under question has seen enough of a transition in ownership to overcome a substandard time frame for cycle completion. This explains why "V"-tops and bottoms take place so quickly—they typically involve much heavier than normal volume, meaning that a large percentage of the crowd was coerced by the price action to alter their investment holdings.

Consider the following simple example: A stock rallies from $100 to $110 in three months and then spends another three months completing a triangle that terminates at $105. The stock market explodes higher after that, and the firm's shares soar to $123.15 in another three months. This is the 1.618 extension target for wave 3 compared to wave 1. Wave 4 retraces 38 percent of the third wave, taking the shares to $116.22. Wave 5 then starts. The price jumps 10 percent in three weeks to $127.84. Wave 5 equals wave 1 and equals wave 3 here. But, the time frame is short—three weeks compared to three months for the two previous impulse waves. Additionally, there have not been any price extensions to this point and volume is just average.

The market *could* turn at this point. There is certainly nothing absolutely wrong with the pattern. Prices have traversed five waves, and there are no overlaps. However, typically at least one leg has an extension, and the fact that there has been neither an extension nor equality in time between wave 5 and the other waves would lead me to be on the lookout for a correction of the move and then a continuation to at least the 1.618 extension of wave 1. Anytime you attain a key target, however, you must be on the lookout for signs of a reversal. If prices collapsed quickly and in an impulsive pattern on strong volume, I would be quick to alter my expectations and look for a good place to enter into short positions.

## FIBONACCI DAY COUNTS

When I compute time horizons for market turns, I typically use day counts. Intraday price action is too inexact. For example, if you are looking at a 15-minute chart, you really do not know at what point during that 15-minute period prices turned. Although the same is true on a daily chart, the noise level inherent in such a short-term chart makes accurate timing more difficult. Although you can alleviate this problem by looking at a one-minute chart, I would assume that most of us do not have a pair of Cray Super Computers in our basement constantly running and computing time and price targets for us. Even if you do have the computers, you will surely lose much of your eyesight and all of your sanity attempting to track the markets from both a time and price perspective from that short of a time frame!

There are many opinions on how to count days. I have found the most reliable method is to count actual trading days. I have seen some use calendar days. That is certainly easier since you can just use your Excel spreadsheet functions or straight calendar functions in a programming language. Unfortunately, just because it is easier to do does not make it more correct. Patterns develop based on time and price. I can see a valid argument for including unexpected off days due to war or natural disasters, but even that is questionable. Actual trading is needed to be able to measure market psyche and market action. If you cannot measure it, I do not see why you should include it in a day count.

It is true that there will be times when the day counts match up perfectly for calendar-based time periods, and there might be some markets where this is a characteristic. The analyst should never stick too long to any preconceived notions, even if they come from a book. One of the keys to successful trading is to listen to the market. Just because I say to use actual trading days, if you see a market that regularly turns based on counts using calendar days, forget about what I said for that market, and use the evidence in front of you!

After many years of working with the markets, I constantly am amazed at how often the stock, bond, and currency markets unfold in patterns that are related to the Fibonacci number sequence. Although there is great danger in believing that what you see as a natural order is merely coincidence,[3] as long as you carefully and objectively trade and do your analysis, you will be able to identify profitable trading opportunities and determine the proper time and price cycles for each and every security or derivative product that you trade or invest in.

Although day counts work the best, if you are working in very long time frames, it might make sense to look at week or even month counts. A market might turn after 55 weeks, or 12 years (144 months). Certainly, it is worth checking to see if a channel or price target is approaching and if your indicators are warning of a loss in momentum whenever one of these time frames approaches. The analyst who does all his or her homework will be best prepared to act when the market makes its move. I have found over the years that Fibonacci day counts often coincide with other time cycles or technical signposts. This can lead to what I call *power points*. Even if a major trend does not reverse, there is often at least a temporary change in market activity. Sometimes it is a reversal, sometimes it is a consolidation, and sometimes it is an inflection point where the trend actually accelerates.

## SUMMARY

In this chapter we studied how to use the Fibonacci number sequence in your Elliott Wave–based analysis. We discussed retracements, projections, and day counts and gave you a basis of how to apply these methodologies. Most importantly, we discussed how and why these tools might work, and how to recognize when your analysis is right or wrong. We also focused on how to act when the market confirms, or fails to confirm, your ideas.

Chapter 4 briefly covers some thoughts about applying Elliott Wave Theory to highly cyclical markets, such as the bond market and currency markets. Unlike equities and many commodities, these markets do not have a long-term upward price bias. Stocks have tended to rise over time due to a combination of inflation and technological innovation. Currencies and bonds are not affected by these exogenous factors in this way. Because of this difference, applying Elliott over longer time frames can be challenging and requires special consideration. Chapter 4 also reveals situations where the 5–3–5–3–5 basic order can fail for individual stocks, or even the equity markets.

# CHAPTER 4

# Interlude— Does Elliott Work Outside of the Stock Market?

You may have noticed that I have drawn examples throughout this book from the major asset types: stocks, bonds, foreign currencies, and commodities. Since the title of the book isn't *Applying Elliott Wave Theory Profitably in the Stock Market*, the title of this chapter is somewhat rhetorical. That said, I've already attempted to remove the five waves equals a bull market and three waves equals a bear market terminology from your lexicon. The proper thought process is that the market moves in five-wave patterns with the current degree trend, while correcting or consolidating the current-degree trend either via a three-wave move or with a triangle. If you follow this maxim, there should be no question as to the efficacy of applying EWT, regardless of the market in which you are trading or investing.

The reader can skip this chapter with no real loss of continuity. It is more theoretical and has little application to day-to-day trading decisions. However, you may find it useful when studying and analyzing very long term price patterns across multiple asset classes.

## ELLIOTT DOES NOT REQUIRE PRICES TO RISE FOREVER

Why is there still a bit of controversy over applying Elliott outside of the stock market? Most of it is because those who are not particularly well versed in Elliott still believe that a market must continuously and forever traverse five waves up and three waves down. If that is the case, then it seems a bit difficult to apply Elliott in a very meaningful manner to the bond or currency markets. This thinking is patently incorrect. If the market has completed a full five-wave cycle and reached a new high, then we look for retracements back to zero, not just the latest five-wave cycle. The common complaint that Elliott requires ever higher prices over time then breaks down. Although I do not necessarily agree with some of the more dire forecasts suggested, at the time this book was written during mid-2002, for U.S. equities going forward[1] the mere fact that the actual Elliott reasoning would permit the Dow to tumble more than 90 percent, should remove the general belief that prices must rise forever for Elliott to work. Although it is certainly true that even if the Dow fell to 1,000, that is more than double the high set in 1929 and 25 times the 1932 low; that also would represent a loss of more than 90 percent from the highs set in 2000 by the venerable index and would mean that from trough to trough the annualized return would be less than 5 percent per annum. A similar view has allowed the Nikkei 225, the Japanese stock market index, to fall more than 80 percent from 1989 through 2002.

In this author's opinion, there is still a weak link in how the EWT is depicted. Although price action with the trend is correctly described as being five waves, this leads to a major disconnect in the classic depiction of the stock market. That is, the price action still must be shown as five waves higher and three waves lower, and all price action must be linked over centuries to show a complete picture. Unfortunately, price history does not go back that far, so authors have estimated true stock market activity by linking the U.S. stock market to British equities. They reasoned that prior to some point in time, the British economy was the world's largest and was thus a fair representation of "the" stock market. I am not convinced that it would even have been fair to depict the U.S. stock market as "the" market during its heyday in the late 1990s. Although well considered, given the overall basis for what EWT truly represents, the break points where the analysts choose to move from one index or currency to another also lead to a discontinuity in what the charts actually represent.

Elliott Wave Theory, as is the case with all chart analysis, represents a sum of the thinking of the crowd of investors and traders at any given moment for that particular market. Even in this day and age of speed-of-light global communications, the various national stock markets do not move in lockstep, nor do their fixed-income markets. Currencies gyrate, moving up and down relative to each other. Although the general direction is often similar, the magnitude of daily, weekly, and monthly changes varies wildly. The German DAX fell more than 70 percent from its peak in 2000 to its low in early Q4 of 2002. The U.S. Dow Jones Industrials had still not lost even 40 percent of its value, the U.S. S&P 500 was down 50 percent, and the U.S. Nasdaq Composite had shed more than 75 percent from its peak value. Given these wide differentials, I find it very difficult to substantiate any concatenation of U.S. stock prices to British stocks, especially during a time when the global economy was far less homogeneous than it is right now.

The author believes that a slight modification of how waves are characterized eliminates the problems introduced by an unfailing dedication to a never-ending series of 5–3–5–3 moves. Remember, R.N. Elliott developed his methodology based on the stock market. He really did not have extensive long-term price data. Stock prices have tended to rise over time. This was and is likely to remain the general trend for equity valuations. Some have posited that stock prices rise due to inflation—that is, prices tend to rise over time. Although we have certainly lived in a mostly mildly inflationary environment, there have been substantial bouts of deflation in recent history and Japan has seen generally falling prices for nearly a generation now. Inflation is not the answer.

## EXPLAINING RISING EQUITY MARKET PRICES: IT'S NOT JUST INFLATION

Stock market prices have risen for hundreds of years in general. Although product and services prices have risen as well, inflation does not provide a sufficient reason for the higher stock market valuations. Consider that high inflation often results in economic slowdowns. When prices are rising, wages typically lag inflation. When this occurs, the stock market tends to pull back rather than rally. Although this is not true during periods of hyperinflation, such as has been witnessed in some of the South American stock markets, those economies, which are often largely dollar-based, have not risen in dollar terms and still have risen less than underlying inflation. Unlike the somewhat arbitrary decision to switch from British to U.S. indices, applying a currency-based adjustment to economies in which many spenders hoard foreign currencies as a hedge against inflation, the value of the index in another currency's terms may make sense.

Even if inflation was a factor in stock market prices, that would not make equities special in their application to Elliott. Inflation also affects the bond market—high inflation raises interest rates and causes lower prices. Investors require higher interest rates if inflation accelerates when they lend money—which is what they are really doing when they buy a bond— since the value of their principal lent decreases as inflation increases. The relative inflation level from one currency arena to another is also believed to have an effect on exchange rates through purchasing power parity.[2]

What is different about the stock market, as compared to the bond market, commodity market, or currency market? Less than you might think is the real answer. A major underlying cause of generally higher stock market prices has been technological innovation. Technological innovation allows companies to be more efficient in their production of goods and services. This will tend to widen the spread between what it costs them to produce a product or service and what they can charge for that product or service. It also has a negative effect, at times, on commodity prices. As it becomes cheaper to produce a raw material, more competition enters the market, increasing supply. Unless demand increases as well, prices will fall. In the case of true technological innovation, prices might not fall if the competition cannot match the technology. Technology may also be behind the fall in inflation (also known as disinflation) in recent years as new products offer more perks for the same money or less. The method that most governments employ to compute inflation leads to deflationary-appearing statistics, since the governments attempt to compare like products. Any improvement to a product is thus discounted from a product's price, even though the final cost to the consumer may be unchanged. For many years, the introductory price for a well-equipped personal computer system hovered near $2,000 even though prices for older components fell substantially. This gave a misleading impression of falling prices even though, to run the most current and advanced applications, you would have needed to regularly upgrade your computer for the still standard $2,000 price tag.

In the end, higher productivity due to innovation does tend to increase the value of the manufacturer, which in turn raises the firm's stock price. This is the only place where innovation has a direct and immediate impact. Since the trend, for hundreds of years, has been to innovation, recently at an accelerating pace, the general trend in stock market prices has been higher. This has resulted in what I believe to be the incorrect assumption that upward price adjustments are always five-wave patterns, whereas bear markets must always develop in three-wave legs.

## THE 1929–1942 DEPRESSION ERA TRIANGLE

The thinking discussed above has resulted in many Elliotticans coming up with difficult-to-stomach wave counts for the period just prior to, during, and after the Great Depression. I have seen this period deemed a triangle. This is something I have a very hard time with. While one *might* be able to make a pattern-based argument for the triangle theory, it does not fit in with what a triangle is supposed to mean—typically, a continuation pattern of a larger trend. Although prices ultimately did return to their upward trek, to call the Great Depression a consolidation does not in any way, shape, or form meet the crowd theory and sentiment-based analysis that is the ultimate framework for any type of technical analysis. The 1929–1942 period was not a minor correction. It represented a cataclysmic shift in how people lived, how governments protected their citizens, and how equity assets were priced. Although one can invoke the fractal nature of price movements, as explained by EWT, the sentiment part of the story still doesn't fit. There is no justification, from that perspective, no matter what the chart *looks* like, to call that period a triangle.

The basic premise for EWT has been, in the case of the stock market, that bull markets developed in five-wave patterns and bear markets in three waves. What does one do in the currency markets? Price action which is bullish for the U.S. dollar is bearish for the Japanese yen. One idea I've seen floated is to use the currency of the larger economy. What happens when the economies are similar in size? And, why should you use the larger currency? Maybe it should be the more volatile currency, since that is what would, by definition, drive most of the exchange rate's price variation? In the case of bond yields, there is absolutely no reason to use five waves up for bull periods and three waves down for bearish periods. There is no general multigenerational direction for interest rates that I can see. They rise and fall in a cyclical manner. I can see no reason to believe there should be a long-term evolution in any particular direction for interest rates.

## ELLIOTT WAVES FOR ALL MARKETS

After considering these many factors for many years, I have come to an interesting conclusion. This idea is not wildly different from work published by Tony Plummer[3] back in 1991. He suggested that prices mostly moved in three-wave patterns, but allowed for five-wave moves in certain situations, which roughly equated to the conditions as they might apply to an EWT-based impulse move. My main point of deviation from what Tony suggests simply places the five-wave move as a major part of the market's framework. Human nature appears to take longer to recognize a major trend, so when it occurs, it seems to take five waves for it to complete. Therefore, price action with the trend will normally develop in a five-wave pattern. However, corrections against a dominant trend should complete in three waves, or via a triangle.

Note that this does not preclude use of zigzags in your analysis. A zigzag is a correction, but the a wave and the c wave represent the price action at that moment in that degree as being the current trend. There is no reason why one or both legs in the direction of the current trend cannot develop in five waves. However, if the trend of next larger degree had reversed, then I would expect the general direction of prices to result in five-wave patterns in the new direction and three-wave patterns against it.

This does not really change anything. As long as technology advances and mankind does not bomb itself into oblivion, I would expect that equity market prices will continue in their long-held 5–3–5–3–5 bias of generally rising prices. However, if disaster ever befell the world to the degree that innovation halted for a period of generations, I would expect that five-wave patterns would develop in the direction of lower prices. If there had been an active and documented stock market during the Middle Ages, I would have expected to see three-wave cycles to higher prices and five-wave cycles to lower prices. If Elliott was alive at that time, he probably would have concluded that bear markets trace out five-wave patterns and bull markets complete in three waves.

This idea also fits almost perfectly with the way prices seem to develop in the bond and currency markets. When there is no strong overriding trend, prices should both rise and fall in three-wave patterns. This would roughly relate to range trading, double threes, triple threes, triangles, and other consolidative ideas within a standard Elliott Wave framework. As soon as a more lasting trend develops, prices should start to trace out five-wave patterns in the direction of the larger trend, and should correct that trend via three-wave price action.

The main difference I propose from classical EWT is that if the underlying trend was to reverse, I would expect price developments in the opposite direction to show a 5–3–5–3 pattern. This means that you might not always be able to link moves from one period to the next, with or without X waves. It does not make applying the Elliott Wave Theory any more difficult. When these changes occur, they will be due to major and possibly cataclysmic alterations in the way the world, individual nation-states, or geopolitical areas exist and behave. Most reasonable time frames will see patterns develop as they always have. The tools you already use—trend lines, Fibonacci extensions, moving averages—will continue to work. Even retracements will apply, although you might need to change exactly what it is you think you are retracing, and you will have to understand that "something is different this time" so that you look for the proper wave count on a larger scale.

There are other instances in which this idea also holds. Consider a company that has built up a strong and successful business over many years. It shows steady growth and technological innovation throughout. Then, it misses a beat, or actually, a whole symphony. The technology in which it specialized no longer is favored, and it is late to the ball in the new favored technology. The firm's management either never reacts, or reacts too late. The price reversal for that stock will not appear as a bear market at all. There should be no reason to believe that the change in direction is a correction of previous excesses. The trend for that firm is fundamentally down. That means you should look for losses to develop in five waves and not in three. Corrections or bull periods for that stock will then trace out three-wave patterns—unless the company rights itself and successfully

**FIGURE 4.1**    Polaroid (daily, close only). *SOURCE:* Poser Global Market Strategies, Inc.

purchases or develops innovations that permit it to profitably compete in the new business world.

There are two recent examples of this situation. One is Polaroid Corporation (see Figure 4.1), the venerable instant camera company. Polaroid's cameras never competed favorably with standard film, but were used mostly by amateurs who wanted immediate gratification or maybe wished to give an immediate gift to Grandma and Grandpa. Sadly, this American icon of ingenuity never reacted to the digital age and did not properly perceive the threat from digital cameras, which could not only provide the same instant response, but also permitted the owner to touch up the picture and remove annoying things like red-eye or poor exposure. When that seismic shift took hold, the true trend was down for the stock, and its losses had to develop in five waves. Also note how, even as the price of Polaroid's shares trebled from 1990 to its high in 1998, the pattern was sloppy at best—three waves.

The story has been similar for Xerox Corporation. Another high-growth stock from a previous generation, Xerox also failed to properly react to and embrace the new digital economy. While many stocks soared into the year 2000, Xerox tumbled more than 70 percent from May 1999 through December 1999 in a clear five-wave pattern (see Figure 4.2). After a brief rally into March 2000, it collapsed again, tumbling more than 80 percent from its minor recovery high before the year was out. By December 2001, in less than 19 months, Xerox's share price tumbled to as low as $3.75 from an all-time high of $63.94.

As of the time this book was written, there had been some promising signs in terms of Xerox's price patterns. While most stocks sank to new lows on multiple occasions throughout 2002, Xerox only fell as low as $4.20 in October 2002. The pattern down still allows for one more new leg lower, but the divergence in performance between Xerox and the overall market bodes well for the firm. It is too soon to tell whether the ultimate bottom of the stock is in or not, and whether the next major move higher will be in five waves or three. However, for the time being, a five-wave fall is countenanced by the change in fundamentals. If the company manages to find its way back into the pack, there would be no reason why the next uptrend could not see the stock return to the typical five-wave pattern higher and three waves lower, *even though it would mean that a five-wave pattern lower developed on its own, without another matching five-wave cycle.* Remember, five-wave patterns, based on standard Elliott rules, cannot stand alone except when they are part of wave C of a 3–3–5 correction or consolidation.

The one problem with this approach is that you must depend on your understanding of the asset under study if you are going to have a clue as to whether you should be looking for a reversal after three waves, or a fourth and fifth wave. This is one reason why I do not recommend using a purely technical approach to the markets. Whether it is the simple act of being

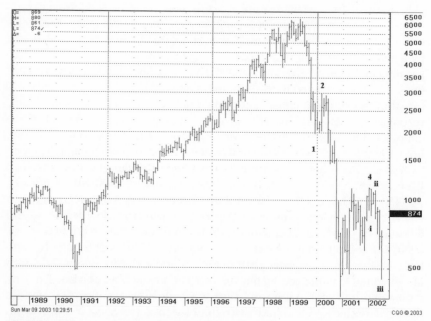

**FIGURE 4.2**  Xerox Corporation, monthly

**FIGURE 4.3**   USDJPY, quarterly

informed as to when a company is due to release earnings or the government is set to announce quarterly gross domestic product (GDP) or monthly employment data, the investor or trader who does his or her homework first can be prepared to not just react, but to be proactive in the face of what could otherwise become an adverse situation.

What actually is quite fascinating about this approach is that it also can give you further insight into the global fundamental situation. Consider the quarterly chart shown for the USDJPY (U.S. dollar–Japanese yen) exchange rate in Figure 4.3. Although the dollar has been moving sideways to higher vis-à-vis the Japanese currency since early 1995, the gains have appeared to be wholly corrective. Although wave counts still suggest there is room for the American currency to rally past JPY160 in the next two years, there is little or no evidence to suggest that the dollar will not fall to new lows versus the yen in the next 5 to 10 years. (For an alternative interpretation of the USDJPY situation, see Chapter 6.)

If the dollar had shown more strength or given a hint of an impulsive rally, I would be willing to forecast that something had changed, that we should look for five-wave rallies higher for the USD versus the JPY, and that the bottom in 1995 represented the end of a secular USD downtrend versus that currency. It certainly would have been very easy to make that pronouncement. After the world spent a generation lauding the Japanese way of doing business, it discovered that the Japanese were fallible as well. A severe bubble in real estate and equity markets sent the Japanese economy into a tailspin that was still active some 13 years after the stock market topped there. While U.S. and other equity markets rose 20 percent per annum in what is called the greatest bull market ever, Japan's equity market sank into near oblivion.

Ethnocentric and patriotic breast-beating could easily lead the uninformed observer to suggest that the Japanese way of doing business was wrong after all and that America, or at least the West, had the "right" way. I am certainly not making any political or ethnic statements in these pages, but rest assured that the long-term uptrend for the yen remains firmly in place. While the U.S. dollar may very well double or triple from new lows due late in this decade or early in the next, I do not see a fundamental reason to believe that the very long term–oriented investor should be proclaiming victory versus Japan Inc.

As you can see, there is a lot you can tell from a chart. Admittedly, it would be impossible to come up with the above brief analysis without understanding the geopolitical climate, as well as something about international trade and both the Japanese and American economies. The analyst needs to understand both the technical and fundamental underpinnings of the U.S. and Japanese economies and their stock markets. That my forecast still calls for substantially lower prices in U.S. equities in the next five years, even as Japan's stock market finally bottoms, adds to my confidence in the above analysis.

One final chart further highlights how a sea change in how the world works can alter the way you should count your wave patterns. Look at Figure 4.4, which shows 10-year U.S. Treasury note yields going back to 1962. Through much of the 1950s and into the early 1960s, inflation was barely known in the United States. The economy grew steadily in the post–Korean War era, with little inflation and a moderate budget deficit, which was actually in surplus during the mid-1950s. Then the Vietnam War came, and the United Stattes, with one brief exception in the late 1960s, ran larger and larger budget deficits while inflation rose steadily.

The chart data do not include yields from the early 1950s. Yields were slightly lower at that time than they were when the chart begins. Including that information, I can make a fairly decent argument for a five-wave advance as yields rose with inflation and budget deficits from the mid-1950s into the early 1980s. After that, the U.S. Federal Reserve made inflation a top priority, and for the next 20 years, inflation fighting became a key policy of the U.S. and other central banks, creating a disinflationary, and in some cases, a deflationary environment. As this chapter was written, yields had begun to rebound, although a possible final yield low in a large terminal

**FIGURE 4.4** U.S. 10-Year T-Note yield

triangle, shown on the chart between the converging trend lines, might still be expected. Note that, including this one final yield low to come, one can make a pretty good argument for yields to have risen in five waves from the mid-1950s to the highs in 1982 and then to have fallen in five waves since that time.

The classic Elliott Wave interpretation would require a five-wave fall in yields, which is what appears to be developing. However, it would also have needed a three-wave advance in yields from the 1950s lows. This is because a bull market in debt issues means higher prices, which run in the opposite direction of yields. Although one could argue that the pattern from the 1950s yield lows was a three-wave affair, that is not how I see it. Also, with multigenerational yield highs present in the early 1980s, unless that yield high was part of an irregular correction, there would also be a need for a three-wave correction higher in yields followed by another 70 percent or so fall in yields in a five-wave pattern, since five-wave patterns in bull markets, do not stand alone.

Attendant to this new approach is a need to understand the world around you. The Elliotticians or technical analysts can no longer fool themselves into believing that they can just look at the charts and divine what is about to occur. A thorough understanding of what you are analyzing and of the factors that move those markets is of paramount importance. Unfortunately, by removing one of the foundations of EWT, it would seem that I am removing something that all analysts could count on: the alternation of five-wave and three-wave cycles. Although technically that may be true, note that many charts that do not use this principle have wave counts that require all sorts of questionable tactics to work out properly. They typically do not fit at all with a reasonable market psyche or sentiment, nor do they appeal to the actual condition of the market they are tracking. Since, at least to the author, that is one of the great strengths of EWT, failure to apply it that way is a far greater problem than a revision that actually only comes into play when there is a major change in how a market works.

Of course, the great danger with this kind of thinking is that you will use such actions to say that "it is different this time." It rarely ever is. I do not envision a return to the dark ages of civilization, or negative techno-logical innovation, which would be required to remove the 5–3 bias in equity prices. Other, more cyclical markets are likely to stay that way, keep-ing their large wave patterns mostly a series of three-wave moves. This revision also fits far better with the author's idea that EWT is a tool and not the Holy Grail. The successful Elliottician should employ Elliott along with classical technical analysis techniques, sentiment analysis, and fundamental research in producing superior trading and forecasting results.

# CHAPTER 5

# Building an Elliott Wave Trading Plan

The first three chapters of this book gave you the basic tools that should allow you to apply the Elliott Wave Theory to your trading and investing decisions. Virtually every imaginable EWT-based pattern was discussed and outlined, with real-world examples from multiple markets and asset classes. Chapter 4 covered some additional ideas, which while not absolutely required, may be useful for readers of this book who trade or invest in the currency, commodity, or fixed-income markets, and as shown in the chapter, even the stock market. That chapter focused more on very long term relationships, however, and typically will not come into play in most trading and even investing decisions.

In this chapter, we build on the EWT patterns highlighted earlier, along with some of the hints and generalities discussed regarding the overall nature of technical analysis, fundamental research, and the markets as a whole. As I have attempted to convey throughout this book, EWT is just one tool that the investor or trader can use in determining how he or she will allocate capital. Every time an asset's price changes, a trade is made, or time passes, an opportunity arises for you to add more information to your databanks and hopefully better confirm, or possibly revise, your positions. You must constantly go back and compare market action with your original assumptions to determine whether prices are developing as expected. Even if your original ideas were not exactly correct, prices might be moving in a way that allows you to keep your current positions with little or no change.

Sometimes, the markets will provide little additional information, and at other times, the action, or lack of it, will tell you to stand pat. The information imparted might suggest that your initial general idea was correct, but that you might need to revise your timing or exact price targets. If you are trading options, even a small change in the timing of a move, or where you expect a price cycle to end, can substantially alter your risk/reward profile. The salient point here is that you must constantly monitor your positions against your assumptions. If anything changes, you may need to take action. This does not mean that if you are holding a stock for an assumed period of 5 or 10 years, you need to have a chart open on your desktop all day long and worry about each and every tick. You might not even need to review price changes every week if your plan is to hold over a long enough time period. I would check the fundamental news to ensure that there has not been a sudden and seismic shift in the fundamentals (takeover, new competition). It is important to understand what kinds of shifts in price and sentiment are relevant to how you are positioned. If you think the market for a stock is entering a new phase, you need to ensure that it is developing according to plan on a regular basis. If you are swing trading for a time frame of a week or two, you probably should check on your progress several times throughout the day.

By the end of this chapter, you will be able to develop a trading plan, with the help of a series of forms that you can use to formulate your strategy. You will need to enter information into these forms to help you justify your decision-making process. You must take responsibility for your actions, and the only way to do that is to, as much as possible, define what actions you should be taking and why you should be taking them. If your assumptions are wrong, then you must immediately respond to changing market conditions and know how you should act, depending on where the market is going compared to your expectations.

Handing you a form with information to fill in will not help a whole lot unless you understand how and why each item exists on the form. In this chapter, I take you through a step-by-step process, showing you how you should go about your analysis in preparation for taking a position. Your work is not done once you've taken your position—it has only just begun. You must define how you will monitor your trade or investment, constantly update your assessment, and take any action based on whatever new information you have gleaned from the market.

## WHAT TIME-FRAME WILL YOU TRADE?

There actually is one more piece of information that you need to determine before you can start your analysis. You must determine the time frame you wish to trade. By this, I mean, will you be trading to hold positions for just a few minutes, hours, days, or longer? Will you be looking for major moves that could take weeks, months, or years to develop, or will you be scalping off one-minute charts? Will you be leveraged, trading futures, options, or currency markets, or will you trade only long equities? You must make these decisions so you can limit your universe of possible tradable items and, from there, further sift through and eliminate those assets or liabilities that do not fit into your personal profile.

## KNOW YOUR RISK PROFILE

Your personal profile describes your level of risk aversion, your need for immediate satisfaction, and the kind of returns you are looking for compared with the losses you (or your spouse) are both willing to and can afford to take. You must know yourself before you can trade. What kind of drawdowns can you afford, and more importantly, how much are you willing to accept? Do you have the patience to wait for a months-long pattern to develop, or are you likely to let your losses run and then cut your profits short? Do you need the excitement of trading a technology sector stock on margin, which might trade in a 10 percent range every day, or is your comfort level only able to handle buying two-year Treasury notes for cash? You *must* answer all of these questions—honestly—before you can begin to trade.

The set of questions posed above is essentially the subject of a book or many books on the psychology of trading. It is well beyond the framework of this effort. However, I will attempt to cover some of the practical results of this kind of review as we step through building a trading plan in this chapter, and then actually trading a series of real markets in the next chapter.

## COMPUTER-GENERATED WAVE COUNTS

Screening multiple markets for profitable setups is beyond the scope of this book. Pattern recognition software that identifies Elliott Wave patterns does exist, but the technology is in its infancy. There has been a good deal of research completed by Richard Swannell of Elliott Wave Research Pty. Limited in Australia. That firm has taken reams of data from people donating computer time from their PCs so his firm could analyze intraday and long-term data from multiple markets using advanced pattern recognition software. Although I cannot vouch for how perfect the computer-determined counts are—and computers certainly cannot factor in the human element nor have they been programmed to cover intermarket analysis—the project has certainly raised the bar in Elliott Wave research and should further legitimize the methodology. The computer program that Elliott Wave Research sells—The Elliott Wave Analyzer 3—will review a portfolio of charts and provide you with what it believes to be the best trades available based on its wave count determinations. There are also many other, non-Elliott portfolio screeners you can use—moving average breakouts, momentum confirmations, relative strength, CANSLIM,[1] and hundreds of others. For the time being, I will assume that you've made a decision as to what it is you want to trade, and will then take you through the various steps you must complete to get from the desire to trade to actually putting a position on, monitoring it and taking your profit (or loss).

In the next section of this chapter, I will cover the steps you need to go through to arrive at your trading decisions. The first step will be to review the basic ideas, in a step-by-step fashion. Then I will build our first trading plan by following these guidelines. We will create a form for you to fill in as we develop the plan. The form is not meant to be constricting. You might want to add or delete information or change exactly what you review depending on the time frame you are trading (multiyear investments and day trading ideas will require different levels of research than swing trades will, for example), but the form will provide you with a general outline as to how you should prepare yourself for taking any position.

## LOOK AT YOUR POTENTIAL TRADE IN MULTIPLE TIME-FRAMES

Throughout the book, I have tried to get you into the proper frame of mind for developing a trading plan. Although some will tell you that EWT is some sort of all-encompassing system, I am not a big fan of raising any methodology to cult status. While I would agree that EWT may very well be the best tool available to you, reading the wave counts correctly is not all that easy. While every freely traded and liquid market should develop in proper Elliott fashion, you might not get the count correct. That is why I suggest you consider other information and look at the market from several different time frames.

For example, why should you look at a monthly or quarterly chart when you are swing trading? There is greater noise in the chart patterns the shorter the time frame you look at. Review the chart of almost any market, and you will find that trends seem far clearer on weekly and monthly time frames than they do from a daily or an intraday perspective. What is interesting is that newsletter writers will tell you that although the trends look clearer on weekly or monthly time frames, you cannot trade off that information because they are too long term and your stops need to be too far off. This is not true. What they are actually telling you is that they cannot sell any newsletters by recommending those kinds of trades because the kinds of people who purchase newsletters are looking for large gains in short periods of time, and also expect a constant barrage of ideas if they are going to spend a lot of money on a weekly commentary. There is absolutely nothing wrong with trading and investing from a multimonth or multiyear perspective, and even if you are not planning on doing that, understanding what the larger trend is will help you to develop a better and more accurate trade or investment strategy.

Looking at the bigger picture is only half the battle. As we review the steps in building a trade plan, you will see that I recommend reviewing three or four different time frames. Often, the best trade entry levels will come from looking at a shorter-term chart. This will allow you to more accurately determine your entry point. However, there is a risk with that kind of research. If you are the type of person that worries about the perfect entry level and are not willing to buy or sell unless you can get the exact price you want, you risk missing your trade completely. I have seen people consistently lose money by entering limit trades when the market approaches their buy or sell levels. For that matter, I also see them do the same thing when stops are hit, which makes even less sense. If you are wrong, you should not hold the position, period.

## GET THE FUNDAMENTAL AND SENTIMENT PICTURES

Of course, simply analyzing the charts over multiple time frames is not enough. As I cover in greater detail below, you need to review the news. You should know what has just been released, and what is due to come out. You should also try and get a handle on market sentiment. Some ways to do this can be from listening to the news and watching interviews. Other good tools include sentiment surveys, implied volatility in the options markets, and put/call ratios. Once again, sentiment-based trading could be the subject of a book, or at least several chapters in a book, and will not be covered in great detail here, except with regard to the Elliott Wave patterns. Finally, you should review your charts from the perspective of other technical tools and indicators. Are prices near an important trend line, retracement level, or moving average? Is a triangle or wedge forming? Is there a momentum divergence? You should consider all of these factors with your wave count, because they could help you time your entry and exit more accurately.

## KEEP AN OPEN MIND

Remember, one of the keys to profitable trading is to understand when you are right or wrong. You must constantly assess and reassess your position. Although I do not countenance widening stops, you will often need to bring stops in closer, or even exit a position long before your stops are hit. One of the beauties of trading with Elliott is that you can easily make money when you are wrong. You might expect a third wave rally, when in fact you are still in a correction. The market might move in your favor, but if prices do not show increasing momentum and volume, you will know that you are not in a third wave and that you probably should take profits quickly, since ultimately, prices will fall below your purchase level.

You can only execute that kind of trade by being flexible—accepting the information that comes from the market regardless of any presupposed ideas of what should happen. You do not need to wait for your stops or a retracement to be hit. You do not have to wait for a moving average to cross or for MACD (moving average convergence divergence, a technical price momentum indicator) to give you a sell signal. You need not wait for a trend line to break either. If the market is not trading as expected and is saying that prices are going to reverse against you quickly, get out now. Don't wait!

## GETTING STARTED

Before you can trade, you must gather some basic information and do a bit of research. The steps are briefly listed below, and will be presented in greater detail as we develop our trading and investing forms.

*Step 1: Preparation and initial research:* At this point, you must determine exactly what securities you wish to trade. You will take a general overview of the markets under consideration and determine exactly which security or securities you wish to trade. As soon as you have identified the security, gather all of the basic information: name, ticker symbol, type (equity, debt, derivative), and where it trades, and enter this on your form.

*Step 2: Long-term data review:* While you might have a predisposition to a short or long trade, you must remove any such thoughts from your head. The idea is to develop an unbiased strategy based on all the facts available to you. Your first analytical step will be to review a long-term chart—long in relation to the time frame you wish to trade—and attempt a wave count on it. This will provide you with the longer-term price bias. You should also identify several major support and resistance levels. These may come from retracements, price projections, trend lines, or prior highs or lows. Your final step is to write down the long-term trend.

A note on time frames is warranted. I have defined several time frames, ranging from intraday out to investing for multiyear moves. There is usually little information in annual charts, so recording analysis on these charts is likely not worth the effort. However, it may still be worth looking at 10, 20, or more years of data to determine long-term support and resistance levels. The idea behind looking at multiple time frames is that it allows you to better identify the risks and rewards available in the trade or investment you are currently considering. You probably will not be trading in these time frames, but looking at them will tell you how sensitive you should be to market movements against you. If the security you are looking at is in a long-term uptrend, but you believe the short-term swing is down, you probably should trade a smaller position, or with a tighter stop, in case the larger trend returns to dominance during your trading time horizon.

*Step 3: Sharpen your time frame focus:* Once you have completed your initial long-term outlook, you will move to the next lower time frame. This will permit you to get much closer to identifying possible trade entry points, as well as stops and targets. At each step of the way, you must ensure that all of your wave counts and projections are consistent. Although you might have a bullish medium-term outlook and a bearish long-term forecast, your wave counts must reflect that this bullish medium-term expectation is based on a correction of a longer-term downtrend. You should write down key support and resistance levels for this degree of detail, and you might want to include a bullish or bearish bias for this time frame as well. One key reason for determining a bias at every time frame is that the amount of money you decide to risk will necessarily be related to the overall trend. If you are buying for an intraday rally, but the daily, weekly, and monthly charts are bearish, you should probably only risk a small amount of money. However, if all trends are up, you can consider a more substantial position.

*Step 4: Trading time frame analysis:* At this point, you will develop a first pass at your trading strategy. Do not be fooled; it is not yet finalized. However, at this juncture, you will move to the next lower time frame, your trading time frame. From here, in conjunction with the key support and resistance levels you identified in prior steps, you will describe your trading strategy. This strategy must include:

1. Entry level.
2. Requirements for entry. Price is not enough. Include volume indications, momentum, trend lines, or completed or pending wave counts to give a clear and precise set of criteria. Assume that you are not the person trading and that somebody else must understand your instructions. Be clear, concise, and precise.
3. Target level.
4. Stop level.
5. Requirements for success. This is very important. If you are buying a breakout, you might want to include that prices should accelerate higher on strong volume. If you get a breakout but volume remains low, it might mean that the breakout is a head fake. Describing how the market should trade, which is an important part of Elliott Wave analysis, can allow you to turn a profit even if your wave count and bigger picture idea are wrong.

*Step 5: Review charts one time frame lower:* You should always look for a trading edge. If you look at an intraday chart, for example, when you are attempting a short-term swing trade, you might find a pattern on the hourly chart that would proffer a better entry level than you could achieve otherwise. Maybe you were looking to sell a break down lower. If you use a closing level on the daily, you might decide to sell at the next day's open. However, a quick review of the 60-minute chart might show an initial five-wave down move now completing. You would then adjust your strategy to sell at a 38 percent or 50 percent retrace of the just completed down move. You would also include in your entry requirements that hourly volume should be lower than it was during the breakout.

*Step 6: The details:* If you expect to make money trading, you had better do your homework. Although technical analysts will tell you that all available information is in the charts, there is lots of information that requires you to read between the bars. Sometimes, these actions might be too small to even cause a blip on anything but the shortest-term charts. When such actions occur at that level, they may be indistinguishable from noise.

There is also information that cannot be known. While very long term wave counts or technicals will not likely be altered by a single news release, the parameters for your trade can easily change from such information. Here is a short, but not necessarily comprehensive list of factors you should check before implementing your strategy:

1.  Review the charts of other similar securities. If you are trading Intuit, you might want to check out the Microsoft chart. If you are considering buying soybean futures, you also might want to look at soybean oil futures. Sellers of oil futures might wish to look at Exxon-Mobil or Schlumberger. Bond buyers should look at the stock market, and dollar sellers might be interested in knowing what the gold charts look like.

2.  Know the upcoming news. If you are considering the purchase of U.S. 10-year Treasury notes, you should be checking for economic releases, or for speeches by members of the U.S. Federal Reserve Bank. An investor in equities, be they individual stocks or indices, should know when key companies will be announcing earnings, making conference calls, or presenting at important conferences.

3.  Know the seasonals. Although less important, you should know whether the market you are trading typically rises or falls during the period you plan on trading. Although overall patterns are far more important, since seasonalities do not always work and may change over time, a seasonal tendency that is different from your forecast should lead you to lower your capital at risk.

In short, you should have a list of all major releases and announcements which are expected for any position you hold. If a major release is due, you might want to consider holding off until the information is out.

*Step 7: Monitoring:* Congratulations! You've done your analysis, your price was hit, and you now are the proud parent of a brand new position, or your research says that there will be a trading opportunity soon and your plan is complete. You are far from done. With every tick, there is new information. You do not have to follow every tick (unless you are day trading), but a regular review schedule should help you to avoid any major surprises. Too much information for very long term investments is dangerous, because you might react to noise, but for short-term trading, regular observation makes sense. Every price change provides information as to whether the market is developing in the direction you forecast. While you might not need to change your trade if your original forecast was wrong, you should immediately update any changes in your forecast and double check to ensure that those changes do not require you to alter your exit point or stop level. Always keep your original trade plan, and add new sheets as you make changes. This way you can study how you reacted to the market as your trade developed and use each and every trade as a learning experience.

## STEP 1: PREPARATION AND INITIAL RESEARCH

Our first example will use the U.S. stock market as represented by the S&P 500 Index. You can trade this index either via the futures available at the Chicago Mercantile Exchange, via the SPDRs® exchange-traded fund (ETF), or via the iShares® ETF. I will assume that you decided that you wish to swing trade this market, looking for a move of 5 percent to 10 percent. Before you can trade, you need to determine what kind of time frame a 5 percent to 10 percent move typically takes. My research shows that the historical three-week volatility of the S&P 500 has been fairly steady, vacillating around 5 percent. A 60-day time frame takes historical volatility up toward the 10 percent region. This means you should expect to hold a position from 3 to 12 weeks to reach your 5 percent to 10 percent total return goal, assuming a nonleveraged position.

My normal recommendation is to consider at least three charts and often four:

1. The time frame you wish to trade
2. One periodicity higher
3. One periodicity lower
4. One very long term chart

Given the volatility of the S&P 500, I would use daily charts for the trading time frame. It is not likely that anything shorter than a 30-minute chart would add value to your decision. You should use a weekly chart to go one time frame higher. In this particular case, since the stock market has been falling for three years and in many cases is testing levels last seen more than five years ago, a monthly chart might make sense. Even a quarterly or annual chart might be of some use. When you do your analysis, you should start at the longest time frame first.

## STEP 2: LONG-TERM DATA REVIEW

In this case, I probably would look at a monthly chart initially. If it appears to give enough information, I would then take the knowledge gathered from that chart and take my research to the next level. Please note that this analysis was written live. That is, I used data as they were coming in during November 2002, so this is how I actually would make a trading or investing decision. That means that this section will be written over several days or weeks, as the price action plays out.

The first thing you should do is to determine where the market is compared to its recent trading range. At about 871, the S&P 500 is near the midpoint of the trading range seen over the past five months.

### Check Historic Price Levels

Your next step is to go back and see if there are any important historic price levels that prices have recently infringed upon. Upon examination of the chart, you would find that the double bottom set in October 2002 at 768.63 and 775.68 in July 2002 were near the middle of a three-month consolidation that the index traded in from February 1997 through April 1997. The bottom of that range is the most interesting level since the stock market has been falling for the past two years. That low price was 733.54.

### Look For Retracement Levels

The next two points I would look at are retracements from a key low, as well as retracements back to zero. The 62 percent retracement back to the 1987 crash low, which is shown in Figure 5.1, is at 726.97, which is quite close to the April 1997 nadir noted above. A 50 percent fall from the all-time high came in at 776.44, which was briefly broken both in October and July. The 62 percent drop from the highs comes in near 593.20, just a shade

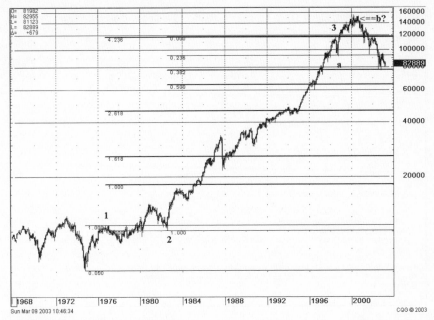

**FIGURE 5.1** S&P 500, monthly

beneath the 1996 low of 597.29. I have included additional levels on the form shown in Figure 5.2 (see page 104).

Do not forget to look at prices above the market. At this point, you have not made any decision on where prices are going, and you need to determine key levels both above and below where the market is currently trading. Some levels I chose also are shown in the form in Figure 5.2.

## Attempt an Initial Wave Count

You need to produce a readable chart with at least your initial go at wave counts. These counts will give you a basis for where you think the market currently stands from a long-term perspective. You also will be able to start placing information on your trading/investing form. We will build this form piece by piece, as I go through the analysis. Each form will include basic information, such as the asset you are trading, as well as charts, key price levels, and strategies. I strongly urge you to print the forms out, along with your charts, since many software packages will rescale charts and will completely remove expired futures and options contracts from their systems. By printing the pages out, you will have a printed and computer-based record of your analysis.

---

### Applying Elliott Wave Theory Profitably -- Trading and Investing Form

**Identification Section**

| | | | | | |
|---|---|---|---|---|---|
| **Name:** | Steven W. Poser | **Security Symbol:** | SPY | **Price:** | 891.00 |
| | | **Security Name:** | S&P 500 Cash Index | | |
| **Date:** | 11-Nov-02 | **Exchange:** | AMEX, ECNs | | |

**Version:**    1.0

**Long-Term Analysis Section**

**Long-Term Support Levels and Descriptions**

768.63 October 2002 low
733.54 April 1997 low
726.97 62% retracement back to the October 1987 low
701.97 Where wave-v down would be 1.618 times wave-I down
646.00 50% retracement back down to 1982 low

**Long-Term Resistance Levels and Descriptions**

944.75 Low set in October 2001, following terrorist attacks
965.00 High set on recovery in August 2002
1063.86 38.2% retracement of labeled wave-iii lower
1176.97 High of rally following post-terror attack low, set in January 2002

**Type of trade (intraday, short-term swing (intraday to several days), swing trade (several days to a couple of weeks), medium-term (weeks to months), long-term (months to years):** swing

**Long-Term overview**

In major bear market for nearly three years. Possibly entering final phase of bear market. Wave-count suggests in or due to begin 5th wave lower with targets below the double bottom set in July and October 2002.

---

**FIGURE 5.2**    S&P 500, long-term

## Write Down Your Expected Trade Type

At this point, you should write down what type of trade you wish to make. The form shows the basic types I am including, though you can use whatever terminology you feel comfortable with. In this book, I will use intraday, short-term swing, swing, medium-term, and long-term. Intraday is day trading. The trader is looking for small moves, possibly via leveraged positions in futures or options, although trading volatile stocks in large size could also suffice. Short-term swing trades include positions held for several hours to several days, in general, though a week or more is possible in the case of quiescent securities. Swing trades include positions held for several days to several weeks, whereas medium-term trades may stretch out over many months, but usually will be several weeks to a month or two. Long-term trades can cover full bear market or bull market cycles.

## Write a Brief Long-Term Analysis

Once you've decided what kind of trade you want to make, quickly write down a line or two describing the long-term situation. Even though you will not be trading from that kind of time perspective, if you need to change this portion of your analysis, you will almost certainly need to revise your actual trading strategy and probably will have to take some sort of action on any positions you hold. Typically, any positions you hold should be exited long before you need to change the long-term picture. As you continue your analysis, the key will be to ensure that all time frames are consistent. In the example shown, I note that prices might be entering a fifth wave lower. Your trading strategy will likely address whether the market is there or not, and what to do if you are short and the market signals that it is still in wave 4.

The focus of this form is to put together, in one place, all the background information to make a trading or investing decision. You will eventually write down what must happen for success, and list possible causes of failure. In some cases, you will have sections that cover factors beyond the charts. You must do your homework whenever you trade or invest. Purchasing a stock just prior to an earnings announcement or a court ruling is okay, if you know about the risk and have factored it into your trading or investing scheme. What is wrong is entering into a position without doing your research and getting blindsided by such an occurrence. There are enough ways to get caught off guard—lawsuits, CEO arrests, terrorist attacks—you must take control of what you can by doing your homework.

Now that you've entered a brief analysis of the long-term monthly picture and recorded it on your trading form, let's move down one level and review the weekly S&P 500 chart. This chart is getting us very close to the analysis we will ultimately undertake to produce our trading goals. You will be able to see patterns that have developed during the past year or two, and should also take note of shorter-term patterns, retracements, and Fibonacci price projections. You might also want to do some rough work at weekly time cycles, though for swing trades, I would probably want to look more closely at day counts rather than weekly time projections.

## STEP 3: SHARPEN YOUR TIME-FRAME FOCUS

As you drill down in your analysis, a trading strategy is likely to start to coalesce in your mind. This becomes especially apparent if the chart patterns give you a strong conviction about the future direction of the security you wish to trade. Although levels on the weekly chart will often not be key to your final trading parameters, they will give you a good framework when you are ready to put together your final entry and exit criteria.

Our review of the S&P 500 trade under discussion (see Figure 5.3) shows that prices made a new low in October 2002. That new low was less than 1 percent beneath August's nadir. The weekly chart does not show enough detail to determine whether or not prices completed a five-wave fall

**FIGURE 5.3**   S&P 500, weekly

to the October low, though my first impression is that the drop was only three waves down. That would imply a 3–3–5 flat under development since the July 2002 low was achieved.

There are arguments for prices having completed their drop—that is, if you can find a five-wave count lower. The low at 768.63 was very close to the 762.78 target you would get if wave v down was 1.618 times the size of wave i down. But, the first wave was very short, and when that happens, I often look at the relationship between the size of the first three-wave move as compared to the distance traveled by wave v. Typically, wave v approaches 62 percent of the size of the first three legs, and should not exceed 100 percent of that distance. The 62 percent of the first three waves' target is down at 718.88.

What is clear at this juncture is that there are two possibilities for the medium-term outlook: (1) The S&P 500 is in a flat correction, which means that from the current price in the low 870s, there is room for gains into the low to mid-900s; and (2) a bottom is in, which means that a rally well past 1,000 is possible. This would mean that if our stated goal was for a 3 percent to 5 percent gain, you should be leaning very heavily to looking for a place to buy the S&P 500.

Our stated goal is for a 5 percent to 10 percent move. That means that the idea to buy might not be as clear, although the current trend is definitely higher. The bottom line is that our analysis is not yet over, and we will not be able to complete our trading strategy until we dig deeper into our analysis (see Figure 5.4).

A few more items are worth noting before shifting to the daily chart view:

1. Momentum did not confirm the lows. This is certainly not enough of a reason to say the market has bottomed, but it should put you on alert.

2. Market sentiment was not terribly bearish at the bottom, making it difficult to believe that a final bottom is in. The volatility index, VIX, did not come close to where it stood at the August low.

3. Studies by Lowry Reports show that major market bottoms rarely occur without volume breadth showing several 90 percent down days, with a turn confirmation requiring 90 percent up days. These studies are based on the NYSE data. These criteria were not met during the past two months.

4. Bear market rallies are typically fast and furious, and bear market bottoms usually occur amid total disgust and disinterest in the markets. Neither was the case in October.

5. Timing is becoming important here as well. The whole fall for the first three waves took 18 weeks. As of the last week of October, if this was wave iv, the consolidation would already be 14 weeks long. At the bottom, the correction was 11 weeks, which was already quite long.

---

**Medium-Term Analysis Section**

**Medium-Term Support Levels and Descriptions**

866.81 50% retracement level between week of 19-Aug-2002 high and week of 7-Oct-2002 low
828.37 Low price during second week of the recovery off the 7-Oct-2002 low
768.63 Low set week of 7-Oct-2002
762.78 Where wave-v would be 1.618 times wave-i if the week of 19-Aug high was wave-iv and not as labeled.
718.88 Where wave-v is 62% of the size of the first three waves of the drop from the start of wave-i.

**Medium-Term Resistance Levels and Descriptions**

918.66 76.4% retrace back to high set week of 19-Aug-2002 from low set week of 7-Oct-2002
924.02 Retest to 19-Aug-2002 high set week of 9-Sep-2002
926.98 Down trend line resistance from mid-March 2002 peak, falls about 7.50 points per week
957.95 Where c=a
965.00 High set week of 19-Aug-2002

**Medium-Term Overview**

Classic pattern could suggest double bottom, but barely breaking July low leaves risk for flat. Timing shows that if this is a 4th wave, getting long in the tooth, but have seen extended 4th waves before. Could turn into triangle, but that would require wave-iv to wind up becoming far longer in time than it took for first three waves to complete. As labeled in chart, most likely outcome appears to be flat. With 62% retracement back to Aug. high already exceeded, watch 76% retracement level, trend line, and c=a point and old high. While momentum, as expected, diverged at the lows, there is no clear impulsive wave count to Oct. bottom. Note that although the current trend is up, typical bottoming behaviors are not present.

**Bias:** Bullish

**FIGURE 5.4** Medium-term analysis section

However, I have seen many extended fourth-wave moves. The markets are pain maximizers, and there would be few things that would cause more pain than convincing investors that the bear market was over, only to collapse in a month or two to new lows from near August's high.

## STEP 4: TRADING TIME-FRAME ANALYSIS

This is where we will start getting down to the nitty-gritty. Since we are going to be looking at a trade that should last at least a few weeks, the daily charts will be paramount. Patterns that are not discernible on the weekly charts will show up in a daily view. We will, in the next step, look at hourly charts to help improve our entry and exit levels, but by the time you complete step 4, you will have at least an initial pass at your actual trading strategy.

### Review Everything You've Done So Far

The first part of your trading time-frame analysis should include a review of what you have written in your trading plan thus far. You probably have several points that will need further study. In this case, we still do not know if the fall from the August high was five waves or three waves. We also do not have any wave counts written down since the bottom was made in October. Although we have a stated bullish bias for the medium-term outlook, it is not yet clear whether there is enough upside potential at this juncture to enter into a long trade.

With prices below 900 and with my previously stated analysis that the most likely outcome would be a flat, there is little reason to be bearish short term. However, my big picture analysis is for generally lower prices. I could never recommend a trade to look for new lows, which is my overall forecast, if I saw room for a rally of as much as 10 percent. For this reason, I would probably develop a two-pronged strategy that would depend on my appetite for risk (see Figure 5.5).

The current trend is up, as I discussed in the prior section. As you will see on the form, the risk/reward opportunity for a long trade is poor if you are looking for a swing trade, which is my stated goal. My longer-term view is for lower prices, but from current prices, with risk to the August 2002 highs near 965, sales would be ill-advised.

There are some very interesting day counts worth noting. First of all, the rally from the July low to the August high took 21 days to complete. The drop after that spanned 34 days. Note how it took longer for the fall to complete than the rally. This could also be a sign that the bottom was not an impulse move, which is one reason why I see the October low as a b wave in a flat. However, bear market rallies do tend to be very fast, so I would not take an enormous amount of solace from that one fact.

**FIGURE 5.5** S&P 500, daily

If the market is going to continue its timing, I would expect the current wave c of this correction to take at least 21 days. Note that all day counts are trading days. This comes to November 7, one day after an FOMC (Federal Open Market Committee) meeting. With a high expected the day after the meeting and given the fact that the market does expect a rate cut, that timing would confirm the idea that the Fed will cut rates, although it does not necessarily provide any insight into how much the Fed will ease.

I would thus look for a reversal around November 7, give or take a day. You must ensure that there is a completed wave count before you put a sale on. If there isn't, then I would look for a turnaround on November 25. Not only would that be 34 days from the October low, but it would also be 89 days after the July low. I might give this turn date a bit more leeway since it is already a fairly large number of days. Also, since I am expecting a top and given that seasonals around the American Thanksgiving holiday are positive, I could fathom gains continuing until after the holiday weekend. Again, sales are not possible without a turn signal.

With this analysis completed and partially reflected on the forms (you do not need to put every point in, but the more the better so you can refer to the information easily in the future and understand what your decision process was), you can now start to build an initial trading plan (see Figure 5.6).

Our initial go at a trading plan will include:

- Requirements for entry
  - Timing
  - Pattern
  - Technical considerations
  - Fundamental considerations
- Expected entry price
- Stop level
- Requirements to stay in the trade
- Target level

---

**Trading Time-Frame Analysis Section**

**Short-term Support Levels and Descriptions**

866.81 50% retracement level between week of 19-Aug-2002 high and week of 7-Oct-2002 low
828.37 Low price during second week of the recovery off the 7-Oct-2002 low
768.63 Low set week of 7-Oct-2002
762.78 Where wave-v would be 1.618 times wave-i if the week of 19-Aug high was wave-iv and not as labeled.
718.88 Where wave-v is 62% of the size of the first three waves of the drop from the start of wave-i.

**Short-term Resistance Levels and Descriptions**

918.66 76.4% retrace back to high set week of 19-Aug-2002 from low set week of 7-Oct-2002
924.02 Retest to 19-Aug-2002 high set week of 9-Sep-2002
926.98 Down trend line resistance from mid-March 2002 peak, falls about 7.50 points per week
957.95 Where c=a
965.00 High set week of 19-Aug-2002

**Timing**

8-days      Since 10-October low
34-days     From high in August to low in October
21-days     From low in July to high in August

**Trading Time-Frame Overview**

Thre trend is up and there is no denying that right now. Unfortunately, with 34 points down side and with the 76% retracement to the August 965.00 high only 27 points away at 918.66, there is no good and safe long trade. Plus, I have an overall longer-term negative bias. For this reason, I cannot make a long trade.

Timing points to possible turning points on November 7th, 21 trading days after the low, and November 25th, which is 34 days after the October low. My strategy therefore will require something negative to happen around that time frame.

Alternately, I would accept a negative signal with a completed pattern at any time near that time period. However, with the Fed meeting on November 6th, I would think twice about any trades before that time.

**Trade Plan**

| | |
|---|---|
| **Trade entry:** | Enter short S&P 500 at the open on 7-November |
| **Stop level:** | High of rally if market opens lower on 7-November.<br>If market opens higher on 7-November, allow for 2% stop above entry.<br>Reset stop at end of day to that day's high if market closes at least 1% below intraday peak. |
| **Entry requirements:** | Must have completed five wave pattern to highs, or be very close to one such that a 2% rally from entry would not trigger the stop noted above. |
| **Target:** | New low beneath October 10, 2002 nadir at 768.63 |
| **To remain in trade:** | The drop from the high must be impulsive, as in five waves. Failure to drop below 16-October low of 856.28 within five trading days would not be consistent with an impulsive fall and would suggest that I either close the position or substantially tighten stops. Lack of five wave intraday patterns lower should result in either closing the position or quickly trailing stops. |

---

**FIGURE 5.6**  Trading time-frame analysis section

Given our prior analysis, there is no good trade to enter into right now. The short term, though bullish, is not set up for a good entry. I typically look for a 2:1 risk/reward ratio between my stop level, entry price, and profit target. As you can see from Figure 5.6, the risk/reward for a long trade is only about 1:1, though admittedly, there is further upside potential. Although I noted that there is no good trade to enter into right now, I can provide a strategy for later entry based on the longer-term wave counts. Let's review some of the key points here:

1. The short-term trend is higher.
2. The medium-term and long-term trends are lower.
3. The FOMC meets on November 6.
4. There is a day count that calls for a turn on November 7.
5. There is a day count that calls for a turn on November 27.
6. The 76.4 percent retracement back to the August high is 918.66.
7. My market forecast is for a flat correction (five-wave) off the October low.

Given that information, the main idea would be to create a short trade based on timing and price patterns. Since I am looking for a turn on November 7 in reaction to the FOMC meeting, then the entry level would be timing-based as long as the price pattern appears complete. If it does not, entry would not be allowed. Stops would probably be set initially based on retracements to the August high, or on a pattern or shorter-term wave-based projection while the main target will be to new lows.

Here is an initial go at a trade plan:

1. Enter short S&P 500 at the open on November 7.
2. Stop level will be the high of the recovery so far, if the open is down on November 7; otherwise, allow for a 2 percent rally from entry point. Reset stop to daily high if market closes down at least 1 percent from the intraday high at end of day.
3. Requirement for entry: Pattern as of the morning of November 7 should be a completed, or nearly completed, five-wave move within the stop parameter noted in point 2 above.
4. Target: new lows beneath the October 10, 2002, nadir at 768.63.
5. Requirement to stay in the trade: Fall should be impulsive. Failure to fall below October 16 low of 856.28 within a week would suggest closing position. Lack of five-wave intraday patterns lower following entry should result in either closing the trade or quickly trailing stops lower if the market moves down.

Now that we've taken a first shot at a trade strategy, we need to further refine it. One way to do that is to look at shorter-term charts. This might help us to determine more exact entry, stop, and target levels.

## STEP 5: REVIEW CHARTS ONE TIME-FRAME LOWER

Since we just looked at a daily chart, we should use either a 60-minute or 30-minute bar or candlestick representation. Some analysts do not like to use a 60-minute chart because the final bar of the day only represents 30 minutes of trading. However, I feel that for these purposes, 30 minutes is a bit too short term. Also, the final half hour of the day sees extremely high trading activity and can stand on its own. Therefore, I will use a 60-minute chart in Figure 5.7 for this analysis.

As you can see from the chart, my wave counts show that prices may have already begun their final five-wave rally. However, the amount of time spent moving higher is rather short, and the price gains are still short of where I might expect the market to move. At the time the analysis was made, the Federal Reserve was scheduled to meet early the following month (November 6, 2002). Speculation was rampant that the Fed would cut rates. The only question was by how much. There are also day counts

**FIGURE 5.7**  S&P 500, 60 minutes

that suggested the market could turn lower on November 25, 2002, since that would be 13 days after the Fed meeting.

The low-level analysis in Figure 5.8 does not add a whole lot of information this time since the index appears to be midway between what could prove to be some very important price levels and triggers. What the chart

---

**One Time-Frame Lower Analysis Section**

**Intraday Support Levels and Descriptions**

885.35  Recent early morning high on 17-October, currently being challenged
866.58  Low set early on 18-October, if still in wave-(v), this could have been the bottom of wave-iv of wave-a of wave-B
856.28  Bottom of wave-(iv). If five waves complete, then needs to fall below this level in impulsive fashion. Count unlikely.
845.27  If this is irregular wave-(iv) still active, then 38% retracement level of wave-(iii).
844.39  Gap from 14-October to 15-October

**Intraday Resistance Levels and Descriptions**

900.69  High of recovery so far, set late in the day on 21-October.
918.56  76.4% retrace back to high set week of 19-Aug-2002 from low set week of 7-Oct-2002
925.89  If wave-(v) active, where wave-(v) equals 62% of the distance traveled by wave-(i) through wave-(iii).
931.80  Down trend line resistance from mid-March 2002 peak, falls about 1.60 per day.
965.00  High set week of 19-Aug-2002

**Intraday Analysis**

Sloppy pattern moving higher since labeled wave-(iv) either means that market is in bullish pattern and this is an irregular fourth wave still active, or that this is a diagonal wave-(v) which is about to fail. At this juncture, given that prices are still well below the 918.56 76.4% retracement, and that even with the recent slowed momentum, the index is making higher highs and higher lows, I would stick with a more bullish interpretation. Note also that timing suggests that prices can rally for another two weeks, until the FOMC meeting on 6-November. At worst, it appears as if we range trade until that time. This analysis also highlights the importance of the wave-iv low at 856.28 on October 16, 2002. I can add an additional alternate entry to the trade plan below.

**Trade Plan**

**Trade entry:**          Enter short S&P 500 at the open on 7-November

**Stop level:**           High of rally if market opens lower on 7-November.
                          If market opens higher on 7-November, allow for 2% stop above entry.
                          Reset stop at end of day to that day's high if market closes at least 1% below intraday peak.

**Entry requirements:**   Must have completed five wave pattern to highs, or be very close to one such that a 2% rally
                          from entry would not trigger the stop noted above.

**Target:**               New low beneath October 10, 2002 nadir at 768.63

**To remain in trade:**   The drop from the high must be impulsive, as in five waves. Failure to drop below 16-October low of
                          856.28 within five trading days would not be consistent with an impulsive fall and would suggest that
                          I either close the position or substantially tighten stops. Lack of five wave intraday patterns lower
                          should result in either closing the position or quickly trailing stops.

**Alternate Trade Plan (do not execute both plans!)**

**Trade entry:**          Drop below 856.28 (wave-iv). Enter on 38% retrace back to recent high

**Stop level:**           0.01 above 76.4% retracement back to high from completed five wave fall from that high

**Entry requirements:**   Must have completed five wave rally from wave-iv low and five wave fall from that high

**Target:**               New lows

**To remain in trade:**   Drop after entry must be fast and furious since the implied count is a third wave. Failure to fall
                          quickly and sharply on higher volume should lead to closing the position, even if profitable.

**FIGURE 5.8**  One time-frame lower analysis section

does highlight is that the low at 856.28 on October 16, 2002, might be critical. I have this labeled as wave iv. If prices complete a five-wave advance off that point, any drop below wave iv would clearly signal a reversal. Therefore, I can add an additional tactic to my trade plan: Sell S&P 500 on a drop below 856.28.

Requirements for entry:

- Five waves completed higher from 856.28.
- Five waves completed lower to 856.28.
- Sell at 38 percent retracement back to the high.
- Stop 0.01 above 76.4 percent retracement back to the high.
- Target will be new lows beneath October 10, 2002 bottom.

## STEP 6: THE DETAILS

I could probably give you a list of 100 items you need to check and track before you actually make a trade. However, if I give you too much to follow, I could inflict analysis paralysis. This sickness leads you to find so many ways in which your trade could go wrong that you never actually place it. The key to all this work is to minimize surprises. All the research in the world cannot guarantee that you will make a profitable trade. Trading and investing are risky business. The only way to ensure that you do not lose money is to buy government bonds and hold them to maturity (ignoring inflation risk and default risk). Your job in the details section is not to become some sort of modern-day financial Sherlock Holmes. Rather, you should make one final pass through the first five steps and then consider the following additional items:

- Create a calendar which shows the following information:
  - Key government releases from the current date out to at least a week after your expected holding period. Show the prior month's result as well as market consensus, where available.
  - Major corporate earnings announcements expected during the same time frame noted in the government releases item above. You should show last quarter's results as well as those of the same quarter a year ago. If available, include the consensus estimates as well.
  - Exchange holidays.
  - Dates or times that you might not be available.
  - If you are buying a security that pays a dividend, then list these as well since you will have to adjust your stop, entry, and exit levels lower by the amount of dividends paid on the ex-dividend date.

- If your trade plan shows a delayed entry, continue to monitor the markets and specific security in case the pattern changes. You'd hate to miss the entry you were forecasting just because your strategy said to wait for a certain date. For the current example, I would be extra vigilant on November 2 when the monthly payroll and unemployment data are to be released.

Your details section (see Figure 5.9) will essentially be free-form. Part of it will be a calendar. You might want to use Microsoft Outlook or some other calendar program to list all relevant items. Of course, you can just enter each item into an Excel spreadsheet, which is the example shown in Figure 5.9. If you use something passive like an Excel spreadsheet, I suggest you give yourself a reminder to check your spreadsheet every morning prior to market open and highlight the items you believe to be most important on that list.

Some of you might be wondering why I did not add a third strategy. That strategy would say that you should sell any time that prices complete a full five-wave cycle higher from the October 10, 2000 low. To a degree, you would be correct in suggesting that should be part of the trade plan. However, I've already included a count for the first four waves, and I cannot really provide a great deal of detail on what the rules would be for entry and exit at this point. If this opportunity arises, however, hopefully I would (or

---

**Details**

| Date | Time | Release |
|---|---|---|
| 10/28/02 | after close | Dell (DELL) earnings and conference call |
| **10/29/02** | **before open** | **Proctor and Gamble (PG) earnings and conference call** |
| 10/31/02 | 10AM | October ISM Purchasing Managers Report |
| **11/1/02** | **8:30AM** | **October Unemployment rate and non-farm payrolls** |
| 11/4/02 | after close | Verizon (VZ) earnings and conference call |
| **11/5/02** | **after close** | **Election Day - could be important as control of Senate is up for grabs** |
| **11/6/02** | **2:15PM** | **Fed Reserve Open Market Committee (FOMC) meets to decide on interest rate policy** |
| 11/6/02 | after close | Cisco (CSCO) earnings and conference call |
| 11/7/02 | after close | Yahoo (YHOO) earnings and conference call |
| 11/7/02 | before open | Disney (DIS) earnings and conference call |
| 11/7/02 | before open | Qualcomm (QCOM) earnings and conference call |
| **11/7/02** | **any time** | **COMPUTED POSSIBLE TURN DATE (21 trading days from the 10-October bottom)** |

**Other important items to track**

Trend line drawn on intraday chart
Look for five wave completion and five wave rally lower after that which takes out 856.28
Prefer momentum divergences on 60-minute and even daily chart at high
Prefer rally above 918.56 before market turns lower
Prefer low volume during rally phase and increased volume as prices turn lower
Prefer falling implied volatility (VIX, VXN) as prices rise and increase as prices reverse

**FIGURE 5.9** Details section of trade plan

you would if you were trading it) notice it, and catch it during the monitoring phase (step 7 below).

There are other reasons that I did not include the five-wave completion as an alternative trading strategy:

1. There is a limit to how much you can track at one time. I assume that you are not trading just one security. If you have five different ways to enter a trade, you'll never get it all correct, and you are likely to miss signals. Additionally, one reason for creating a trade plan is to build confidence in your research. It is difficult, at least from where I sit, to have a whole lot of faith in your research when you have too many different scenarios from which you can trade.

2. From an Elliott Wave perspective, note that the research calls for a major price reversal. I am much more comfortable with price reversals when they occur with proper timing, very near reversal day counts. Failure to turn near a calculated timing point decreases the probability that the turn is real. You might sell at the end of the first wave of wave 5, selling way too early and then missing the real opportunity at a later date. You will probably be all primed to trade once you've completed the trade plan, and I think there is a real risk of jumping the gun. That is why I left that idea out. If you go back and look at Figure 5.7, you can possibly make out a completed five-wave pattern from the wave iv low, but it is way below my preferred minimum retracement above 918, and I want to avoid getting in too soon. Remember, the analysis calls for a flat correction, which would even permit gains to or slightly above 965, while downside potential is into the low 700s.

## STEP 7: MONITORING

That sure seemed like a lot of work. You might think that you're done. Your preferred strategy says that you should sell on November 7 and that is more than two weeks away. Your alternative plan requires a drop below 856.28 and although that is not too far from current levels, all you need to do is enter an alert into your computer system to let you know when the S&P pierces 856.28 support. NOT!

You have now filed your trade plan and are ready to go. However, as prices develop, new patterns might become apparent that would lead to you put a trade on before the date noted on your trade plan. It would certainly be tempting to sell a day early, on November 6, at least once the FOMC makes its announcement and if prices start to fall sharply. You would then place your stop probably at the high to date. Of course, you still would not want to

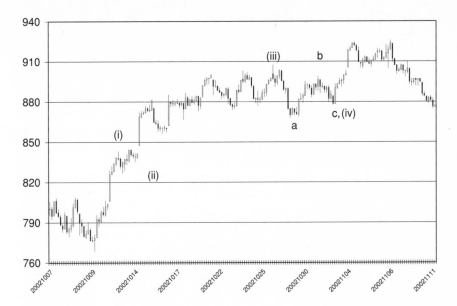

**FIGURE 5.10**  S&P 500, 60 minutes

be a seller if there was not yet a completed five-wave pattern to the highs from the October 10 low.

Another possible scenario would be a completed five-wave advance even before the Fed announcement. I discussed that possibility earlier. The details section above lays out some of the signposts to look for that alternative.

Look at Figure 5.10. Our alternative choice to sell below 856.28 did not play out; prices never got close to that level and continued to rise into my computed turn date. As you can see, I revised my wave counts. The top set on October 28, 2002, was reached in three waves. Therefore, I changed my label to make that wave b of what should then be an irregular wave iv. The drop to the low on October 29, 2002, was arguably five waves, which is required for wave c, completing wave iv. Place these changes in the monitoring section.

The rally to the high at the time of the FOMC decision is arguably five waves completed on November 6. Aggressive traders could have shorted here, but that was not in my trade plan. I waited until the open on November 7. (I am using an open price of 914.00. The official open on the S&P 500 was 923.19, but that is because the index is reported based on the prior day's close. The only way to short the S&P 500 is to either sell futures or an S&P 500 ETF. The 914.00 price used as the shorting level is an approximation based on where these securities traded at 9:30 A.M. on November 7,

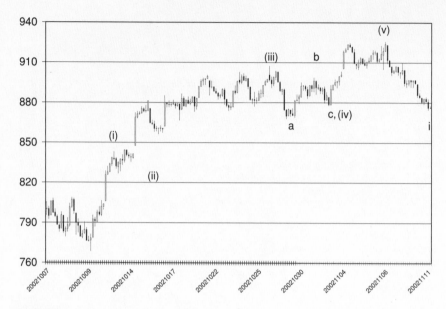

**FIGURE 5.11**   S&P 500, 60 minutes

2002.) The trade plan calls for a stop initially set above the high to date, or 925.66 set on November 6.

As per the trade plan, at the end of the day I reset the stop to 914.00, which was the day's high price in Figure 5.11. Continued monitoring shows a possible five-wave completion at the low on November 13, 2002, at 872.05. However, the pattern is not very clear, and it could have been three waves. The intraday momentum divergence at the low has me leaning to the five-wave count. This means I can update my stops to place them above either

---

**Monitoring**

10/29/02 Revised wave count, moving wave-iv to low set today. Rally to high (wave-b) was a double three.
11/6/02 Possible five wave completion at FOMC meeting at 925.66. Prepare to enter at open tomorrow.
11/7/02 Entered at open price of 914.00. As per trade plan, stops placed at high to date, or on break above 925.66.
11/7/02 Stop reset to entry level since that was day's high as per trade plan, on close.
11/13/02 Possible five wave move lower completed at 872.05. Move stop to just above 61.8% retrace back to high (905.19).
11/15/02 Stop triggered.

**Trade Review**

Since wave patterns were not all that clear, it might have been reasonable to track stops more closely. However, given the size of move forecast, about the only change I would have made is to have changed my stop to just above the initial fall from the high on November 6th at 900.51. This is because it is not clear that the 872.05 low was truly five waves, and above 900.51, we would have an overlap of the first leg down, thus invalidating the impulsive count lower and implying that new highs should be expected.

**FIGURE 5.12**   Monitoring

the 61.8 percent or 76.4 percent retracement back to the 925.66 high. Since I am expecting a drop to new lows, the move should be fairly sharp. Therefore, I would place my stop above the 62 percent retracement level, or at 905.19. That stop was triggered on November 15. In the end, the analysis was incorrect as prices continued higher. However, continued monitoring allowed you to make a profit anyway.

## When the Trade Is Done

You also might want to include a review of the trade to see if there was anything, with 20/20 hindsight, you might have changed. See Figure 5.12 for one possible interpretation.

## SUMMARY

At this point, you should have a pretty good feel for what it takes to complete a trading plan. I went through the many steps required to get a good strategy together. This includes multiple time-frame analysis, reviewing related markets (or stocks or sectors), and tracking important news and data releases. However, one of the keys is to continuously study the markets. Never assume you are correct. The market never really closes. Even when the exchange is not trading, there is news, and investors and traders are updating what they would buy or sell a security for. That means that you must be prepared to update your trade plan at any time based on the chart patterns and news, as you read it. Remember, ego does not make you money.

A surprise announcement might force you to throw hours or days of work out the window. It is better to trash your idea than to stubbornly stick with it and throw away your money instead. The example I gave you is a case in point. The analysis was incorrect. The stock market did not embark on a run to new lows, but because I kept up with the news and the chart patterns, I was able to exit the trade with a small profit even though my analysis was ultimately incorrect.

The next chapter builds on what we've learned here. I show you more trade plans and how to do it over several markets. The main reason for this is so you can see how I put everything together when making a trade. I will put my thoughts on paper so you can see the things you need to look at when making a trade.

# CHAPTER 6

# Tying It All Together

By now, you should be comfortable with what the Elliott Wave Theory is and how to recognize wave counts and patterns. You also should have a pretty good idea how to incorporate non-Elliott analysis into your work. Although many Elliotticians and technical analysts point out that all information is already in the charts, surprises still occur. If you can develop a deeper understanding of what fundamentals are currently driving the global stock, bond, and currency markets to produce the patterns you currently see, then you will have an advantage over other investors, traders, and analysts if and when the lay of the land changes.

The natural order school of EWT suggests that Elliott goes beyond the stock markets. It implies that you can predict social cycles as well using Elliott along with other long-term cycle theories such as the Kondratrieff Cycle. One of the top practitioners of this is Robert Prechter Jr., who is also the person who brought EWT to the forefront of technical analysis in the 1980s when he first forecast that the Dow would reach 4,000 as the rest of the world wondered whether the index would ever be able to manage a foothold above 1,000. His recent book *Conquer the Crash: You Can Survive and Prosper in a Deflationary Depression* (John Wiley and Sons, June 2002) leans heavily on extrapolating bearish patterns in the global markets into a much larger international economic crisis.

The next chapter will build on what we've learned here. I will show you more trade plans and do it over several markets. The main reason for this is so you can see how I put everything together when making a trade. I will put my thoughts onto paper so you can see the things you need to look at when making a trade.

I noted earlier in this book that I do not use Elliott as a way of forecasting the world since I have no desire to take it beyond its use as a tool for forecasting trading market prices. However, there is nothing inherently incorrect about what Mr. Prechter and others are doing. There is little doubt in my mind that the market forecasts in Mr. Prechter's book are only possible in a deflationary depression. Although I do not have a similar forecast right now, his counts are an alternative scenario in my mind. The reader is free to try and determine what various market scenarios mean to the global economy, but this book's focus is on how you can learn to trade and invest in any market environment by applying EWT in conjunction with other forms of technical analysis, side-by-side with economic, fundamental, behavioral, and other types of market-oriented research.

This chapter will tie it all together. I am going to provide a series of analyses of various markets, from intraday out to multiyear forecasts. I will leave it to the reader as an exercise, in some cases, to transfer my analysis to the trade plan form developed in Chapter 5. In other cases, I will do the work for you. I am also going to give examples from multiple markets so you can get a flavor for how you might need to actually perform your research. I will include other forms of technical analysis, as well as fundamental and economic research in strategies I develop. I will also make note of situations that might require you to apply the modified wave structures covered in Chapter 4 (a fundamental change in the outlook for a stock forcing a break in the wave counts allowing consecutive five-wave patterns, and markets that are cyclical and thus not exhibiting long-term five-wave/three-wave structures, but three-wave/three-wave cycles instead).

## THE BUBBLE BURSTS: INTEL CORPORATION

I am going to start off with Intel Corporation. Intel's personal computer processors have been, in my opinion, the cornerstone of the PC and therefore by extension, the Internet revolution. Without PCs, the Internet would likely have remained an esoteric and loosely knit menagerie of computer nodes mostly hooked up to American universities and research centers. I can remember sending electronic messages across the ether back in the late 1970s when I was a Computer Science and Mathematics major at New York University. At that time, the network was essentially an offshoot of Arpanet, which was tied to the United States Department of Defense.

In its early years, Intel was a little-known, small semiconductor company. The stock was trading a bit above $18.00 per share when this chapter was written. On a split-adjusted basis, that compares rather favorably with the $0.02 the shares of the firm were worth when it went public in 1972. That is 9,000 times their value. Unfortunately for investors, that $18.00 price is less than 25 percent of what it reached at its apex in September 2000, when it touched $75.81! The October 2002 low of $12.95 represented levels not seen in more than half a decade.

The bull market gurus who continued to recommend Intel in 2000 hung their hats on the fact that Intel was a great company. Unlike some who think its time has passed, I still see the firm as a leader, despite its enormous size. With hundreds of firms always aiming to dethrone it, Intel has continued to produce the best combination of value and reliability in the industry. However, even now, priced at nearly 50 times earnings, Intel appears to be more than a little bit expensive. Of course, if this is the end of its falling earnings, then given that earnings could easily double or triple in the next couple of years, *if Intel's price remained unchanged,* one could argue that it is fairly priced right now (see Figure 6.1).

Intel's share price will not remain locked in at current levels if the market smells a recovery. Interestingly, though I would like to suggest that the company's share price will not rocket next time around, if the five-wave advance completed in 2000 was wave I, then the next leg higher, wave III, should theoretically be even more expansive. That said, if we add just a touch of reality to the situation, you will quickly realize that another 35,000- to 40,000-fold increase in Intel's share price is none too likely. Remember, the company went from a no-name to a global leader in technological innovation. Although the next leg is almost certain to see new highs well beyond the old $75.81 peak, I wouldn't be counting on selling Intel for $200,000 per share in 2020!

The real question right now is whether or not Intel has seen its bear market low with its October 2002 bottom at $12.95. If Robert Prechter Jr. is correct and we are only in the early stages of a multiyear deflationary depression,

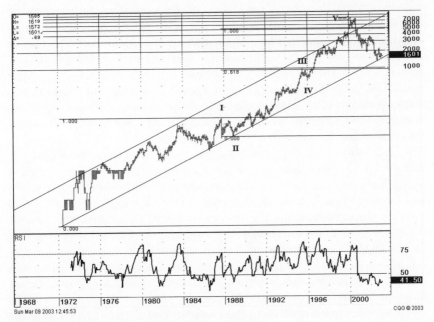

**FIGURE 6.1** Intel Corporation, monthly, semilog

the answer is a resounding NO! The monthly chart shown does not provide enough detail to see if the low set in October gave us a completed five-wave pattern lower. However, I can tell you that the $n/(n+4)$ Fibonacci ratio near 0.146 would target a low of $11.06, and if wave c equals wave a off the highs, then I can compute a bottom price of $9.20. Without looking at the charts in greater detail, I am at least slightly concerned that Intel, which rallied from $12.95 to $22.09 by early December 2002, might make yet another new low. At $9.20, that would be an 88 percent drop from its peak!

How can a great company fall 88 percent? Easily. Remember, the price of a stock is an interest in the future earnings stream of the company. In fact, some researchers have suggested that you can value a firm's stock price as an option on its earnings (per share). That would certainly account for the huge volatility in the company's stock price. If the earnings potential for Intel falls substantially, so will its price. Also, remember that at its peak, Intel had a price to earnings (P/E) ratio of about 90. That means that you had to pay $90 for every $1.00 in earnings. That is not a sustainable valuation, unless interest rates sit near 1.00 percent. Unless there are major changes in the global economy, 1.00 percent interest rates are just not consistent with earnings growth or corporate pricing power.

If you believe Intel is a great company and you expect it to outperform its rival, Advanced Micro Devices, Inc. (AMD), then you can still make money by holding a long position in Intel and a short position in a like dollar amount of AMD. However, if the U.S. and global economies sink, you can be sure that the share prices of both Intel and AMD will fall from their current lofty levels. Try counting waves on the ratio of Intel/AMD as an exercise.

You cannot avoid the vagaries of the market by just holding long positions in stocks. There are very few stocks that have a consistently negative correlation to the direction of the stock market. Few companies can increase their earnings during major economic downturns, and even if they do, investors are less prone to throw money at riskier assets when the economy is faltering. Being short a stock does not mean that you think the company is poorly run or that it will not make money. It does mean that you believe that the price that the stock of the firm currently changes hands at is too high relative to its future earnings potential coupled with other, largely exogenous factors. These factors include the expected direction of the U.S. stock market, the U.S. economy, prices (inflation), and interest rates. It also includes the competitive landscape and the relative health of the firm when it is compared with other companies in its industry and sector, as well as the overall global economic and financial outlook. Although some of these factors cannot be measured quantitatively, they should factor into your trading and/or investing decisions.

Now, back to my analysis of Intel's stock chart. To this point, I have not mentioned my time frame. However, I am sure, from the fact that I started

---

**Applying Elliott Wave Theory Profitably -- Trading and Investing Form**

**Identification Section**

| | | | | | | |
|---|---|---|---|---|---|---|
| **Name:** | Steven W. Poser | **Security Symbol:** | INTC | **Price:** | | $18.05 |
| | | **Security Name:** | Intel Corporation | | | |
| **Date:** | 12-Dec-02 | **Exchange:** | Nasdaq NMS, ECNs | | | |

**Version:** 1.0

**Long-term Analysis Section**

**Long-term Support Levels and Descriptions**

$16.91 Prior month's low (November 2002)
$13.67 Long-term channel support line, rises about $0.26 per month
$12.95 Low since high in 2000, set in October 2002
$11.06 14.6% Fib ratio target
 $9.20 Wave-c = wave-a target off highs

**Long-term Resistance Levels and Descriptions**

22.09 High of bear market rally set in early December 2002
26.70 Gap resistance from June 2002 (not visible on monthly chart)
36.78 2002 high, set in January
47.88 High in November 2001, top of bear market rally following bottom in September 2002

**Type of trade (intraday, short-term swing (intraday to several days), swing trade (several days to a couple of weeks), medium-term (weeks to months), long-term (months to years):** medium-term

**Long-term overview**

Bear market rally likely completed at December 2002 high. Target area focuses on $11.06 at best and could be somewhat worse than that. Economic data coming in mixed right now, and stock market seasonals are slightly positive, but huge rally from lows leaves little upside potential. Only concern is trend channel which could provide substantial support, as it did at the bottom in October.

**Bias:** Bearish

---

**FIGURE 6.2** Intel, long-term analysis

with a monthly chart that shows the firm's history back to 1972, that you have presumed that I am thinking of at least a medium-term trade. Note that I've also proffered some initial long-term analysis, suggesting that Intel's share price will ultimately rally far beyond its September 2000 peak at $75.81. Please review Figure 6.2, which includes the Identification section and Long-Term Analysis section of my Intel trade plan.

Since the monthly chart gives me all the detail I need, in this case, there will only be three levels of analysis. For a medium-term trade, there is no real reason to look at very short term price action. My initial price targets suggest that Intel will tumble nearly 40 percent, and possibly approach a 50 percent haircut before a real bottom is in. However, the monthly chart does not give a detailed enough picture to discern whether the November high at $22.09 represented the end of the whole bear market rally, or if there could possibly be another leg higher.

You might ask, "Why not just sell here? Your forecast is for a drop of more than $7.00 per share. That's a long way to go!" That is certainly a good

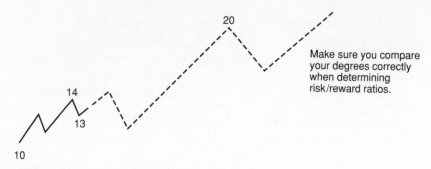

Make sure you compare
your degrees correctly
when determining
risk/reward ratios.

**FIGURE 6.3**   Watch your risk/reward ratios.

observation. But, as I noted above, until I review the charts in greater detail, I cannot be sure that Intel won't first rally past $22.09. I really doubt that you want to sit short through a 25 percent rally! I like to put trades on where my target level, compared to my stop level, affords at least a 2:1 risk/reward ratio. I know what my reward is, but I don't know what my risks are yet.

A quick note is warranted here regarding risk/reward ratios. Look at the stylized drawing in Figure 6.3. The thick line represents prices that might have already occurred for this theoretical example. The stock has risen from $10 to $14, has just dipped to $13, and is starting to rise again. The dashed lines represent forecast targets for future parts of the projected active five-wave bull cycle for this security. A quick glance might lead one to suggest buying at $14, targeting at least $20 per share. You might be tempted to place a stop even at $13 per share, the prior minor fourth-wave low. That would give you a 6:1 risk/reward ratio. Is that realistic? The answer is almost certainly not.

Look at the projections. You are trying to trade two different-degree wave patterns. The third wave should take prices to or even past $20, but the current five-wave rally is not yet completed. Prices might reach $15 or so, but are likely to correct before embarking on their rally to $20. A 62 percent retracement of a move from $10 to $15 would take the price below $12! A $13 stop would get hit. I don't think it makes sense to enter into a short position when the downside risk is 15 percent, as it may very well be here. Remember, a second wave can even retrace 100 percent of the first-wave rally. Although that might not be likely, it is clear that a purchase at $14 with a $20 target probably has a risk/reward ratio closer to 2.5:1, and not 6:1.

I have to admit that I am constantly amazed at how some newsletter writers advertise their products. They feed into the hope, desire, and greed of investors who want to get rich quick and advertise trading recommendations that they claim have risk/reward ratios in the neighborhood of 10:1. If that really existed on a regular basis, it wouldn't be so hard to trade. I am not sure there is ever a 10:1 risk/reward ratio. You might perceive it, but you are probably blocking out a risk or wave count that you do not want to see. In general, the probability of avoiding a stop on a trade that shows an apparent risk/reward ratio of anything substantially beyond 3:1 is very low.

Although the metrics are not the same, you can think of trading very high risk/reward ratios in the same way as buying far out of the money options with very low deltas. Buying an option with a delta of 0.10 means that the vast majority of options traders do not think that the security will finish in the money. They expect the option will expire worthless. Your analysis might show otherwise, giving you an edge. However, the probability of your being correct on a large percentage of those types of trades would be very small. Fat tails in the distribution of stock market returns might allow you to ultimately be profitable, if you don't run out of money first. Unfortunately, that is not a very good strategy for consistent returns, or for longevity in the trading game.

As I drill down to the medium-term time frame seen in Figure 6.4, which is what I consider my trading time frame for this example, I can see that there might be some problems with the idea that this stock has completed its bear market rally. Although it is clear to me, from separate analysis, that the broad stock market has likely seen its best levels for a

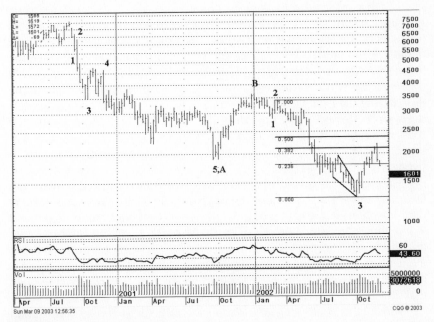

**FIGURE 6.4** INTEL, weekly

while—as in the S&P 500 should make a new low beneath the October 2002 bottom before rallying past the early December 2002 high—Intel shows a somewhat different pattern. Intel's bottom in October 2002 was about 20 percent beneath its July low. In contrast, the S&P 500 bottomed only about 1 percent beneath its worst levels from July. There are several possibilities to consider:

1. The early July low was actually the end of wave 3 of wave C.
2. The early August bottom was the end of wave 3 of wave C.
3. The October low was the end of wave 3 of wave C.
4. The October low was the end of wave b of an irregular wave 4 of wave C.
5. The October low was the end of wave C.

The first two choices could be considered consistent with choice 4 or choice 5, depending on further analysis. I would need to determine the wave structure from any interim recovery high to the October bottom to declare what the wave count was to that point. That will require further detail, during review of the daily chart.

Let's take a look at some more information on the chart before I move to the next level of detail. Since this is my trading time frame, I want to at least make a first cut at a trading strategy. To do that, I need to get a better idea of what is the most likely wave count.

As you can see, I drew in a possible diagonal triangle as prices approached their October lows. Given that third waves are usually very impulsive, the only likely way that you could get a diagonal would be if the low hit was the end of a five-wave structure. Volume signatures also could suggest a five-wave pattern completed. Turnover increased throughout the drop during the first part of the summer, which you would expect during a third wave. However, the final drop did not see as high volume until the week that Intel actually bottomed. That would be a sign of a capitulation of sorts. This would favor the idea that the stock has already completed a five-wave pattern lower.

The story is not all bullish. Other factors worth considering include the fact that momentum confirmed the price lows. I usually like to see momentum divergences at the end of a major move. That said, there might be a momentum divergence on the daily chart, which I will check at the next analysis level. The weekly time frame may be too long to offer a reliable momentum reading here. Finally, the rally since Intel bottomed has not been on very strong volume. The other bearish factors come from the fact that downside price targets noted earlier have not yet been met.

With all this conflicting information, it is difficult to develop a very good strategy. At this point, I would lean slightly to the bearish story, but more because of the S&P 500 chart, which was discussed in Chapter 5, than the Intel chart. Couple this with the stock's still very high fundamental valuation, based on its P/E of nearly 45. With that in mind, I can only give a generalized strategy: Sell Intel at the 50 percent retracement higher of any completed five-wave move lower from the December 2002 high. Place stops $0.05 above the 62 percent retracement of that move. Please see the summary information in the Trading Time-Frame Analysis section of the trade plan shown in Figure 6.5.

As you can see from Figure 6.6, my concern over being too bearish with regard to Intel's share price was well founded. The chart patterns, though not 100 percent clear, apparently show a complete five-wave pattern lower to the October 2002 bottom. Why do I say this? The list of reasons is substantial. Although later price action could change my perspective, the arguments in favor of a five-wave fall from the January 2002 high are overwhelming: (1) Wave 3 was a nearly perfect 2.618 extension of wave 1; (2) momentum was virtually at its worst level at the third-wave bottom; (3) momentum had a large divergence at the wave 5 low; (4) volume spiked as if in a capitulation at the final low; (5) volume rose as prices increased from October through the start of December; and (6) Wave 4 was irregular while wave 2 was a zigzag, an example of alternation.

The price gains from the lows in October appear to have completed in five waves, although that count is not as clear as I'd like it to be. Losses since the high at the start of December look to be a nearly complete five-wave pattern as well. The preferred wave count from the start of 2002 is shown in Figure 6.6. The alternative count would still show the first three waves down as labeled, but would make the October low an irregular wave b within a larger wave 4 that would have ended at the December high. Such a deep irregular fourth wave is not particularly common, and would imply extreme weakness to come. However, such extreme weakness is a bit difficult to justify given that Intel rallied more than 70 percent from its October low to its December high.

This revelation requires a change in the strategy I presented in my trading time frame analysis. As presented now, the bias is negative only for a swing trade, and even then, not from current levels. The longer term seems to pose substantial risk that Intel has actually seen its low, even if the S&P 500 does achieve a new low.

Remember, every company does not have to make a new low for the S&P 500 to make a new bottom, and there is no 100 percent guarantee that my projections for the S&P will prove to be correct. Furthermore, even if they are, remember that my forecast is for that index to only manage a small new low on the order of something from a few percent to probably less than 10 percent beneath the prior low. Also note that the expected

## Applying Elliott Wave Theory Profitably – Trading and Investing Form

### Identification Section

**Name:** Steven W. Poser    **Security Symbol:** INTC    **Price:** $18.05

**Date:** 12-Dec-02    **Security Name:** Intel Corporation

**Exchange:** Nasdaq NMS, ECNs

**Version:** 1.0

### Long-term Analysis Section

**Long-term Support Levels and Descriptions**

$16.91 Prior month's low (November 2002)
$13.67 Long-term channel support line, rises about $0.26 per month
$12.95 Low since high in 2000, set in October 2002
$11.06 14.6% Fib ratio target
$9.20 Wave-c = wave-a target off highs

**Long-term Resistance Levels and Descriptions**

$22.09 High of bear market rally set in early December 2002
$22.99 High in mid-June 2002, top of 4th wave rally of 3rd wave fall
$24.86 50% retracement to 2002 high
$27.68 62% retracement to 2002 high

**Type of trade (intraday, short-term swing (intraday to several days), swing trade (several days to a couple of weeks), medium-term weeks to months), long-term (months to years):** medium-term

**Long-term overview**

Bear market rally likely completed at December 2002 high. Target area focuses on $11.06 at best and could be somewhat worse than that. Economic data coming in mixed right now, and stock market seasonals are slightly positive, but huge rally from lows leaves weak upside potential. Only concern is trend channel which could provide substantial support, as it did at the bottom in October.

**Bias:** Bearish

### Trading Timeframe Analysis Section

**Short-term Support Levels and Descriptions**

$16.91 Prior month's low (November 2002)
$16.44 61.8% retrace back to October 2002 low
$15.11 76.4% retrace back to October 2002 low
$12.95 Low since high in 2000, set in October 2002
$11.06 14.6% retracement Fib ratio target

**Short-term Resistance Levels and Descriptions**

$22.09 High of bear market rally set in early December 2002
$22.99 High in mid-June 2002, top of 4th wave corrective rally of larger 3rd wave down
$24.86 50.0% retracement to 2002 high
$27.86 61.8% retracement to 2002 high

| Timing | | |
|---|---|---|
| 39-weeks | Since 2002 high in January 2002 |
| 8-weeks | From October low to early December high |
| 2-weeks | Since December high |

**Trading Timeframe Overview**

Bearish engulfing and sharp drop from December high should make bulls nervous. Lack of follow through lower in next two weeks though is more bullish. So far, INTC has not even retraced 38% of the October to early December rally. Low volume on falling prices though is not necessarily bullish as turnover is often weak when prices fall. Add to that typically lower volume during end of year holiday season, makes the drop in turnover even less significant. Strong volume though into the October low is a moderately bullish bit of information as that could have been representative of a capitulation low.

Wave counts is not totally clear from January high. I can make argument for either three waves or five waves lower. If it is five waves down, the final leg was a diagonal triangle. Market rallied almost exactly to 38% retracement of the whole fall from 2002. If there was only three waves lower into the October bottom, I would not see any reason for the market to turn at retracements of the whole drop.

**Trade Plan**

Due to very bearish nature of S&P 500 chart, I still favor lower levels in Intel. However, unless we can get a clearly impulsive (five wave) fall from the early December high, I cannot recommend sales.

**Trade entry:**
Enter short at 50% retracement higher from a completed five wave drop from $22.09. As of now, there is no such pattern.

**Stop level:**
Set stop $0.05 above 76.4% retracement higher from a completed five wave drop from $22.09.

**Entry requirements:**
See trade entry

**Target:**
Minimum is match of prior low at $12.95, but more likely at least $11.06 with $9.20 possible.

**To remain in trade:**
INTC must absolutely accelerate lower on very high volume. Implied vols should expand for Intel options as well. Failure for that to occur means we are most likely in a corrective drop and profits should be taken.

**FIGURE 6.5** Intel, trading time-frame

**FIGURE 6.6** Intel, daily

low is less than 20 percent beneath the index's current level. Finally, although Intel's rally from its October low is most likely a five-wave affair, it is somewhat less likely that the S&P 500 traced out a similar pattern.

Add it all up, and I need to change my trading idea for Intel. Given that the stock has been extremely volatile, and that there is likely significant room for the stock's price to drop in my forecast next leg lower (even if it does not make a new low), I can stay with a short trade, but shorten my time frame. Actually, it is less a shortening of time frame and more a lowering of my expectations for percentage gain. The timing for a bottom is really unchanged. The difference is that instead of looking for a low in the $12.95 to $9.20 range, I am looking for Intel to bottom near $15.11. Short-term counts allow for a bit lower now, probably not beneath $16.44. Sales would then make sense near the 50 percent retracement from that level back to the high at $19.67 with stops at $20.76 ($0.01 past the 76.4 percent retracement). Of course, these levels will be adjusted during the monitoring phase once I've determined exactly where the current short-term five-wave pattern lower actually completes (see Figure 6.7).

As always, defining a trading plan does not put you at the finish line. In fact, it really only places you into the starting blocks. There is still a bit more research that you must do before you really can trade. At a minimum,

---

**Applying Elliott Wave Theory Profitably -- Trading and Investing Form**

**Identification Section**

| | | | | | |
|---|---|---|---|---|---|
| **Name:** | Steven W. Poser | **Security Symbol:** | INTC | **Price:** | $18.05 |
| | | **Security Name:** | Intel Corporation | | |
| **Date:** | 12-Dec-02 | **Exchange:** | Nasdaq NMS, ECNs | | |

**Version:**                 1.0

**One Timeframe Lower Analysis Section**

**Daily Support Levels and Descriptions**

   $16.91 Prior month's low (November 2002)
   $16.65 Low on 19-December
   $16.44 61.8% retrace back to October 2002 low
   $15.11 76.4% retrace back to October 2002 low
   $12.95 Low since high in 2000, set in October 2002

**Daily Resistance Levels and Descriptions**

   $17.56 Overlap with very minor first leg lower ending on 13-December
   $17.68 If expanded third wave, 62% retrace back to start of minor third wave, begun on 17-December at $18.31
   $18.58 Recent minor high
   $19.30 Bottom of first leg lower off 2-December high
   $21.28 2-December high

**Intraday Analysis**

Daily chart requires relabeling of move to the October low. Preferred count is now five waves down. Although the very end of the move is not 100% clear, most of the exogenous evidence, such as volume cues, support that thinking. Also, the rally to the December 2nd high, although also a bit sloppy, appears to have been completed in five waves. This means that although the there is room for further losses, that the bigger picture is more likely to result in major gains in 2003. With Intel now more than 20% off its high set in early December, though shorts remain preferred for the time being, sales are only advisable on a rally after a five wave pattern lower completes someplace below the recent low set at $16.65.
entry to the trade plan below.

**Trade Plan**

| | |
|---|---|
| **Trade entry:** | Enter short Intel at 50% retracement following completion of five wave down pattern from $22.09. |
| **Stop level:** | Set stops at $0.05 above the 76.4% retracement back to $22.09 from low used to compute entry level noted above. |
| **Entry requirements:** | Must have completed five wave pattern to lower than $16.65, preferably by first week of 2003. |
| **Target:** | At least $15.88 to $14.69 (62-76% retrace to the lows) and possibly lower. |
| **To remain in trade:** | Prices must fall fairly quickly. There is a chance this is still going to new lows, but even if it doesn't, we should be in a wave-C which should permit a drop below $16.65 within a few sessions of trade entry. |

**Alternate Trade Plan (do not execute both plans!)**

| | |
|---|---|
| **Trade entry:** | Buy at $14.70 |
| **Stop level:** | $12.94, $0.01 beneath the old low |
| **Entry requirements:** | If Intel never rallies enough for short sale, larger picture bullish leanings suggest purchases at end of an A-B-C correction. Only enter on clear a-b-c with low volume. |
| **Target:** | Rally past $22.09 |
| **To remain in trade:** | Should be fast move higher as it should be a third wave. Volume should be strong as well. Due to powerful turn however in early October, I am not sure that we'd get as strong volume as we did in October. However, watch for formation of inverted head and shoulders and increased volume on a trendline break to higher prices in late Winter 2002/2003 or early Spring. |

**FIGURE 6.7**   Intel, a change of plans

you should gather together any key data releases, holidays, and dividends or earnings announcements that are expected and place them on your calendar. You also need to set up a monitoring section where you can place notes and update trading activity to see if you need to modify your trade plan going forward. This information is shown in Figure 6.8.

---

**Applying Elliott Wave Theory Profitably -- Trading and Investing Form**

**Identification Section**

| | | | | | |
|---|---|---|---|---|---|
| **Name:** | Steven W. Poser | **Security Symbol:** | INTC | **Price:** | $18.05 |
| | | **Security Name:** | Intel Corporation | | |
| **Date:** | 23-Dec-02 | **Exchange:** | Nasdaq NMS, ECNs | | |

**Version:** 1.0

**Details**

12/24/02 Stock market closes early, at 1:00PM NY Time
12/25/02 Stock market closed for Christmas Day
12/31/02 Consumer confidence data and Chicago PMI
 1/3/03 Monthly payroll and unemployment rate report
 1/14/03 Fourth quarter 2002 earnings release
 1/15/03 Yahoo and Apple Computer earnings releases
 2/5/03 Approximate date for next dividend ex-date

**Monitoring**

I initially began writing this section on Dec. 12, 2002 and it is now Dec. 23, 2002. As of now, I have not yet entered into a trade, but we are getting close to one. If prices accelerate lower now, I might need to reconsider and go back to a more bearish interpretation. That is, I would think this is a third wave down. As of now, that does not look likely, and in fact, a bounce after a small new low looks to be the most likely immediate-term outcome.

---

**FIGURE 6.8** Trading and investing form

## THE DOLLAR AND THE YEN

You may recall that in Chapter 4 I spent a good deal of time discussing the idea that certain securities or markets do not naturally trace out long-term five-wave and three-wave patterns. I noted that exchange rates and interest rates tend to be cyclical and suggested that five-wave patterns only occur during strong trends. Short-term price action does develop in five waves and three waves as periodic imbalances in supply and demand result in the well-known Elliott Wave five-wave three-wave cyclicality. However, largely stationary cyclic markets will exhibit mostly three-wave activity for the very long term. By this, I am referring to multiyear periods. My next example will focus on the U.S. dollar (USD) versus the Japanese yen (JPY). As you will see, although there have been several very powerful trends, including the dollar's nearly calamitous drop once it was floated in the early 1970s, the very large patterns have shown series of three-wave moves.

Such price action does further the challenge of Elliott Wave–based investing and trading. Many of the relationships from one cycle to another become less clear, and most likely irrelevant. In essence, it is not clear that one three-wave pattern should be related to another three-wave pattern. Experience shows that there is a relationship, but great care is required to understand both the fundamental and technical driving forces of such markets before blindly applying classic Elliott Wave tools. If there is a shift in

**FIGURE 6.9** USDJPY, monthly, semilog

the economic standing of one country versus another, prior Elliott-based relationships may disappear.

As you can see in Figure 6.9, though there have been several powerful moves, mostly lower for the USD, only the intracycle action has shown five-wave price action. The bigger-picture patterns have all been three-wave legs. The chart is presented in a semilog scale, and you can see that the initial A–B–C down saw wave C terminate almost exactly at the 1.618 ratio to wave A. However, the subsequent A–B–C did not show that kind of relationship, though the second wave C down, which ended in 1995, did find substantial support in the latter half of 1994 around the level where wave C would have equaled 62 percent of the size of wave A.

To say that there is no relevance connecting one swing to another is too strong a statement. Although I am not convinced that as far as the wave counts are concerned, they are important measuring sticks, there is little doubt that the markets do find these kind of relationships in price swings important. For example, the USDJPY chart shows that the percentage drop from the point where the USD floated in 1991 to its 1978 low was almost exactly equal in size to the November 1982 to April 1987 tumble. Although that was nowhere near the final bottom, USDJPY rallied more than 10 percent over the ensuing three months! This kind of tight targeting does not necessarily give us an Elliott Wave meaning, but it does legitimize the general technical importance of swing price targets outside of the Elliott Wave methodology. As I have said many times before, I do not consider the Elliott Wave Theory to be the only valid form of analysis—technical or fundamental. I see it as one of many tools available to the investor or trader. I believe Elliott is one of the most accurate and extensive, but it is far from the only legitimate way to determine valuations in liquid markets.

I am also including the same monthly chart of USDJPY in Figure 6.10, but this time with a linear scale. Although I consider the semilog chart more useful for long-term movements (USDJPY fell from over 350 to under 80) since it accurately displays percentage moves and also allows you to see greater detail in price changes across the whole trading range, it is also a good idea to look at the price charts with a linear scale.

Although it is true that calculating EW price targets is more correct using percentage moves, psychological factors are part of what draws any price chart. The crowd that makes up the markets often looks at the world in discrete price levels. If the dollar falls from 350 to 250 and then rallies back to 300, there will be a large camp that will find it important for the dollar to hold support at 200, since that would represent a 100-point fall from 300, and would thus match the size of the initial fall from 350 to 250. They

**FIGURE 6.10** USDJPY, monthly, linear

would not be interested in the fact that a like percentage drop in the dollar from 300 should have targeted a level closer to 215.

Similarly, trend lines move at different rates on semilog and linear charts. It is worth drawing these lines with both types of charts. As you saw in Figure 6.9, there seemed to be little importance to the semilog trend lines. However, the linear channel lines have actually appeared to act as strong support and resistance over the past 30 years.

I am not going to present the trade plan as a set of attachments for this analysis. As an exercise, you should apply my commentary to relevant parts of a blank trade plan. Remember that you will need to summarize what I write. A trade plan should not be pages upon pages of verbiage. It should highlight your reasoning for being bullish or bearish and you should be able to apply that reasoning directly to a plan of action. The ideas should be well enough thought out so that you will be able to execute them, without emotion, as soon as the necessary requirements you detailed in your plan are fulfilled.

A brief warning is warranted here. Telling you to await a certain set of requirements before entering a trade needs to be expanded upon. It is very easy to adjust your entry strategy to get a result that you want, rather than one that the market tells you. For example, if you are very risk averse and really do not want to make a trade, you might create a trade entry strategy that would be almost impossible to meet, so you would never put your position on. Alternatively, you might feel you've missed an opportunity and wish to enter the trade anyway. You might then try to justify a very poor risk/reward ratio and chase the market, rather than doing a complete analysis and finding a better spot to put on your position.

Now, back to the monthly USDJPY chart. The first order of business is to review the labels I placed and see if they appear justified. For my readers' own edification, you should be aware that I have been on record for several years with a forecast that USDJPY would reach past its August 1998 peak of 147.62 and should probably approach the 170.00 neighborhood. I have written in the past that there was risk even of a substantially more powerful USD rally. At the time that I first wrote about such a move, as the dollar appeared to be making a beeline for sub-100 levels in late 1999, I was pretty much a loner. Many analysts were forecasting a new USD low beneath the 1995 nadir at 79.92. However, I made that forecast before I had developed my idea that cyclical markets might not always display the classic Elliott five-wave/three-wave cyclicality and interwave cycle relationships.

In light of this prior forecast, it is worth noting how I came to that idea. If you look at the wave 2 high in Figure 6.9 or Figure 6.10 from February 1985, you can argue that the low in 1988, shown as 5,A, might actually only have been wave 3. If so, then the 1995 low was the end of an enormous five-wave fall. A mere 38 percent retracement of that 13-year fall would measure to just about 155 and should take 5 to 8 years to complete. At the time this chapter was written, the USD had bottomed nearly eight years ago, so time was running out on that particular forecast.

My current chart, which shows five waves down to the December 1988 low shown as 5,A, also can be questioned. That final fifth wave is certainly substandard when compared with the wave 1 drop, but the comparison on the linear chart is deceiving. On a percentage basis, wave 5,A was very close to 62 percent the size of wave 1, which is fairly common. Therefore, I find the wave count as shown, barring any changes as I drill down to greater detail, to be acceptable and accurate.

There are some important levels that appear at fairly nearby points, even on this monthly chart. The highs in October 2002 and December 2002 were almost identical at 125.65 and 125.70, respectively. Also nearby was the bottom in March 2002 at 126.36, set in the aftermath of the dollar rally all the way up to 135.20. That same general area has acted as a pivot, support or resistance, many times over the past 15 years.

The recent trading activity does pose a risk that USDJPY is forming a continuation head-and-shoulders pattern to lower levels. (Some technicians believe that the head and shoulders is only a reversal pattern, but that is not correct.) USDJPY might be in the process of forming the right shoulder of this formation. The next important resistance levels come from the retest to the 135.20 high near 134 in April 2002, the January 2002 high of 135.20, and channel resistance, currently just below 136. Key support comes from the recent low in November 2002 at 119.11, the July 2002 bottom at 115.52, possible neckline support at 115.34, and the 62 percent retracement back to the 101.27 low from the end of 1999, which comes in at 114.23. The February 2000 111.73 high point might also be worth watching.

As I've said before, I always like to have a fundamental story as well. I have not yet told you what my forecast is, but I can now: Lower for the next few months, but much higher later. I will get into why later in this section.

## Exchange Rate Determinants

There are many theories as to how exchange rates are determined. I do not think there is yet a valid, well-tested, unified theory of exchange rate determination. One idea, called *purchasing power parity* (PPP), suggests that over time, inflation differentials must be reflected in exchange rates. Thus, if there is higher inflation in the United States than in Japan, the USD must depreciate relative to the JPY. At the time that I wrote this chapter, there was a good deal of controversy regarding this idea, as some Japanese officials had suggested that using PPP, the yen should weaken by 25 percent or more from then-current levels. The problem with PPP is that you must pick some starting point as valid from which you can compute the inflation rate differentials. Your choice of starting point changes your PPP value, making determinations based on this methodology arbitrary.

A common theme used to forecast a continually weakening USD is that the United States consistently runs a trade deficit with Japan. The argument for a weaker dollar is that either Americans must buy yen to purchase these products, or that if the United States pays in dollars, that Japanese firms will convert those dollars into yen, thus putting constant pressure on the USDJPY cross. To a degree, this is true, all things being equal. Unfortunately, all things aren't equal. The Japanese economy's bubble burst at the end of 1989, and remained in a deflationary descent while this book was in production. The economy there is not 100 percent open, and banks still had not owned up to the level of their nonperforming loans. The Nikkei-225 stock index continued to fall and had been in a bear market for more than 13 years. Until the perception that the Japanese economy's growth potential is less than that of the United States changes, USDJPY will not collapse, despite the continuing trade deficit. Japanese and foreign investors continue to prefer USD-denominated assets to yen assets.

This leads to another theory that has not held water to date. This theory says that a weak U.S. stock market or bond market should lead to repatriation by Japanese investors. This could become a dangerous feedback loop, since as the dollar weakens versus the yen, the yen value of dollar assets falls. That would result in even more Japanese selling of their dollar-linked assets, causing an accelerated decline in the value of both the dollar and dollar assets. However, even as the stock market has tumbled since 2000, the dollar has held its own. Even with recent losses, the dollar is more than 10 percent above where it stood when the U.S. stock market peaked. It seems as if investors find a falling dollar as an opportunity to increase their holdings rather than fearing a USD collapse. Any change to that perception could push the dollar sharply lower.

I have been reading about this impending doom, especially in the Treasury bond market, for years. I have to admit that with U.S. yields very low now, I am more nervous that foreigners could start pulling their money from the U.S. government bond market. The chart patterns, which I will discuss elsewhere, also show that Treasuries have probably nearly completed their downward interest rate course (which by the way probably means that deflation, though a greater risk than inflation in the short term, is not likely to take hold in the United States).

There is no question that an event that could cause a collapse in the USD would almost certainly lead many investors to pull the plug on USD assets. However, the tight correlation among the global markets means that it would be very hard for other markets to rise, even as their currencies appreciate, thus partially removing the attractiveness of taking losses on their dollar-based holdings. Remember, wealth just gets destroyed as markets crack, and there would be no place to hide anyway. In fact, the less liquid foreign markets might fall further, even though the problem could be dollar-related (as happened from 2000–2002 when most European bourses fell more than the broad U.S. equity market indices). So far, since the U.S. economy is still viewed as being more resilient than Europe's or Japan's, and America remains the dominant geopolitical power, the dollar and dollar-based markets have remained immune to these kinds of risks. That does not mean that won't change in the future.

The chart pattern shows a dichotomy. Although the near term appears bearish, the longer-term outlook, though not necessarily in line with my three-year-old forecast for a weak yen based on a five-wave pattern lower from the 1982 high (see Figure 4.3), still shows potential for substantially higher USDJPY levels (weak yen). Let's take a look at the weekly chart in Figure 6.11 and see what kinds of opportunities appear with that level of detail.

The first thing that should jump out at you in Figure 6.11 is where I have placed wave 5,A in early 2002. It is not at the 135.20 high. This is one of those wave counts that would have been almost impossible to forecast *a priori* (and I guarantee you that I didn't). This is that rarest of price moves, a failed fifth wave. Note that the dollar also failed versus the Swiss franc, and may have also failed vis-à-vis the Euro. I know that it is tempting

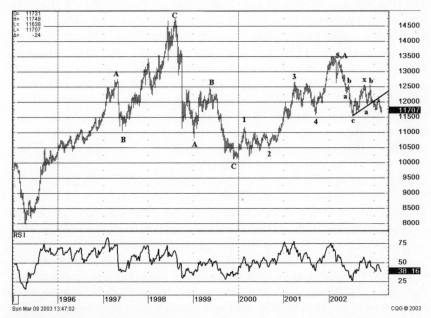

**FIGURE 6.11** USDJPY, weekly

to force a five-wave count to the recorded high, but at least at the weekly level of detail, I do not see it.

A failed fifth wave should indicate upcoming weakness, and it certainly did. The dollar, as of this writing, had retraced more than 50 percent of the rally from 101.27, and though not my preferred forecast, I can see some risk to a move beneath the dollar's 2001 low set at 114.36. Interestingly, however, placing the fifth wave high at the retest to 135.20, at 133.83 in early April 2002, puts me in a different camp than most other Elliott-Wave–based analysts. Those that show that the five-wave cycle ended at 135.20 also have a five-wave count down to the 2002 low of 115.52. That means the three-wave count shown higher since the July low would be a correction that requires a drop below 115.52. Although that is certainly a risk in my preferred scenario, it is not an absolute requirement.

Note that there is an alternative count that avoids the failed fifth wave, but still places the wave 5,A high at 133.83. That result is also achieved if you count the 135.20 high as wave b of a fourth wave of larger wave 5,A higher. That wave count would not change the bigger picture analysis presented here.

The weekly chart gives us a clear short-term sell signal since I would certainly expect a move back down to the wave a low at 119.11. The break of the uptrend line from the July low of 115.52 adds to my negative short-term to medium-term leaning. Note though that wave b as shown slightly exceeded the wave X high, so a huge move beneath the wave a low at 119.11 is not all that likely, unless I find a better wave count as we move to the next level of detail.

To this point, I have done my analysis more from a theoretical perspective, rather than looking at it as a possible trade. However, at this juncture, you probably have enough information to make an initial pass at what your bias will be. My wave count shows that, with USDJPY just above trend-line support and with wave c lower apparently incomplete, the short-term bias should be to lower levels. However, the question now comes down to risk/reward. The bigger-picture outlook might arguably be to higher USDJPY levels, so I will need to look at the daily chart to get a better idea of what kind of trade I should make.

I am looking for a swing trade, and actually consider the daily chart my time frame. Therefore, I will look at a 120-minute chart as well. For most markets, I would use a 30-minute or 60-minute chart, but the foreign exchange markets trade actively for a large part of the 24-hour day, so I use a longer time period even for intraday price analysis.

Figure 6.12 shows that USDJPY is in a third-wave fall, which when it completes I will label as wave iii. Some key support points to watch include the recent USDJPY low at 119.80, the wave a nadir at 119.11, and the 1.618 third-wave target at 118.39. Trend-line support was at 119.98 as of December 26, 2002, and rises 0.04 per day. Resistance levels to watch include the

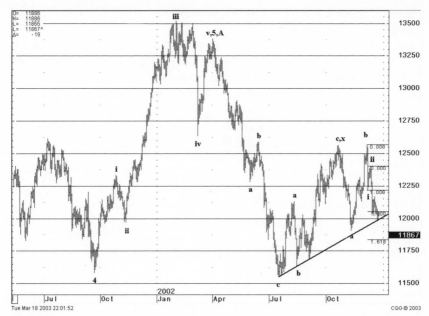

**FIGURE 6.12**  USDJPY, daily

mid-December high at 121.69 and the wave i low at 122.20. A move above 122.20 would be an overlap of the first wave down and mean that the current price action was not impulsive (in the Elliott Wave sense). I would also watch the 62 percent retracement of the drop from 121.69 at 120.97. Much above there would be a bit stronger than I would typically look for. As of now, however, this wave count clearly shows an opportunity for lower USDJPY levels. Wave iii should reach 118.39 and wave v could take the dollar another full point or more lower. With USDJPY currently near 120.44, there is pretty good risk/reward for a short with a stop a bit above 120.97 and a target of 118.39. This strategy is a good trade, though I was really looking for a larger swing than 2 yen. Let's take a look at the 120-minute chart in Figure 6.13 so I can create a more detailed strategy as well as determine an alternative wave count.

The 120-minute chart has led me to revise my short-term wave count. I no longer show wave i as completed at 122.20. Instead, I see that as the end of the first subwave of wave iii, which I've denoted as wave (i). This means that 122.20 is still an important overlap level, but from a smaller subwave. It is not clear whether wave iii is complete or not at this juncture. The rally off 120.24 was an apparent three-wave move on the 120-minute time frame. Although it is not worth taking the whole analysis down to another level of

**FIGURE 6.13**   USDJPY, 120 minutes

detail, I checked the 30-minute chart, and the move from 120.24 to 121.69
looks like a five-wave fall. Therefore, I have labeled the rally to that level
as wave a. The drop to 119.80 after that definitely was not a five-wave move,
keeping with the corrective idea. Prices may be in a triangle or just a standard issue irregular, but either way, the immediate-term outlook suggests
more upside than downside.

   If the dollar is in a triangle, gains will probably halt just shy of 121.00,
which is where the short-term swing target from 119.99 would equal the
size of the initial bounce off 119.80. If this is a wave c, prices could come
close to challenging 122.20. Given that idea, my strategy would be to enter
USDJPY shorts on a rally to 120.90 with stops at 122.21, just above the overlap. The downside target is to at least 119.10, but more likely the wave (v)
equals the wave (i) target of 117.80, which is not far from where wave iii
would be 6.86 times wave i at 118.36. Either way, the risk/reward is more
than 2:1, which makes it a good trade.

   It is important to understand what must happen once you enter a trade
to ensure that the market develops properly. I do not like to stay in a trade
until the stop is hit, but would rather exit early if the market does not
develop as expected. In this case, I would not put the short trade on if the

market falls much below the recent 119.80 low. Also, a powerful rally past the 121.00 level, unless it is part of the completion of a clear five-wave advance whose likely measurements would keep USDJPY south of 122.20, should sound alarms and have you exit your short trade early. Finally, if you enter on an apparently completed wave c five-wave advance, then you can probably move your stops to just above the top of that move. Additionally, the preference would be for an impulsive five-wave move lower to start immediately. Three-wave patterns down would not be considered impulsive and would require you to trail stops very quickly.

I want to go back to the longer-term picture for a moment. We discussed several pages back the old idea I had that the dollar might be in a five-wave drop, with the rally since the 1995 low being part of a fourth-wave correction. Certainly, that remains a possibility, although my theory regarding Elliott Wave would not require five-wave patterns in the foreign exchange markets. However, I also do not preclude such a possibility, and if there was a strong fundamental reason for the dollar to be in a general and strong depreciation mode, then a five-wave drop would be a possibility. As a reminder, I have reproduced the two long-term counts previously discussed for USDJPY in Figure 6.14.

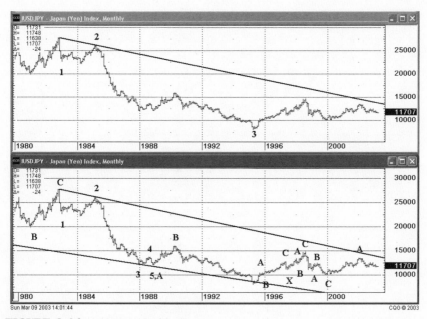

**FIGURE 6.14** USDJPY, monthly, linear

If the dollar is in a five-wave move lower, then there is not much time left in wave 4. Prices have been rising for nearly eight years now. The first three waves down took about 24 years. I can see some risk for the fourth wave to continue for about another year, but not much more than that. The first two waves only took a total of about 4 to 5 years to complete, whereas wave 3 took about 19½ years to run its course. Although I do not typically fret about extended fourth waves, when we are talking about multiyear patterns, I am much more comfortable when the timing makes sense; anything much beyond a 38 percent retracement timewise for wave 4 would be stretching it, and 38 percent of 19½ years is less than 7½ years, so we are already stretched.

With all that said, as you can see from Figure 6.15, there is a chance that we are in a triangle fourth wave. That possibility remains as long as USD-JPY holds the 115.52 low. A strong rally toward the 130 area, where triangle resistance stands, should be possible as well. Interestingly, the longer-term more bullish idea, as indicated by the lower half of Figure 6.14, would allow for a 62 percent retracement of the rally from 101.27 to 133.82, which comes in at 113.71. Below there would be a major concern. Either way though, with the dollar sitting just above 120, the longer-term outlook allows for a

**FIGURE 6.15**  Triangle fourth wave, as long as 115.52 holds

rally at least to 130 and possibly on up to the 140s or 150s if my more complex cyclical theory works out.

This realization leads to a longer-term swing trade. I would stick with the short-term bearish trade, but would look at starting to enter into long-term bullish positions as the dollar approaches the target areas noted above for the daily perspective trade. Either outright purchases or sales of dollar puts as USDJPY approaches the 117 handles would make sense. If the buck keeps falling, as long as the cross holds above the 76 percent retracement back down toward 101.27, which comes in at 108.95, I would be comfortable staying long. The minimum target would be to triangle resistance, which was at 131.75 in January 2003 and falls about 0.30 per month.

I realize that this does not meet my normal 2:1 risk/reward ratio requirement, but my recommendation for such a long-term trade would be to build a position as the dollar falls, so that you average into a full position at a price somewhat lower than the upper 118 target area. Also, you would be partially hedged by your outstanding short trade. The idea of selling an out-of-the money dollar put is also attractive since you receive income for the puts, and because you want to own the dollars anyway longer term.

## HOT CHOCOLATE

The next market I want to look at is the cocoa futures market. I have to admit that I am definitely not an expert on cocoa, and any advice you glean from me here is based purely on the chart patterns. I cannot provide any insight whatsoever into the fundamentals of this market. I strongly recommend anybody who is interested in trading any of the agricultural or related futures markets to spend some time learning about growing seasons and seasonality in these markets. That information can be incredibly important. You might read about a horrible drought and expect your wheat futures to soar, only to find out that the futures you own are based on a wheat season that has not even been planted yet. Another possibility is that your contract might not be priced based on the area where the drought exists, lessening the effect of the lack of rain on your contract.

### Futures Contract Expiration Strategies

One of the reasons that you need to understand this kind of information comes directly from part of the analysis I will show you in the following discussion. As you know, futures expire periodically. Some markets have a contract every month, others every three months, and still others at seemingly irregular intervals. Futures provide a special challenge when attempting a long-term analysis. Because any given contract is usually only liquid for a few months and because a contract might only have a year or two of data available, and sometimes even less than that, the only way to perform a long-term analysis is by concatenating a series of contracts. Most financial futures can also be analyzed by looking at the spot or cash markets for a long-term view, but that will not always make sense in the agricultural commodities.

Different kinds of futures markets provide different challenges when doing this. In financial markets, the shape of the yield curve affects the relationship from one month to another in a futures contract series. You can choose just to splice one contract onto another at expiration, a month before expiration, or even when the next contract starts trading with larger open interest or volume. However, a simple splice might lead to a gap from one contract month to the next, making your indicators, retracements, Fibonacci extensions, and trend lines useless. The alternative idea is to adjust the historical prices from the old contracts so that there is no price gap. This will allow you to continue to use your price targets, retracements, and indicators, though prices prior to the splice point are totally fictional and may not offer true support or resistance. You might even end up with negative prices in your historical data. Despite this weakness, it is the method I usually use. However, I also will look at the data from the currently most active contract as well to see if there are any important price levels directly attributable to that contract.

Soft and agricultural markets provide an additional challenge when concatenating futures contracts. Because of the problems discussed earlier regarding possible different growing seasons or irregular contract placement, there is more than just an interest rate differential involved. In fact, there might be no logical relationship at all from one contract to the next. For that reason, though it may be worthwhile taking a quick look at spliced futures series, I would not use them for price targeting. It might even be dangerous to apply highs and lows for the purpose of wave counts since the adjustments might give a false outlook from that as well. However, if the differentials are large enough, you can probably determine whether or not there have been overlaps.

## Cocoa Chart Analysis

As you can see, there is a very clear five-wave advance completed in cocoa futures in early October 2002. My recollections though had been of a huge and very long cocoa bear market, and I honestly did not know, when I produced the chart, when the losses stopped. I had no real reason to believe that July 2001, which is where the low price occurred in Figure 6.16, was the low of that bear move. Unfortunately, that is how far back the data for

**FIGURE 6.16**   March 2003, cocoa, weekly

the March 2003 futures extend. I decided it would be a good idea to check a spliced chart, and that turned out to be important since cocoa actually bottomed in December 2000 and not July 2001. That means that what I have labeled as wave V on the chart is probably more correctly labeled as wave III with the previously shown I-II-III-IV-V designated as 1-2-3-4-5, III instead. That also means that the current rally that began in late November 2002 is actually a fifth-wave rally in a larger five-wave cycle.

I am actually looking for a shorter-term trade here, but it is always important to understand the underlying trend, which in this case is clearly bullish. It is interesting that at the time I wrote this, there was a good deal of debate going on as to whether or not the global risk was for a return to recession and possible deflation, or whether the U.S. Fed and other central banks were providing so much liquidity, by keeping interest rates low, that there was actually a risk of reigniting inflation. That would be major news since the major Western economies had been in a disinflationary environment (falling inflationary pressures, but still inflation) for more than 20 years. Cocoa certainly does not provide enough evidence, but it would appear that this sweet entry probably has more downside than upside over the next year or two, but that a collapse to new lows beneath its worst levels of 2000 is not likely.

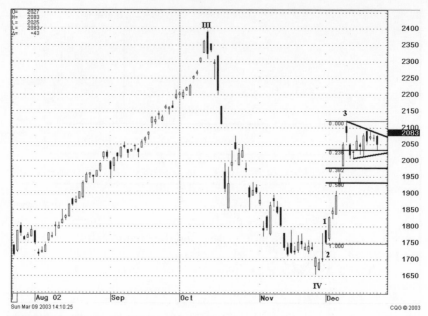

**FIGURE 6.17**   March 2003 cocoa, daily

As shown in Figure 6.17, the daily chart provides a good deal more information regarding the current situation. There was no way of determining the proper wave count since cocoa completed its corrective losses in late November without switching to a daily time frame. The daily count shows a fairly clear three-wave advance completed as of December 10, 2002. The top, which also was an island reversal that quickly got filled, has seen cocoa move into a very narrow range since that time. There are two possible counts since then. One would place cocoa in wave c of wave 4 lower now. This would permit a run to the 38 percent retracement of wave 3, which comes in at $1,978 per metric ton. The idea that appears most likely is that cocoa is in a fourth-wave triangle right now, and is set to complete wave c down (with wave d and wave e to come). Trend-line support rises about $2 per day and is at $2,023 currently with resistance at $2,076 and falling $4 per day (December 24, 2002 close was $2,052). Note that it took 9 days for the first three legs higher to complete and wave 4 is already 10 days old. It appears as if the triangle could extend for another three to four days. The ultimate breakout should be to higher prices.

Note that the proper count is probably that cocoa is completing the fifth wave of the first leg of a larger five-wave rally. Potential for this minor fifth wave is probably not much past $2,150. My preferred strategy is to buy after touching the trend line (triangle support) with stops just beneath that day's low. This should allow purchases near $2,025 or so with very tight stops. The alternative idea would be to buy on a breakout above the triangle, but with the minimum upside potential so close by, I do not consider that to be a viable alternative. Don't forget to check for governmental releases that could affect cocoa's prices as well, such as weather reports and crop forecasts, before you put your trade on.

The fact is that the uptrend is clearly strong. Even with the normal slowdown into year end, open interest continued to expand as prices rose and has been little changed during the recent trading range. Volume has slowed during the triangle, but it is hard to know if that is due to the correction or because it is late December. Although it is probably a combination of both factors, the underlying analysis is that higher prices are likely ahead of us.

The intraday chart shown in Figure 6.18 does not offer a huge amount of additional information. It does highlight, however, that the triangle interpretation is likely the most correct one, and thus removes any ideas about attempting to wait for a deeper retracement to enter into longs.

Although the noted target is quite near the wave 3 high so far, that does not mean that March cocoa will not rally further. If the minor fifth wave extended wave 1 by a 1.618 ratio, the target would be near $2,250. Using the alternative technique of wave 5 approaching 62 percent of the distance traveled by the first three waves, an approximate target of $2,300 is revealed.

**FIGURE 6.18** March 2003 Cocoa futures, 30 minutes

Possible interesting swing trading ideas also may be considered here. Since the $2,394 wave III high is expected to fall eventually, retracements of a completed first wave of wave V suggest good buying opportunities. Given expectations for wave 1 of wave V to end in the $2,150 to $2,300 range, and given the wave IV low of $1,655, any fall below the upper $1,800s provides for an excellent longer-term swing trade. I would rather not buy though until a full five waves have completed to avoid any possibility of the drop from wave III developing into a more complex correction.

## DAY TRADING WITH ELLIOTT

My next two examples will be from the very short term trading and day trading arenas. Trading from very short time frames requires extra attention to detail. Although you probably do not need to look at charts beyond a daily periodicity, you still need to do your homework. In fact, it is doubly important here that you are aware of any important data releases that could affect your trade: government statistical releases, foreign central bank meetings, geopolitical concerns, corporate earnings releases, or SEC rulings to name a few. Any one of these items can cause the market you are looking at to move in a violent manner and take a profit to a loss very quickly.

### Consider Trading Costs before Day Trading

When you day trade, every mistake is amplified. Every penny counts. Slippage, the bid-ask spread, and commissions eat up a much larger share of your profits than they do when you are swing trading. Consider this: The average daily trading range is about 4 percent in the S&P 500. That means the daily trading range in the S&P 500 SPDRs (SPY), which currently trades around $90.00 per share, is around $0.36 each day. Consider a purchase of 100 shares at $90.00 per share. That will cost you $9,000. If you buy at the low and sell at the high, on an average day, that would net you $0.36 per share, or $36.00. Only one problem. That does not include the bid-ask spread, slippage, or commissions. Assume the low for the day was $90.00 and the high was $90.36. Most likely, the best level you could have bought at would have been $90.01 and the best level you could have sold your shares for was $90.35. That lowers your profit to $34.00. Then, you most likely had to pay a commission of about $20.00 ($10.00 to buy and $10.00 to sell), plus SEC fees and possibly even ECN fees. So, now you are down to $14.00 at best. If you had any slippage at all, every penny eats another dollar out of your gains. All in all, the bid-ask spread, commissions, and slippage on such a small-sized trade could consume more than two-thirds of your profits.

What I gave you was a best-case scenario. That assumes you could buy at the low and sell at the high. It is more reasonable to assume you could only capture about half of the daily range. Assuming you used limit orders and did not have to pay extra for them, you would already be in the red.

However, all is not lost. First of all, for day trading purposes, it might be reasonable to trade a larger size. Because most retail discount brokers have a flat fee up to 5,000 shares, your commission takes a smaller bite out of your total size. However, realize that a 1,000-share trade in the SPY eats up $90,000, based on the parameters I gave you. The more shares you trade, the larger your slippage as well. There are some very deep discount brokers as well, where you can pay as little as $0.01 per share or less in commissions. That would make this type of trading more profitable. Even then, on a 100-share trade, commissions and slippage will likely take 20 percent or more of your profits.

In the case of futures trading, you will typically pay from $5.00 to $25.00 in commissions and fees or more per round turn trade. A round turn means both the buy and sell trade. Unlike equities, that is typically how futures trading is priced. You still need to worry about the bid-ask spread and slippage. The difference here is that futures are highly leveraged. You might need to put only $2,500 or so up to control $100,000 of an investment. That means that commission becomes a much smaller percentage of your costs, but slippage and the bid-ask spread are based on the value of the underlying futures and not on your initial margin. You can make or lose a lot of money very quickly in the futures market. I usually try to dissuade people from trading futures unless they have money to lose and are very experienced. You can lose more money than your initial margin deposit, or for that matter, more than all of the money in your account, trading futures. Imagine you bought a futures contract on an equity index that had a value of $100,000. Assume you put up a margin of 5 percent, or $5,000, and that was all of the money in your account. If the index fell 7 percent and you closed the trade there, you would have to write a check for an additional $2,000 to cover your losses. This is because 7 percent of $100,000 is $7,000 and that is $2,000 more than you had in your account. After writing that check, you would have zero in your account!

Electronic trading has made it a lot easier for you to day trade. It has also lowered the barrier to entry. You still need to consider fees for your charting program and for real-time prices (which are not exactly real-time, but are very close) when you try to determine how much you are really making from trading. However, it has become easier to trade and be profitable with the ever-increasing list of low-cost brokers and data and charting packages. To a degree, the cost may have been brought so low that it added to the bubble that ultimately resulted in the collapse of the Nasdaq and helped exacerbate the still ongoing bear market in equities. Too many people who did not have the knowledge or experience found it cheap and easy to trade. Trading is not easy, or there would be more wealthy people doing it. Day trading is orders of magnitude harder!

## Yielding A Profit:
## U.S. 10-Year Treasury Note Futures

My first example will be drawn from the U.S. Treasury market. The most active futures contract for many years had been the bond futures, based on a notional 20-year Treasury bond. However, because most foreign government benchmarks have been issued with 10-year maturities and because the U.S. government halted issuance of 30-year bonds, the benchmark and most active futures contract is now the 10-year Treasury note.

The 10-year futures expire in a March, June, September, and December cycle. The next expiring contract is usually the most active until the first week of expiration month, when the following contract usually goes front month.[1] For example, the March 2003 futures became the most active and front month contract during the first week of December 2002. A discussion of hedging techniques and conversion factors is beyond the scope of this book. See the Chicago Board of Trade's website, http://www.cbot.com, for detailed descriptions of these principles.

Treasury bond market yields offer a window into global investors' expectations of future U.S. economic growth, as well as the health of the global economy. Yields also represent insight into future inflation expectations. Unlike corporate bond yields, there is little or no assumed default risk in U.S. Treasuries. Understanding the multitude of factors that move yields in the Treasury market could fill several volumes. Your job in trading this market requires close attention to any and all economic releases from the United States as well as attention to important releases in Europe, and to a lesser extent, Japan.

## Don't Forget Your Intermarket Analysis

Intermarket analysis is incredibly important when you are set to trade the bond market. This means that you should always keep a wary eye on stock market futures, European debt futures, and to a lesser extent, the U.S. dollar. Central bank announcements from the United States and Europe are also very important. When the United States issues debt, it is in competition with other foreign governments who are also borrowing money from the global capital markets. That means that if interest rates rise sharply in Europe, they likely will increase here. The relationship is not one-to-one, but correlations between American and European interest rates have increased in recent years as the global village has shrunk.

Remember, I am talking about futures here. Although the price volatility of debt futures is far lower than that of most stocks, don't forget that you might be putting up $2,500 in futures margin that controls $100,000 in the bond market. That means a 1.0 percent move in the underlying 10-year note could result in a 40 percent change in your margin. As I've warned before, you can lose more than your initial margin if the price moves against you in a big way. If you put up $2,500 in margin and the futures move more than 2½ points against your position, you will have lost more than the money you already put up and will have to wire more funds into your account (actually, a margin call would happen before the margin was completely wiped out).

Look at the three-panel chart in Figure 6.19. The first chart shows the daily chart for TYH3, the March 2003 10-year Treasury note futures. The next chart shows a rollover adjusted continuous futures chart. The final frame in the montage depicts the 10-year benchmark yield. As you can see from the chart, my warnings regarding the differences between futures charts and cash charts really play out here. The adjusted futures and straight March 2003 futures charts show that this market made a new price high. However, the yield chart indicates that the apparent new highs on the futures charts are very misleading. Yields were more than 20 basis points above their lows set

**FIGURE 6.19a**   March 2003, 10Y futures

**FIGURE 6.19*b***   Adjusted 10Y futures

**FIGURE 6.19*c***   10Y Treasury note yield

in October. Twenty basis points is more than a full point in the futures. That is a big difference—greater than $1,000 for one futures contract. It is important to be aware of this distinction. When I show you some of the support and resistance levels in the trade plan shown in Figure 6.20, I will use approximations for the futures contracts based on the historic yield levels since the futures prices themselves do not tell you the whole story.

As I mentioned earlier, my plan is for a very short term trade, possibly even a day trade. That means I need to find an excellent entry point—be it long or short—from which I can hold a very tight stop and know very quickly whether I am right or wrong. I likely would hold this position from several minutes to at most several days, though it is more likely that I would not hold a position overnight unless I had a very compelling reason to do so. Too much can go wrong when a market is not open, or not active anyway, to overcome the risk/reward of giving away targeted gains on a day trading position.

Since I am talking about a relatively short-term or day trade here and since you will need to be nimble in your entry and exit, I do not feel that it is

---

### Applying Elliott Wave Theory Profitably -- Trading and Investing Form

**Identification Section**

| | | | | |
|---|---|---|---|---|
| **Name:** | Steven W. Poser | **Security Symbol:** | TYH3 | **Price:** 115 17/64 |
| | | **Security Name:** | U.S. 10-year March 2003 T-Note Futures | |
| **Date:** | 30-Dec-02 | **Exchange:** | CBOT | |

**Version:** 1.0

**Long-term Analysis Section**

**Long-term Support Levels and Descriptions**

114 51/64 Low on 30-December-2002
114 18/64 Gap support from high on 26-December
113 48/64 Channel support on 31-December, rises about 12/64ths per day
113 22/64 Start of 3rd of 3rd of 5th on 23-December
112 07/64 Start of 3rd of 5th of 17-December

**Long-term Resistance Levels and Descriptions**

115 22/64 New contract high set on 30-December
115 60/64 Channel resistance, rises about 12/64ths per day
116 09/64 Where wave-iii of third of wave-5 is 1.618 times first of third of five
116 32/64 Approximate level where March 2003 futures will reach the cash yield low
117 22/64 Where third of wave-5 equals 1.618 times first of wave-5

**Type of trade (intraday, short-term swing (intraday to several days), swing trade (several days to a couple of weeks), medium-term (weeks to months), long-term (months to years):** intraday

**Long-term overview**

Calling this long-term is only in relation to the time frame I am trading! Overall direction is bullish. Concern over fact that futures made a new high, and there was little follow through. However, fact is that although futures made a new top, cash was no place near its prior best levels, lessening the importance of the futures break. Still see a couple more minor swings higher in the next month or so, though will require reviewing next level of periodicity to get better idea of day trading opportunities.

**FIGURE 6.20** 10-year Treasury long-term analysis

reasonable to complete the same detailed analysis as you would for a longer-term swing trade. That does not mean you should not do your homework—quite the opposite. Things like data releases will have a far greater impact on your returns in the very short term. A day trade does not require four levels of data periodicity. You should start with a daily perspective and then go down two intraday levels—your trading time frame and a very short term time frame to nail down your buy, sell, and stop points.

The next level of detail that I will use is a 40-minute bar chart. Although 60 minutes is far more common, the trading day, using the pit day session only,[2] in the debt futures does not evenly divide into a full hour. The final bar, if I used a 60-minute chart, would only be 40 minutes. Although this is not the end of the world, it makes trend lines, indicators, and tick volumes suspect. For this reason, I have chosen to use a 40-minute chart. An 80-minute chart would work as well, but I prefer the detail available from the 40-minute perspective.

As you can see from Figure 6.21, I show a completed third-wave rally as of the high on Tuesday, December 31, 2002. Prices fell into the close that day, but there is plenty of room for further losses as the 23.6 percent retracement of wave 3 comes in at $114^{47}/_{64}$ with the wave iv of wave 3 low the next support at $114^{38}/_{64}$. This compares favorably with the December 31 close of $115^{26}/_{64}$ and the intraday peak of $115^{35}/_{64}$. Although my bigger-picture outlook is bullish, the best day trade appears to be from the short side.

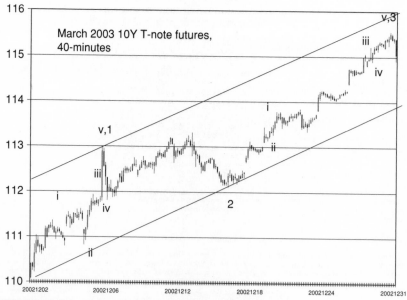

**FIGURE 6.21**   10-Year Treasury trading time-frame

There are other reasons for concern as well. Intraday RSI is hugely over-bought near 81 and also shows a minor divergence. I never like to see divergences in third waves. Additionally, although the wave counts seem complete, wave 3 is rather short. The 1.618 Fibonacci extension target for wave 3 forecast a high of $116^{53}/_{64}$. This adds to the my preference for a trade from the short side, especially from a day trading perspective. With the market closed for a holiday, my first take would be to sell at the open on Thursday, January 2, 2003, as long as prices do not open strongly higher (more than 50 percent back toward the December 31 high). Also, I would be loath to sell on a move much below the initial 23.6 percent retracement target of $114^{47}/_{64}$. I have included this information plus further key price levels in the updated trade plan shown in Figure 6.22. I've also included the Details section, which

---

### Applying Elliott Wave Theory Profitably -- Trading and Investing Form

**Identification Section**

| | | | | |
|---|---|---|---|---|
| **Name:** | Steven W. Poser | **Security Symbol:** | TYH3 | **Price:** 115 17/64 |
| | | **Security Name:** | U.S. 10-year March 2003 T-Note Futures | |
| **Date:** | 31-Dec-02 | **Exchange:** | CBOT | |

**Version:** 1.0

**Trading Time Frame Section**

**Trading Support Levels and Descriptions**

    114 58/64 Low on Dec. 31, 2002
    114 47/64 23.6% retracement of labeled 3rd wave
    114 38/64 Wave-iv of labeled 3rd wave
    114 15/64 38.2% retracement of labeled 3rd wave
    113 52/64 0-2 trend line at open on January 2, 2003, rises about 1/64th per 40-minutes

**Trading Resistance Levels and Descriptions**

    115 03/64 Close on December 31st
    115 26/64 Price from where prices started falling quickly on 31-December
    115 29/64 50% retracement from Dec. 31, 2002 low back to the contract high of 115 35/64
    115 35/64 Contract high set on December 31st

**Trading overview**

The sharp drop late in the day on December 31st heralded trouble, and also gave us a good risk/reward for a possible short trade. The likely wave count says that prices finished a third wave higher. Although the losses had already been fairly substantial by market close, the fact that wave-3 was also fairly short in price traveled raises risk that this was a corrective move which has now ended, making the short trade even more attractive.

**Trade Strategy**

Sell at open on Thursday, January 2, 2003 as long as prices do not open below 114 47/64 or above the 50% retracement back to the high at 115 35/64. That level is 115 29/64. Initial target at least 114 38/64 and more likely 114 15/64.

---

**Details**

Keep a close eye on USD, which has been deteriorating sharply, but is oversold.

Data due on Thursday morning, January 2nd:

Weekly unemployment claims: Prior week was 407,500 and expectation is near 400,000 (8:30AM)
Monthly ISM Report on Manufacturing: November was 49.2% and consensus is 50.0%. (10:00AM)

Other upcoming data:

    1/3/03 Construction spending: November was +0.2%, December expected +0.2% (8:30AM)
            Domestic vehicle sales: November was 12.7mln, December expected around 13.0mln (throughout day)

**FIGURE 6.22**  10-Year Treasury, updated trade plan

shows key news items to watch for. The first few days of the year will not see any major corporate releases, and the weekly claims should not really move the market, but with the dollar oversold and the bond market overbought, the Institute for Supply Management's (ISM) survey of manufacturers' purching managers could be important and has the potential to move the market substantially. With most of the risk to the downside, I would want to have my trade on prior to that release, which is due at 10:00 A.M. EST.

Now that I've put together a fairly detailed plan of action, I want to get inside my trading time frame to nail down my exact trading strategy. Although a 20-minute chart will show more detail, I am talking about an intraday futures trade here, which is highly leveraged, and 20 minutes really doesn't give you all that much more insight into the short-term patterns. Certainly, you can see that prices fell sharply late in the day, and the interesting point now would be to see if there were any wave patterns evident in a somewhat shorter periodicity. Therefore, Figure 6.23 exhibits a five-minute chart of TYH3.

The five-minute chart does clear things up a bit. There was a pretty clear five-wave move off the high early on December 31, 2002. A powerful third wave lower also has likely completed, with wave iv possibly also done. If not, there is just room for a few more ticks higher. The close was $115^{03}$/64, and the 38 percent retracement comes in at $115^{06}$/64. This move seems pretty

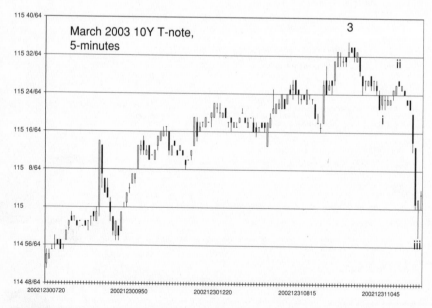

**FIGURE 6.23**  March 2003 10-Year T-note futures, 5-minute chart

powerful and any drop beneath 115 would imply that either wave v down had begun or that prices were in a third of a third lower. If wave iv is already complete, the target for wave v would be near $114^{55}\!/_{64}$ and the 50 percent retracement of the whole drop would only get prices back toward $115^{13}\!/_{64}$. With a powerful third-wave run lower due, it probably pays to look to get short first thing Thursday morning, January 2, 2003, as long as prices don't surge or collapse outright. The detailed trade plan is shown in Figure 6.24.

Note that futures gapped open sharply lower on January 3. I waited for the 8:30 A.M. unemployment claims report, looking for a rally as prices reached and slightly exceeded the fifth-wave targets. However, as soon as

---

**One Timeframe Lower Analysis Section (five minute chart)**

**Intraday Support Levels and Descriptions**

115 00/64 Minor dip since bounce off wave-iii low
114 58/64 Wave-iii low
114 55/64 Possible wave-v target
114 47/64 23.6% retracement of wave-3
114 38/64 Wave-iv of labeled 3rd wave

**Intraday Resistance Levels and Descriptions**

115 04/64 High of bounce off wave-iii low so far
115 06/64 38.2% retracement of wave-iii down
115 11/64 50% retracement of wave-iii down
115 21/64 Wave-i overlap

**Intraday Analysis**

A clear impulse move has developed. Though not shown on the chart, wave-iii lower is well beyond 1.618 times the size of wave-i which implies a possibly more powerful drop beginning than suggested in my earlier analysis. If so, it would behoove us to get on board for a very quick and powerful drop as early as possible. I do not want to enter at too low a level, but the parameters noted in the trading time frame section might be worth stretching if stops are trailed aggressively. Remember, there is a data release 10-minutes after the open. Any rally on that release should be sold as soon as it appears to be petering out, especially if prices first reach the 114 55/64 target. You don't want to be waiting to get short when the 10:00AM data come out if prices are already running out of steam on the up side.

**Trade Plan**

**Trade entry:** Enter short TYH3 early on January 2, 2003

**Stop level:** If five wave pattern already completed, due to gap lower, 1/64th above 62% retracement to the high. If market opens higher, stop should be 1/64th above 115 11/64, the 50% retracement of wave-iii. Do not enter if market opens above 115 11/64

**Entry requirements:** TYH3 must open below 115 11/64, but not beneath 114 38/64

**Target:** At least the 38.2% retracement of wave-3 at 114 15/64

**To remain in trade:** Prices should fall fairly quickly. If five waves completed on open, then we should probably exit trade by late on Friday, January 3rd as main preference is for an a-b-c drop. Even if it is the start of a larger fall, the retracements of a greater than one point drop would eat too much of a day trade's profits.

**Alternate Trade Plan (do not execute both plans!)**

**None**

---

**FIGURE 6-24** 10-Year Treasury, final trade plan

prices slipped beneath 114$^{39}$⁄64, which was the early low, it was clear to me that we were in trouble. The entry price would be 114$^{38}$⁄64, the old wave iv of wave 3 low. There should be stops beneath there, and I would not want to have to fill as those stops were going off because there would be substantial slippage. Stops for the trade would be 114$^{59}$⁄64, ¹⁄64 above filling the daily gap. For those not wishing to risk that much, you also could use a price just above the high set following the weekly unemployment claims report set at 114$^{52}$⁄64. The sharp losses imply either that we are already in wave c down with a very short and shallow second or wave b lower completed on the claims, or that we are in a third of a third. This means we should look for a sharp and powerful extension lower with targets at least to 114$^{32}$⁄64 and preferably to below 114. Remember, overlap does not come in until 113.

Continued monitoring was quite pleasant on this trade as prices fell quickly. The 10:00 A.M. data showed much stronger than expected manufacturing results from the ISM with strong gains in almost every part of the index. The stock market and USD soared and the 10Y had fallen below 114 before 10:00 A.M. as the numbers apparently got out a bit early. Stops were trailed to 113$^{59}$⁄64 by 10:05 A.M. and then to 113$^{37}$⁄64 within another 40 minutes. These were hit as losses slowed shortly after. The five-minute chart for the whole day is shown in Figure 6.25. Note that there is probably still room for further losses, but this is a day trade and after a more than 2-point drop and

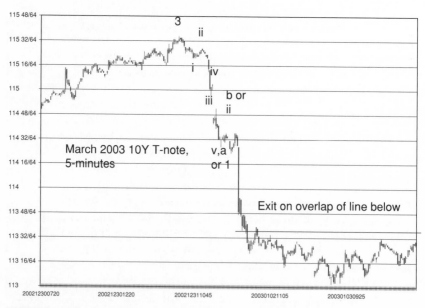

**FIGURE 6.25**   March 2003 10-Year T-Notes, a profitable start

greater than 1-point gain, which is not all that common in a day trade, there is far too much to lose to hold on to the position! I should point out that there is still a chance that this move has not even completed wave a as yet. The sharp additional losses seen following the news at 10:00 A.M. could be interpreted as a third wave within a larger third wave. If that is the case, then prices would need to quickly slide toward $112^{54}\!/_{64}$, where that subwave is 1.618 times the size of the apparent third wave lower. This would need to occur quickly, on Friday morning. Given the large losses already seen, from a day trading perspective, there is more upside/retracement risk than downside possibilities, which is why I feel closing the trade makes sense.

In the end, the idea to close the trade was probably a good one. Although the third wave within a larger third wave may in the end prove to be correct, prices barely moved on Friday. After initial small losses, futures finished slightly higher that session and I certainly would not have been willing to hold a day trade over the weekend given the enormous losses incurred in the futures, leaving little actual trading, and therefore little resistance, above then-current prices.

## Profits Can Be Addictive: Altria Group

My final example will be a day trade or very short term swing trade in the stock market. Most traders are familiar with day trading technology stocks, such as Intel, Dell, NVidia, and their ilk. This is because of their extreme volatility, allowing for large profits (or losses) to accrue quickly. Most technology-oriented issues trade on the Nasdaq, which means that you can usually short them more easily, especially in smaller size, because the more liquid shares also have active and deep markets not only with market makers, but with the ECNs. Since direct-access stockbrokers allow you to route orders to the ECNs, if your short is the next available order and the stock shows an uptick, your short will be filled as long as there are enough shares available for you to trade. This set of circumstances is far less likely on the American Stock Exchange or the New York Stock Exchange (NYSE). Specialists control the trading in those stocks, and very few have deep or active markets on the ECNs. The specialists attempt to keep an orderly market while always, or almost always, earning the bid-ask spread. By providing an orderly market they tend to force orders to congregate at key levels. There are not as many direction changes on a tick-by-tick basis, making it more difficult to sell short in a falling market. On the other hand, the specialists do provide liquidity to the market, and you sometimes will be able to get a larger portion of your trade filled at one price level, thus affording less slippage. On ECNs, you can sometimes buy at the bid or sell at the offer since there are no market makers involved, but if the market is moving quickly, you might suffer substantial slippage in your trade.

Day trading stocks is somewhat different than doing the same thing in futures or currencies. The leverage is much lower, meaning you need a larger move to make a significant sum of money. That said, there is no real need to make huge sums of money on every trade. Steady 2 percent, 3 percent, or 5 percent gains can earn you substantial returns over time. In fact, that is exactly the kind of trade I seek out in my retail-oriented newsletters for my clients. You do not even have to go on margin (you do need a margin account and will have to pay interest on short trades if they are held until settlement). In other words, you would not even be leveraged, if you don't want to be. Most stocks trade in a 2 percent or greater range every single day. Remember, 2 percent for a $40 stock is just $0.80. Although it might not be reasonable to expect to day trade and make 2 percent per day, you should be able to find trades where you can have 1 percent to 2 percent stops with 3 percent to 5 percent targets that can reasonably complete in a period of several sessions.

Despite the much higher volatility in technology stocks, I have chosen every lawyer's dream stock for this example: Altria Group (formerly Philip Morris). Although its businesses are relatively staid (foods, liquor, and tobacco), the constant litigation regarding the tobacco industry's apparent attempts to hide the dangers of smoking has turned Altria (MO) into a widely traded and highly volatile issue. The stock trades on the NYSE, however, so it is controlled by specialists. The company also pays a fairly high quarterly dividend of $0.64 per share, which if you are short at the time of your trade, you will need to pay out of your pocket to whomever you borrowed the shares from to enter into the short position.

To be honest, day trading Altria requires a great deal of research. You need to review the news and current litigation. Although late December is typically a quiet period in the markets, there were several news items released regarding court cases involving the company. Part of your preparatory work would require you to be aware of the recent court decisions. These decisions often lead to revisions of analysts' earnings forecasts as well as changes by the ratings agencies to the presumed credit quality of the firm's debt. This is because a large award in one court can be used as a precedent elsewhere, thus increasing the probability of substantial successful claims elsewhere, which could ultimately harm Altria's long-term viability as a going concern.

Beyond the court cases, you should also be vigilant with regard to dividend payments as well as possible earnings releases. You should review earnings release dates from prior years in case there are no forward-looking schedules on the Altria Group web site. My research shows that MO announced its 2001 earnings on January 30, 2002, so you probably have the better part of this month before earnings are announced. However, you should also check release dates for competing firms and be aware that preannouncements are possible. Finally, court cases involving other tobacco companies are also important, so you should check the web sites of Altria's competition as well for news regarding those firms' legal proceedings.

Figure 6.26 deserves a good deal of attention. It is a very interesting chart since there are many different possible interpretations one could initially come up with, until you spend a bit of time looking at all of the relationships. Once you've spent some quality analytical time on this page, however, you will be able to see why I consider this scenario a very high probability one.

The first five-leg down move that began at the end of May is clearly impulsive. It ended a long period of outperformance by Altria Group. In fact, the company's shares had more than tripled from their low in early 2000, and all the while paid a substantial dividend. Anybody that had shifted funds into Altria in 2000 never even noticed the equity bear market! Although not shown here, because of the time scale that my expected trade should cover, that trebling formed a pretty clear five-wave advance. Therefore, a correction of even 62 percent of the rally from the 2000 low would be possible. That price is $33.63. Altria traded at $57.79 in May 2002. It is also worth noting that the high in November 1998 was $59.50, so despite the strong gains that MO made since 2000, it failed to exceed its all-time high.

**FIGURE 6.26** Altria Group, daily

I realize that some of this information is not shown in Figure 6.26, but your analysis can and should include exogenous key data if you have access to it. Given any preknowledge of Altria Group's performance, it certainly makes sense to get a historical feel for the stock's trading. I've mentioned elsewhere in this book the importance of prior highs and lows, so even though the weekly and monthly charts are well beyond the focus of this trade, it can help put your analysis in perspective. The good thing is that when you've done this once, you need not do it again if you choose to day trade MO again in the relatively near future.

The subsequent wave B retracement would have been difficult to trade in spots since prices recovered in July 2002. Although the wave pattern was not very clear, by late July prices had just about risen to the top of the preceding fourth wave and then started to fall. That level also was very close to the 38 percent retracement of the drop from $57.79. Even though the losses in MO's value were substantial, the short period of time spent retracing those losses, the relatively shallow correction, and the continuously rising volume at that time made the peak in late July seem unlikely to be the end of the correction. Once the stock did start to edge lower, it was abundantly clear that there was little volume or momentum in the losses, meaning that better levels were due. A quick spike ensued, followed by a low-volume retracement and then a further five-wave move into the August 20, 2002, high of $52.00.

The top at that time was a bit more than 1 percent above the 62 percent retracement of the whole fall, which had it coming in at $51.38. Although volume did increase some as prices rose, turnover did not match what was reached as prices hit their prior minor peaks in late July and early August. This, coupled with a fairly clear zigzag completion, should have had swing traders looking for renewed losses.

Traders did not have to wait long. Altria's share price fell more than 5 percent from the prior session's high as volume almost doubled the next session. Wave C was almost certainly under way. Stops could sit just above the prior high. The ensuing five-wave decline came on fairly strong volume and with a clear wave count. There was even an extended third wave in the middle of it all, coupled with a pair of gaps that had yet to be filled by the time the stock finally bottomed on October 10, 2002. This was the day that virtually every major stock market index in North America and Europe hit their 2002 low.

You also should note that although prices continued to fall into October 10, volume started slipping and there was a momentum divergence as well as Altria hit its low. These two points are very important because they should immediately dissuade you from labeling the price bottom as wave 3 (and therefore the bottom in July as wave 1). Third waves typically show increased momentum and volume. Add to that the fact that the drop from

August to October was not as large as the May to July fall, either in percentage or gross point terms, and it becomes clear that Altria Group completed a classic A–B–C zigzag on October 10.

With a zigzag complete, you should have become fairly bullish on Altria's stock. It would be reasonable to even look for a new bull market trend to start in the company's shares. However, given that the very long term picture suggests lower prices would still be possible going forward, I would be leery of anything more than good swing trading opportunities. This is exactly what occurred as prices rose in a zigzag to a peak in late October on low volume. The initial losses from what I have labeled as wave A appeared to be developing into a bull flag, but the subsequent top in early November failed to exceed the wave A peak, leaving the count off the lows a corrective three-wave affair. Happily, the overlap at wave a at the turn of November likely would have eliminated any but the shortest-term bullish trades and more likely than not would have had you flat or short as Altria tumbled more than 6 points from $42.98 to as low as $36.90 on November 12, 2002!

With the collapse on November 12 completed, I would have been looking for a possible consolidation followed by a new drop for a fifth-wave fall. In other words, I'd be looking for a new wave A as the start of a second zigzag fall that began with the high on October 23, 2002. The small two-day rally off the November 12, 2002 low failed to achieve even a 38 percent retracement of prior to turning lower. EWT traders could have entered shorts with stops at the November 14, 2002 high. Ultimately, they would have gotten stopped out as new lows were not forthcoming. The next rally took prices past the 38 percent retracement of that November 12 loss, and volume had begun to increase a bit, suggesting that there was a chance that MO's stock would continue to recover some.

With those thoughts in mind, you can start looking for a couple of different possibilities. The initial three-wave rally to the October 23 peak might have been an X wave. However, I would have then expected a new low after that move, or at least a five-wave leg lower to create the first leg of a zigzag. Although a three-wave move followed by another X wave is a possibility, we would need another three-wave drop to complete the pattern. At this point, there is no way of telling how to label the initial rally to October 23, 2002, or the three waves lower since that time. With the three-wave rally and subsequent three-wave drop, a triangle X wave also becomes a possibility.

A rally past the 62 percent retracement of the three-wave drop from the October 23 peak would largely eliminate the probability of a more complex double three lower. A five-wave rally would eliminate the triangle theory. Both of these occurred. In the final analysis, the most likely count is what I show labeled as an A–B–C flat. This is most likely also an X wave, meaning a new three-wave drop, preferably to new lows, has likely begun as of the top set on December 26, 2002. Note that this also took place on low volume. Turnover also has been increasing as prices have fallen since that date.

I have to admit that when I did the initial work, I tried very hard to see if I could find a five-wave count to the low on October 10, 2002. I even drilled down to the 30-minute chart to see if anything jumped out at me. In fact, if you had not done that, I would recommend that you review the next level of detail to ensure you did not miss another leg in the cycle since a five-wave fall would have made sense at that juncture. My initial count was to place wave X at the high on October 23 until I realized that the rally from the November 12 low was pretty clearly five waves. Of course, there is still a small chance that the high on December 26, 2002, was wave a of a larger a–b–c rally, but I find that unlikely at this juncture.

The 30-minute chart in Figure 6.27 may show a completed five-wave drop as of the low late on January 3, 2003. The lack of detail does not provide us with enough information to determine the exact count, and I will almost certainly need to look at a five-minute chart to be sure. Volume did increase late in the day as prices rose, but turnover tends to be strongest in the first hour and last hour of trading, so it really is not clear if the improved volume was just a normal daily pattern or an improved outlook. Without the benefit of Monday morning's price action, my strategy would be to have a

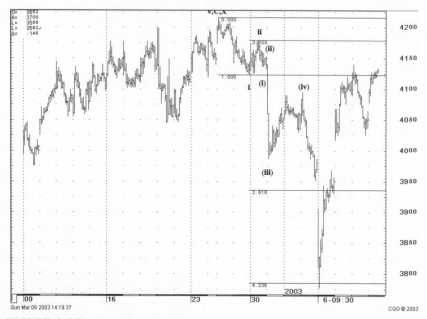

**FIGURE 6.27** Altria Group, 30 minutes

buy order as of the open on Monday as long as prices opened between the late day high from Friday and the 76.4 percent retracement back to the low set that day. A move beneath that low would signal a short trade as wave (v), iii would then be confirmed completed with wave v down then underway.

A quick look at the five-minute chart starts to favor the idea that wave (v),iii is not yet completed. The stock looks to be in a fifth wave lower of this larger wave (v). The two main targets would be $39.36 and $37.85, which are the Fibonacci extension targets shown in Figure 6.28. Although short-term price action seems to favor the higher-priced solution, because wave iii in Figure 6.26 should preferably witness a confirmation from downside momentum, I would not eliminate risk to the deeper fall.

This additional information allows me to hone in on a more detailed strategy. The detailed five-minute chart shows that a rally above $39.90 would eliminate the very short term down move. Therefore, purchases are possible from $39.71 on up to about $39.91. Much past there would leave little room for immediate-term profit. The main choice though is to play this stock from the short side. Sales remain preferred on any open below $39.71. However, a gap open beneath Friday's low of $39.52 would be dangerous. If it was too close to the 2.618 extension target at $39.36, I would keep a tight rein on the position. Any pair of consecutive five-minute bars with higher highs and higher closes would probably have me close the position. I also

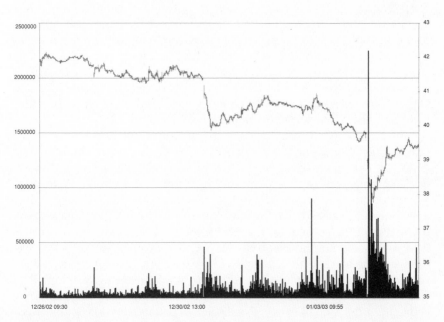

**FIGURE 6.28**  Altria Group, 5 minute. *Source:* Poser Global Market Strategies, Inc.

would not permit the shares to move more than 2 percent against my position. An open below $39.36 would be a sign of a more powerful move down and could target $37.85.

In the end, Altria stock opened at $39.05, below the 2.618 extension. It had a tick up to $39.05, but within 45 minutes reached the 4.236 extension target at $37.85. There was one small rally of a bit greater than 1 percent, which would not have met my criteria for exiting. Once the 4.236 target was reached, I would have tightened my stops using the same criteria noted earlier: Two consecutive five-minute periods of higher highs and higher closes, as long as prices had risen at least 1 percent from the lows already reached. That would have been achieved at $38.14 by 10:25 A.M. You would have sold at $39.05 for better than a 2 percent gain in less than an hour. There is still potential for a move lower, but with the rest of the stock market soaring, I was too nervous to hang on longer. This turned out to be a good idea since MO was threatening to fill its gap by midday on January 6, which would have left this trade in the red!

## SUMMARY

This chapter presented you with multiple examples that showed you the myriad of factors that you must consider when you trade using the Elliott Wave Theory. Different markets require different considerations. When trading the stock market, not only must you consider the standard economic and political headlines, but also you need to follow earnings releases and warnings from the company you are trading, along with those from its competitors. On top of that, you always need to worry that an analyst at a major brokerage firm will change his or her rating on the stock, or that one of the credit agencies could upgrade or downgrade the firm's debt rating. I won't even get into surprises from the legal front.

Anybody who tells you that you can just look at a chart and forecast the prices is not telling you the whole story. The chart patterns are the most important item in my research, but to trade without considering and understanding what can go wrong is putting yourself at risk. If you manage money for others, then you also are not meeting your fiduciary responsibilities. One of the keys to making money in the markets is risk management. If you do not understand how and why you could lose money on a trade, then you should not put that trade on. There are too many things that can change in the markets that, no matter how hard you try, still are capable of surprising you. Sometimes they will help, sometimes they will hurt. You cannot defend against lightening bolts out of the blue, but you can prepare yourself for the kind of events I've discussed throughout this book.

# CHAPTER 7

# The Psychology of an Elliott Wave–Based Trader

I write several newsletters that are marketed to both institutional traders and investors, as well as to individuals. Those sitting on trading desks at the brokers, banks, mutual funds, and hedge funds that buy my reports never ask me about my trading record. They understand that it is their job to make the trading decisions. They also comprehend that before they can make an informed choice on buying or selling, when, and for how much, they must do the necessary research. Part of that research may be to have the drone of CNBC or CNNfn on in the background all day long. More of it is simply talking to other traders at their company or their counterparts at other firms. They may also scour the Internet for stories that could possibly have an effect on what they are looking to trade. Finally, they might pay somebody like me to get their opinions on what they think the market will do next. Their job is to trade; my job is to tell them what I think is going to happen and why I believe it will occur. They are paying me for my opinion. Of course, many like to see a track record of my past recommendations since they don't want to waste their already busy day reading work from somebody who is inconsistent (I was going to say somebody who is never right, but that is just as valuable as an analyst that is always correct).

What is interesting is that individuals often have much different reactions. They are much less trusting of people who try to sell them a market newsletter. I guess that is because the newsletter business really is not regulated and, unfortunately, there are plenty of people out there who are less than honest about their track records. In this day and age of computers, it is way too easy to falsify your record. Customers are not interested in all the highlights on your website showing the great calls you made over the years. They understand that the author has probably made thousands of forecasts over the years and that it does not take a great deal of accuracy to gather enough super recommendations to fill a few screens on the Internet. I have even heard of true scam artists who will send out e-mails with opposite forecasts to half of their lists and then publicize the correct one. When choosing a newsletter, I strongly recommend that you seek verifiable track records and ensure that the author belongs to a professional organization that has an ethics requirement, such as the Market Technicians Association (MTA) or the Association for Investment Management and Research (AIMR).

One request that I often receive from individuals is to see my trading records. They actually want to see my personal brokerage statements over time to see whether or not I've been profitable in my own trading endeavors. Unfortunately, they do not realize that I cannot possibly trade every position I suggest and that the only way to truly measure my performance is to track every trade recommendation I make. They also do not realize that I write many newsletters for different audiences. Some are interested in long-term trades, others are day traders. Some readers are looking for highly leveraged ideas, which if they are correct can make them a lot of money in a short period of time, whereas others seek slow and steady returns. Each group has a different risk/reward profile, so to ask for my track record without understanding to whom each idea is relayed, means little. Add to that the simple fact that there is a big difference between recommending trades and actually making them, and you can understand why an audit of my brokerage accounts would tell you very little about what to expect when you subscribe to my newsletters. My personal risk/reward preferences might not exactly match any of the reports that I write.

There is another reason not to ask authors for their trading records: Unless they are actually managing money (which I do not), you probably do not want newsletter writers to take positions in the issues that they recommend. This adds baggage to the trade and makes it more difficult for the analyst to provide an unbiased opinion. Although my reports do give clear buy, sell, and hold recommendations, there is plenty of latitude for revising my forecasts. It is a lot harder to make a change when it is your money on the line. If the writer can make a clear decision, just based on an investing or trading methodology, coupled with a sense of fiduciary responsibility to readers, he or she should be able to effectively manage revisions to any trade already suggested in the newsletter.

## TRADING AND ANALYSIS ARE TWO DIFFERENT THINGS

One common retort to the previous reasoning is that I probably do execute some of the trades recommended in my reports. Since I must be cherry-picking the best ones, my trading record ought to be superior to what is published. Unfortunately, it is not so simple. If I truly knew which recommendations were going to be the most profitable ones, I would provide only those to my readers. I just don't know *a priori* which trades will work and which won't. True, using the Elliott Wave patterns, I might have a feel for what patterns are most probable, but that does not directly correlate to choosing the best trades. Add to that the simple fact that it is not always so easy to listen to your own advice, and you can start to understand why it is impractical to expect newsletter writers to hand over their trading records to prospective clients.

I am very honest with anybody who asks me: I am much better at telling other people what to do than I am at telling myself. It is something that few people can understand. The ability to have ice in your veins and follow your own advice is one that few have mastered. It is not so easy, or more people would be able to make money doing it. There is a world of difference between telling people what to do and actually doing it yourself. Beyond that, there is also a much different perspective in trading your own money—which you use to buy food and clothes and pay the mortgage—than trading capital from a large bank or from investors who have asked you to manage their investments. I have worked side-by-side with and know several traders at large banks and brokerages who could regularly make 100% or more on capital at risk every year for these firms, but when it came to trading their own money, they lost money on a regular basis. They could not trade their money with the same size or with the same risk/reward profile as they could the bank's.

## KNOW THE PSYCHOLOGY OF INDICATORS

The preceding preamble should make the importance of psychology to trading very clear to you. Any time you have an indicator, you should question its psychological significance. Why should a moving average crossover work? What does a momentum divergence mean with regard to the crowd behavior that is behind the liquid trading markets? For example, how is Welles Wilder's average directional index (ADX) computed and how does that relate to market psyche? These questions, most of which never seemed to have clear-cut answers to me, are what led me to adopt EWT as my primary form of research for my clients. I needed to put price, volume, and indicator action into a behavioral framework before I could ever feel comfortable forecasting the market.

That does not mean that I believe indicators do not have a place in your work. I've discussed several times in this book the use of momentum divergences and have mentioned other indicators as well. Lower momentum as prices attain a new extreme means that the most recent move was made with a lower degree of commitment from those who helped push prices to that new level. I always look at indicators with an eye on how they reflect what the "market" is thinking. The minute I let myself slip from that perspective, my ability to correctly forecast the market drops precipitously. I used to write computer-based trading systems using indicators, and was very successful at it, but I could not get myself to follow the systems' recommendations because I could not really understand why they worked from a market psychology point of view. I do understand why EWT works, and as long as I am willing to accept what the market is telling me, I usually make the right calls.

I have attempted throughout this book to provide practical ideas on how to trade. Elliott Wave Theory can be overwhelming. I have been using it as my primary analytical and trading tool for more than a decade, but I learn something new every day. There are nuances within nuances. You can easily get caught up in minutiae. However, as long as you remain focused on understanding how and why the market is moving in a given direction, you can filter out all the noise and hone in on profitable trading.

## CONTROL YOUR EMOTIONS

If you get just one thing out of this book, it must be that you are not smarter than the market. However, it also is not smarter than you. There will always be unforeseen events—gaps that turn a profitable trade into a small disaster. When that happens, look at the chart and make an informed decision. How does the news, and the related price action, change your analysis? How much further against you can this position go? Never start hoping, because hope has nothing to do with the market. The market does not care what your position is. There is no glee when you record an enormous gain or book a loss that wipes out your trading capital. Savvy traders prey on those who hope because just when there is no more hope is when you will fold, and that will often be the end of the move against you. You should not find it surprising that the crowd capitulates together. That is what leads to reversals, when there is nobody on the other side of the trade anymore. You can avoid getting caught in traps like that by understanding how to quickly determine the opportunities in any trading or investing situation.

## KNOWLEDGE AND INTELLIGENCE ARE NECESSARY BUT NOT SUFFICIENT FOR GOOD TRADING

What does it take to become a good trader? Hopefully, this book has satisfied one of those requirements, which is knowledge. You do not have to know anything about EWT to be profitable in your trading. There are many other useful methods that will make you money consistently, but I personally find EWT to be the best tool for my work. This book shows you how to apply Elliott to your trading, but knowledge is not nearly enough to make money trading.

When I speak to people about trading, they are consistently amazed that I do not own a small island in the Carribean. I have an excellent record calling the markets, and they cannot understand how it is that I have not leveraged those forecasts into at least a small fortune. Although intelligence always helps, you must be able to apply that intelligence. When I was in college getting my undergraduate degree in mathematics, I once had a graduate student as instructor for a class I took. He was absolutely brilliant in his field of study, but that did not mean that he could teach, nor did it mean that he could go out into the real world and apply his knowledge. He was incapable of relating a theoretical concept to its application in the business world. He could only see the theory; he could not apply it.

The smartest people are not always the best in any given endeavor. Often, intelligence acts as a barrier. You think you know how something works. It prevents you from seeing the whole picture or allowing you to visualize the different ways things work. If great thinkers always accepted the boundaries that they were told existed, many of the world's greatest discoveries and innovations never would have gotten off the drawing board.

## SEPARATE YOURSELF FROM THE CROWD

To become a successful trader, you must allow yourself to believe that it is possible to make money simply by understanding how and why crowds react to certain stimuli. This is the essence of the new field of behavioral finance. Although technical analysis is the application, behavioral finance essentially tries to understand why technical analysis works. There is no way to determine what a single person will do in response to a given set of stimuli, but crowds are somewhat more predictable. Psychologists do a much better job of predicting crowd behavior, with all its peer pressures, than they do of figuring out what an isolated person will do in reaction to the same set of stimuli. This is what technical analysis and behavioral finance attempt to quantify and measure.

Elliott Wave Theory fits perfectly into that kind of scheme. It is all about market sentiment. Every wave has a characteristic signature, and that signature can be directly related to the market's psyche. If prices do not develop in a way that is consistent with a wave count, then you know that your wave count is incorrect, or that something has caused the market's psyche to be altered. The biggest challenge in all of this is that you always must remain open to new information. Also, somehow you need to separate yourself from the market sentiment and just read the charts and interpret them (along with the news and how that is affecting the price and volume action).

## TRADING SYSTEMS

I have seen many books written about how to make money trading. Most of them seem to focus on using trading systems. These works suggest that you will be able to either buy or program a system that will be profitable. I find this absolutely incredible. I have written several systems that have made money, but the amount of time and money that you will spend developing a system is prohibitive. And, since most systems are optimized, they usually will only work for a period of time and typically are effective in a tiny subset of all the markets in which you might wish to trade or invest.

The reason why these books focus on trading systems is because the systems make the decisions for you. You are supposed to be able to blindly accept what the system tells you regardless of the news you hear and the way you interpret the charts. Unfortunately, shutting out the rest of the world is not so easy. Even if you overcome the incredibly high hurdle of actually developing a trading system that is both profitable and exhibits low enough drawdowns to fit within your risk/reward profile, you must be able to execute every trade the system recommends. Most people attempt to pick and choose which trades they think will work and ignore the rest. However, by doing that, you are defeating the very reason why you bought or developed the system in the first place.

I am not saying that systems do not work. There are people for whom system trading is perfect. They are very comfortable listening to a computer's advice. Those who develop the systems and then implement and trade them probably can and will have an easier time following their own system's recommendations, since it was their own thought processes that created the system. Unfortunately, they probably will be less willing to question when the program needs to be tweaked since it is very difficult not to have an ego with regard to your own creation. By the time you recognize that your system is no longer functioning profitably and within your personal comfort level, you likely will have suffered a far greater drawdown than was planned.

Purchasing trading systems may be the right thing for some individuals as well. However, if you are at all cynical over why you should buy a newsletter, I would strongly urge you to question why somebody is selling a profitable trading system. Although the psychological barriers still exist in implementing decisions made by a computer program, they often are easier to overcome than other ingrained habits. There always are companies available to the entrepreneurial capitalist that are willing to provide seed capital to a well-thought-out and apparently profitable system. If the system writer has not been able to entice people to invest with him, why should you? At a minimum, you should require verifiable records of the system's track record. Do not accept theoretical results. They are meaningless and are usually based on optimized results. If the only results that are available for the system you are considering are theoretical, I would strongly urge you to pass on it. You should also be able to get a money-back guarantee. Otherwise, I would not even waste my time evaluating a system. There are no get-rich-quick schemes out there no matter what all the shiny brochures say.

## UNDERSTAND WHY YOU ARE PLACING AN ORDER

In my opinion, most people will be able to make more money if they understand why they are putting on a position. That is why I always include fundamental research in my work. It is not very easy to tell clients that they should buy or sell a stock, bond, currency, or commodity because a trend line broke, a moving average crossed, a third wave just began, or a momentum divergence was just confirmed. If you can point out that market expectations are shifting to a slowdown in the economy and that the specific stock you are looking at is in a sector that is usually among the first to be affected by recessionary forces, and then add that it broke a five-year-long trend line, you will be in a much better position to catch your investor's attention. If investors can understand why they are making a trade, they will find it much easier to stick to and follow your advice.

Even better than having clients follow your advice is the ability to show your clients how to make money on their own, which is what this book is about. The preceding six chapters gave you all the important rules and regulations of EWT. I also presented detailed examples of how I go about doing my research. I've attempted to intersperse tips and techniques for some of the markets that I am most familiar with as well. Armed with this knowledge, you should be able to start training your mind to be able to trade profitably using Elliott.

The key to profits with EWT is to always remember and understand what the driving forces are in the market you are trading. Know where there has been volume and at what price points. Try to understand where money has gone into the market, because when prices start reaching those levels, that is where those on the wrong side of the trade start feeling angst. Never forget that every wave pattern, whether it is based on a five-minute chart or a monthly chart, carries a memory with it. It is a memory of those who bought and sold at past levels. It is a memory of those who do not want to give back, on an already profitable trade, more than a certain percentage of those gains. It is a memory of what investors and traders believe is the current nexus of supply and demand, which is often represented by a trend line.

## UNDERSTAND WHAT YOU TRADE— THE CHARTS ARE NOT ENOUGH!

Your job as an Elliott Wave–based trader or investor is to go beyond just marking 1-2-3-4-5 and a-b-c on a chart. The patterns are not nearly enough. If you go back into history, you might want to consider reading a newspaper to see and understand what was the news of the day at that time so you can gauge what people were thinking. I am constantly amazed at how Elliotticians will invent astoundingly complex and incomprehensible wave counts in an attempt to make everything work together. They totally ignore the mood of the times when they do this. I saw people comment that the stock market's gains in the late 1990s were corrective because they could not see an impulsive wave count. Although that might have been true for the last few months of the bull market, anybody proffering that sort of advice is not staying with the spirit of Elliott's methodology. We have just lived through one of the greatest investing bubbles in history. How anybody could suggest that when an index rallies almost 100% in a matter of months, as the Nasdaq composite did from late 1999 into early 2000, it is not an impulse move, especially given that people were climbing over each other to buy these stocks in increasing volume, is beyond me. Although the very end of the move may have been an irregular top, much as we saw in 1929, I can see no way of supporting the idea that the greatest bull market in history was anything but part of a five-wave affair. Similarly, the proposition that the crash of 1929–1932 was part of a triangle is equally preposterous to me. Triangles were defined by Elliott as consolidations, not all-out market annihilations.

## DON'T FORGET YOUR WAVE CHARACTERISTICS— MAKE SURE YOUR COUNTS ARE CONSISTENT WITH MARKET SENTIMENT

To trade successfully using EWT, you must take these types of considerations into account. If you need cut and dried signals, you will find that Elliott is not for you. However, although pattern and wave identification are somewhat qualitative, as long as you understand what is required for your trade to be correct and are willing to accept being wrong, you will be successful using EWT as your primary trading decision tool.

To wrap this all up, here is a list of dos and don'ts for you to follow when you use EWT for trading or investing:

- DO read the newspaper to understand current forces driving the market.
- DON'T ask other people what their wave counts are.
- DO listen to the news to help you determine market sentiment.
- DON'T consider your sentiment as being more important than market sentiment.
- DO write your trade plan down.
- DON'T change your trade plan without reviewing everything that you've already written.
- DO define your expected time frame and the wave degree that you plan to trade.
- DON'T cut your profits short by exiting a position that is acting according to your analysis by lowering the degree you are trading.
- DO trail stops as long as they make sense within the same trading degree.
- DON'T ever widen your stops.
- DO intermarket analysis.
- DON'T exit a position because another position was wrong.
- DO understand all of the characteristics of every wave.
- DON'T make Elliott Wave more complex than it already is.
- DO find your comfort level for portfolio volatility.
- DON'T put more at risk than you can afford to lose.
- DO fully label your wave counts to one degree lower than your trading time frame.
- DON'T change your counts as an excuse to avoid making a trading decision.
- DO allow market information to guide you in your continued market monitoring.
- DON'T allow noise to take you out of a well-thought-out strategy.

## SUMMARY

Your work is never done. Every single time you pick up the newspaper, turn on your television, or look at a chart, you will probably learn something new about the markets or about yourself. This is the essence of Elliott Wave Theory. Since it is all about market sentiment and crowd behavior, as soon as you can understand how you interact with the market and how the market interacts with you, your trading will improve. Elliott will help you do exactly that because, by understanding how and why things work, you will be able to separate your hope, fear, and greed from those of the market. You will recognize when there is a sea change and be able to move past all the platitudes and clichés you see, read, and hear from the media and instead do your own, more thorough research and analysis. And, once you learn, through trial and error and repetitive practice, you will become a profitable, very profitable trader by employing the Elliott Wave Theory in your decision-making process.

Good trading!

## CHAPTER 8
# Future Waves

I have vacillated, ever since I embarked on this project, regarding the idea of providing a chapter forecasting the future direction of the markets. Although more than one book on Elliott Wave has included such prognostications, this book's aim is more to show you how to use Elliott in your trading and investing than to be a vehicle used to advertise my market prescience. A chapter telling you that the Dow Jones Industrial Average or the S&P 500 was either going to collapse by more than you ever imagined, or that the stock market was set to rise in a parabolic manner, really did not fit in with my idea of what was important for this book. A forecast chapter is great for headlines, and if the forecast is correct—and different from what others have to say—it will certainly help sell the book and my newsletters, which I am sure is not lost on the fine publisher of this tome. However, I did not want to include such a chapter, because I felt it really did not add much to the point that I was trying to get across to my readers.

We live in interesting times. The global stock markets have entered their most negative phase since the Great Depression of the 1920s and 1930s. I use the Elliott Wave Theory as a tool in my trading, and I do not consider it to be directly predictive of global trends. That said, the stock market reflects a certain mindset. A prolonged drop in equity market values represents a general lack of confidence in our own ability to run our lives, businesses, and governments. Robert Prechter Jr. has taken this to a higher level, coining the term *socioconomics*, which applies Elliott Wave Theory to the application of forecasting society itself. Prechter believes that human thought and society act and interact collectively in somewhat predictable patterns. Long-term cycle buffs argue that the Kondratrieff Cycle predicted a collapse in the stock markets, along with war and famine for the end of the twentieth century. Although the timing may have been off by a few years, the current world order certainly makes that a risk in the early twenty-first century.

Economists tend to deride this kind of thinking. They correctly point out that we do not have nearly enough data points in the history of the world to accurately test any hypotheses regarding long-term cycles such as proposed by followers of Kondratrieff, or very long term Elliott Waves.

There just are not enough 100-year cycles that can be matched up with any kind of trading data to validate such a hypothesis. To be sure, the cycle timing is fuzzy at best. Many of the most bearish forecasters have been screaming for a bear market in stocks from the middle or late 1990s and missed the greatest run-up ever in the equity markets. Timing is everything when it comes to the stock market, and their timing was awful.

I have seen some analyses that point out that if you had been dollar cost averaging throughout the big bull market, this most recent collapse in values would leave your portfolio in the red. Bear market pundits love to point this out, although they neglect to highlight the fact that if you had shorted stocks in the late 1990s, you probably would have gone broke by the time the bear market finally began. You would have made some money if instead you bought bonds, since yields generally fell, but the right asset allocation to anybody with a longer time horizon was to be in equities pretty much until the end of the surge in early 2000. The rejoinders from the permanently bearish camp just do not ring true and merely represent 20/20 hindsight.

The current world situation, with the broad U.S. stock market down nearly 50% from its highs, the technology-laden Nasdaq off more than 75%, and several European bourses down 60% or more from their peaks, does tell you something about our global village. Without a doubt, especially in this day and age of the Internet and light-speed communications, the linkages among the various international stock and bond markets are instantaneous. Although individual short-term patterns differ, there is not a major stock exchange that is not affected by the global mood (see Table 8.1).

**TABLE 8.1**   Losses from Start of Bear Market to Lowest Level as of December 31, 2002

| Stock Market Index | Percentage Loss from High |
|---|---|
| Dow Jones Industrial Average | 35 |
| S&P 500 | 48 |
| Nasdaq Composite | 78 |
| Germany DAX | 69 |
| London FTSE-100 | 48 |
| Paris CAC-40 | 62 |
| Hong Kong Hang Seng Index | 46 |
| Japan Nikkei-225 (since 1989) | 79 |

Is this kind of international psychic depression predictive of the kind of strife present in the world right now? Is the sun about to set on America as it did on Great Britain, Spain, Rome, and Greece before? Is the terrorist threat merely a reflection of the current international mood? Certainly, war and famine have been predicted by long-cycle advocates and the coincidence is more than a little bit unnerving. I do not believe that anybody seriously believes that the fall in the Dow is predictive of global strife and the rise of militant religious sects. The point is that the bear market reflects global conditions and the feelings, hopes, angst, and anger of the masses.

Although past bear markets did not always result in such tectonic geopolitical shifts, you must understand where we are in the cycles to help determine if such risks do exist. The bear market of the early 1970s (see Figure 8.1) did not result in the kinds of risks we currently are faced with. We did see the oil embargo around that time (the stock market actually had already bottomed), but our position in the wave counts at that time was much different. In fact, that leg represented the end of a negative period in the charts. Much of that time did coincide, however, with the Vietnam War.

One of the problems that I've had with the recent forecasts of social and political Armageddon from the Elliott Wave perspective comes from the place we currently sit on the long-term charts. I see the U.S. stock market

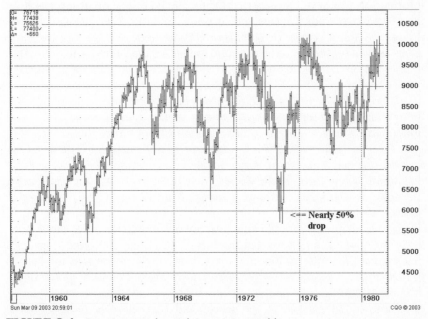

**FIGURE 8.1** Dow Jones Industrial Average, monthly

as being in a fourth wave, which I do not equate to financial or social Armageddon. As you may recall, I have railed against the idea of using hundreds of years–long charts to justify a count. Although there is logic in the splicing of gold prices to British stocks and then later on to U.S. equities, the actual changeover points and price action around those periods are somewhat arbitrary. I understand the reasoning in that the authors who have done this have attempted to create a cycle framework that represents the mood of those in control of international finances going back hundreds of years. These titans of the financial world are the same people that have helped to mold crowd psychology, and so these charts, according to their authors, accurately reflect international long-term cycles.

The biggest problem is that the charts are not truly predictive. The choice of when to switch from gold to British stocks to American equities was only known after the fact. It might be that the end of the world is not about to come, but merely that Japan or Korea is waxing and America is waning. Future books on the subject may show an international stock index, or the Nikkei-225, starting from 1989, 2000, or 2010, rather than the S&P 500 or Dow Jones Industrials Average.

Does all this mean that long-term outlooks are not plausible? The answer to that is a resounding no! There are more than 100 years of data available for the Dow Jones Industrial Average, and there is theoretical information going back nearly that far for the S&P 500. We also have more than 30 years of daily prices since currencies floated freely, as well as hundreds of years of prices for gold. Interest rate data go back into the early 1900s as well for the United States and longer for the United Kingdom. And, in my opinion, comparing market price cycles to economic data, which in some cases go back more than a century, is a key tool.

There is no doubt that one requires centuries of information to determine equally long-term outlooks, and it is also important to know and understand where we are in that framework to optimize the accuracy of your forecast. However, given the amount of information available to the analyst, one can make some very educated and accurate assumptions that will permit you to forecast the global stock, bond, and currency markets for the next several years without leaning on artificially constructed price series.

In this chapter, I provide you with my outlook for the U.S. stock market, the Japanese stock market, and the U.S. dollar. Although there is a chance that the United States' place as the only superpower may not last, as of now, the U.S. markets represent an enormous share of the global pocketbook. Add to that the simple facts that U.S. equities are the most developed and liquid market in the world and that there is more detailed information available for American assets than any others, and you can see that there is also a bit of practicality in providing forecasts on these markets. Unfortunately, the same level of detail is not available for the continental European bourses or for those markets more recently organized in Asia, Africa, and South America. Furthermore, I am not prepared to take my forecasts to the next social level and predict the end of the preeminence of the U.S. stock and bond markets, although I have little doubt that there is a strong and valid relationship between the two.

In an attempt to keep this chapter educational, as well as offering you some insight into where I expect the markets to move in the next few years, I provide you with both my forecasts as well as alternative views. I explain how and why I favor a particular count, and what would need to happen to favor my alternative (or some other not yet divined) wave count. I warn you now that my forecast almost certainly does not exactly match those of other Elliott Wave analysts. As an additional learning tool, I also bring many non-Elliott tools into the discussion. Sometimes, seeing wave counts can be a challenge. I will attempt to show you how classic technical analysis, indicators, and candlestick patterns can help you to better do your analysis. I will also relate fundamental economic data and sentiment numbers into the analysis. Although I am not going to create trade plans for this chapter, feel free to build them yourself!

It is always important to develop a relevant framework for your research and trading strategies. When day trading or swing trading, this involves getting into a great deal of detail regarding individual economic releases, corporate announcements, and short-term technicals. You need to look at intraday charts, minor trend lines and moving averages, and reactions to speeches by politicians and central bankers, as well as analyze the developing price patterns. It certainly is important to know and understand what the larger price patterns are as well.

In this chapter, I am looking at multiyear patterns. Although the actual Elliott Wave rules are unchanged, the framework is much different. My research for this chapter includes an understanding of the global economy and the history of bubbles (since that is what burst in 2000), as well as an understanding of the causes and effects of war, since the U.K. and America were at war with Iraq at the time this chapter was written and the long-term battle against terrorism could also be considered similar to war.

I look at several markets in this chapter. While equities are sexy, they weren't always all that interesting, and if the bear market continues for another few years, they probably will not be very interesting again (which, of course, will be the time to buy them). But, I also am going to look at the bond market, and the currency market. All of these markets are related. I will expand a bit on this as we review the fundamental landscape that existed in the first quarter of 2003.

## BUT YOU'RE A TECHNICAL ANALYST— WHY ALL THE ECONOMICS?

Many technical analysts scoff at looking at and understanding the fundamental factors that are behind the markets. They claim that the charts show everything anyway, so why should you worry about these "details"? What such proponents fail to fully appreciate is that a forecast is always at risk of being wrong. Knowing what could go awry gives you an advantage over the competition. Technicians claim that reading the charts is based on market psychology. Although a chart pattern, or reading the tape, has an indelible effect on my sentiment with regard to the market, I cannot, with a straight face, say that it does for Joe or Jane Investor. The average market participant is swayed by corporate performance (or, in this day and age, malfeasance), and such "unimportant" factors as the economy and how it affects their wallets. Although this is built into the chart patterns and creates a feedback loop, sudden seismic shifts can and will change the market psyche, and therefore the patterns themselves.

All of these factors help to create a mindset, which is ultimately what draws our charts. Although proponents of long cycles and socioconomics are probably ultimately correct in suggesting that even very long term social and business patterns are predictable, Hari Seldon, the fictional nexus of Isaac Asimov's *Foundation* series, warned us that any forecast is merely a probability and the longer the term that the forecast covers, the greater is the risk of that forecast being wrong. In the science fiction world, some of the forecast errors were generated by mutants. In the real world, random events, criminal activity, and simple individual acts of human nature can derail developing patterns and probabilities.

I am not in any way, shape, or form arguing against some of the pioneering work in long-term forecasting. I am merely stating that doing it in a vacuum, without understanding cause and effect, is only doing half of the job. Use everything that you possibly can to improve the probability of being correct, and you will become a standard bearer of accuracy.

## THE STATE OF THE WORLD—2003

There is no doubt that the advance in the global stock markets, which accelerated in 1994, and then shifted into an even higher gear in 1999, was a bubble. Technical analysts had become the Chicken Littles of the financial community. When more stocks started falling than rising (the advance/ decline, or A/D, line began falling) in the spring of 1998, many chartists warned that the stock market was due for a fall. Actually, the word "fall" is probably a bit too soft, as most technicians were calling for a bear market.

We all looked pretty smart in the summer of that year as the Russian debt crisis and the Long Term Capital Management (LTCM) debacle unfolded. You may recall that LTCM decided that there was no need to do anything but put together a bunch of equations that they believed fairly represented the global financial markets. Very sadly, they forgot to consider the fact that the markets are human, and therefore, they are not always rational. They also forgot that economists cannot accurately forecast any set of economic data, or interest rates, or the direction of stocks. And yet, LTCM thought that they could model the world in a detailed enough way such that hugely leveraged so-called arbitrage positions could never go awry.[1]

U.S. equities tumbled 20% in a matter of just over two months. We technicians were all busy patting ourselves on the backs for an awesome market call. Unfortunately, in an unofficial poll taken on October 6, 1998 (albeit a very unscientific one), the day after stock prices bottomed, less than 10% of the technical analysts questioned thought that stocks had bottomed at that point. So, even most proponents of the sharp drop at that time did not properly see the signs of a market capitulation and bottom. Less than two years later, the Dow Jones Industrial Average had risen nearly 60% from its depths and the Nasdaq Composite went into orbit, almost quadrupling in that same time. Many analysts fought the rally tooth and nail, and looked for the return of the bear market at virtually every minor correction or consolidation.

I admit to you that on October 6, 1998, I was not one of the brave few who had figured out that the stock market had in fact bottomed for the time being. However, I was probably the only person on this planet who correctly forecast the Fed's surprise between-meetings rate cut on October 15, 1998. Prices had been at the low of the day, and were falling, just prior to that announcement. A look at Figure 8.2 shows that a move much lower likely would have started to turn sentiment somewhat more negative again. As soon as the cut was announced, the sharp rally that followed told me that we were in for a rocketship ride higher.

Before the Fed cut rates, the market looked as if it was ready to roll over and start a new leg down. I have always been a strong believer that the U.S. Federal Reserve, via Alan Greenspan's stewardship, was strongly aware of the importance of market psychology and technical analysis. In fact, I have often suggested that though not the best, Mr. Greenspan is certainly the most important technical analyst on the planet. Central banks use technical analysis all of the time. They always want to know what the market is thinking before, during, and after any rate move or foreign exchange intervention. Market psychology has always been a key variant to the

**FIGURE 8.2** Dow Jones Industrial Average, daily

Greenspan Fed. Why else did he raise the consumer sentiment surveys to exalted status by indicating that he watched that information very closely?

If you are still skeptical, consider the following, which is published on my web site (http://www.poserglobal.com):

> But, although there doubtless have been profound changes in the way we organize our capital facilities, engage in just-in-time inventory regimes, and intertwine our newly sophisticated risk-sensitive financial system into this process, there is one important caveat to the notion that we live in a new economy, and that is human psychology.
>
> The same enthusiasms and fears that gripped our forebears, are, in every way, visible in the generations now actively participating in the American economy. Human actions are always rooted in a forecast of the consequences of those actions. . . . To be sure, the degree of risk aversion differs from person to person, but judging the way prices behave in today's markets compared with those of a century or more ago, one is hard pressed to find significant differences. The way we evaluate assets, and the way changes in those values affect our economy, do not appear to be coming out of a set of rules that is different from the one that governed the actions of our forebears.

> *Hence, as the first cut at the question 'Is there a new economy?' the answer in a more profound sense is no. As in the past, our advanced economy is primarily driven by how human psychology molds the value system that drives a competitive market economy. And that process is inextricably linked to human nature, which appears essentially immutable and, thus, anchors the future to the past.*

If you do not think that is a strong argument for technical analysis, I do not know how you got so far into this book. Those words came directly from a speech made by none other than Alan Greenspan, on September 4, 1998, even as the LTCM debacle was still unfolding.

As 1998 came to an end, the U.S. and global economies had dodged bullets two consecutive years. First, several Southeast Asian economies nearly ran aground in the summer and fall of 1997, as their equity markets and currencies tumbled as much as 90%. American and European stocks fell also, but those drops, though severe, were merely corrections in a bull market. Then, we were faced with LTCM and the Russian debt crisis a year later. In both situations, Alan Greenspan followed the script he wrote after the crash of 1987 by flooding the system with money, which ultimately sent stocks soaring. Figure 8.3 shows the surge in M3 money supply during these periods. (It is not clear that this medicine will cure the market's post-bubble ills.)

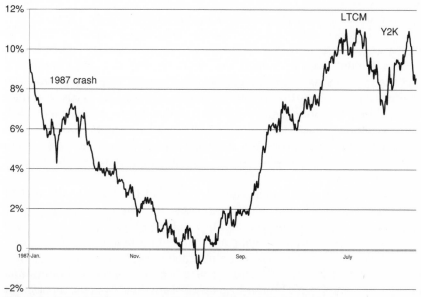

**FIGURE 8.3** M3 money supply percent change versus prior year

Unfortunately, the A/D line clearly was telling us that things were not exactly as rosy as they looked. And Elliott Wave patterns and projections also implied that the end was fast approaching for this great bull market. The economy was too strong, according to many economists, and with the large risk of the Y2K bug ahead, it was anybody's guess as to what would happen next. This fear of Y2K was part of what made this bubble and over-capacity even worse than they otherwise would have been. As a former computer programmer, I was well aware that the bug was easily fixed. Unfortunately, many companies had enormously complex and old computer systems in use, and in some cases, they did not have the original source code available. Without the code, they could not fix their systems without rewriting them. That is both a time-consuming and costly process.

The U.S. Fed, and their cousin central banks throughout the world, spent vast sums of money and time ensuring that the world's financial systems would not implode. Corporations spent money like it was going out of style. They figured that if they were going to rewrite all of their legacy code, they might as well go out and purchase the newest and most powerful computers while they were at it. These systems would almost certainly not be at risk of crashing on January 1, 2000. The same sort of logic was repeated across the globe, but not just for computers themselves. Anything that had a computer in it was fair game: telecommunications systems, engineering equipment, broadcast systems. Everything! Manufacturers built and re-built and upgraded plants as if there was a never-ending supply of money and demand.

There was more. George Soros has written about "the virtuous cycle," and that is what we were in the midst of: spending money as if it flowed like water, and technological advances so great that the science fiction writers couldn't even keep up. Of course, the great panacea for everything was the Internet. As recently as 1996, few companies had a web site. The Internet was a home for so-called computer geeks and nerds. Internet-based e-mail was not considered to be particularly reliable. Even in 1998, there were still some large companies with little more than a business-card presence on the World Wide Web. Although e-mail was becoming more common and popular, it was not ubiquitous as it is today (and has been for at least two years).

This new Internet, which had grown out of the U.S. Department of Defense's ARPANET, and which connected the military with university researchers, was built on the ability to share information quickly and cheaply. Its users gladly and willingly shared information for free (at least if it wasn't a military secret). As the Internet grew, the free data and information concept remained ingrained. It got extrapolated to infinity and beyond. Somehow, we'd be able to get almost anything from the Internet for free, just because companies and advertisers would give goods and information away in the hopes of serving a bunch of annoying advertisements in front of our faces.

The thinking was that distribution was cheap, because you didn't need a lease or have to open a store. That advertising to unseen and unknown people is costly and ineffective was irrelevant as Internet usage was rising exponentially. Nobody seemed to notice the fact that it cost a heck of a lot of money to buy and run the equipment required to handle a large transaction-oriented web site. I know of this first hand. I consulted to a company that planned to build a financial portal built on the advertising model. All you had to do was add ".com" to the end of your corporation's name, and its value increased 10% or more during the bubble's heyday in late 1999 and early 2000.

This was a new economy. Gravity and the business cycle had been repealed. Companies were cheap with P/E ratios of 200. And, why shouldn't you buy shares in a firm whose prospectus said that it had no business plan, but would figure it out once you gave them the money to spend? Don't worry, it said, it will have something to do with technology and the Internet. And, you knew they had to be telling the truth, because the owners had only recently started to shave and the name of the firm had ".com" in it!

Living through this market as a technical analyst was both exhilarating and frightening. Like most chartists, I had read Charles Mackay's famous treatise on irrational exuberance, *Extraordinary Popular Delusions and the Madness of Crowds* (Current publisher Three River Press, 1980; originally published by Richard Bentley, 1841). Commentators and analysts announced that it was different this time. No doubt, the Internet provided an alternate means of distribution, and if harnessed properly, it did certainly lower costs. And, the initial build-out of the Internet was expensive and did mean that technology companies would experience strong growth and profits as they sold the infrastructure. However, the blind greed and avarice with which investors bid up shares of companies that had no profits, and had virtually no hope of every attaining profitability, was as clear a sign as I've ever seen that we were in the midst of a bubble.

Alan Greenspan reminded us what a bubble looks like in that speech I quoted earlier in this chapter. Unfortunately, like so many of us before and since, he did not heed his own advice. The Fed helped make the bubble worse by continuously priming the pump. Maybe they should have sent interest rates far higher in 1999 instead of leaving them low over fear of Y2K. Criticisms of the Fed policy should consider that there was a large risk that Y2K might have become a big problem if the Fed had not opened the spigots and made it cheap for industry to spend and overcome any Y2K problems that were hiding under the covers. Twenty-twenty hindsight makes it easy to question the Fed's decisions, but it still does not tell us whether their vigilance saved the financial system from major Y2K-related problems.

Anybody who even began to suggest that stocks were ready for a bear market was ridiculed. This was a favorite game of some of the personalities in the television financial media. Because their minds were closed to the idea that stocks could ever fall, or that anybody could forecast a market reversal, any technical analyst who came on television to warn that equity markets could very possibly take a huge hit was received with instant derision.[2] When somebody with an opposite view is automatically laughed off the air, you have to know that sentiment is stretched so far beyond rational levels that it is only a matter of time before a reversal of major proportions is lurking in the wings.

The gains made in the late 1990s and into early 2000 were beyond belief. The Nasdaq Composite nearly doubled in less than six months. Remember, we are talking about a market average comprised of more than 4,000 individual issues. I am not referring to a single company that maybe was bought out by a competitor at a large premium, or a biotech company that just made public that their new cancer drug tests had been hugely successful. Consider that in normal times, a buyout might come at a 10% to 40% premium, while a major announcement in the volatile biotech world could lead a company's share price to double or even treble. The gains that we saw in the Nasdaq Composite were more like those seen in penny stock pump-and-dump schemes.[3] The only problem with all these great gains is that GDP growth was not particularly strong during that period, at least when compared to past periods of strong stock market gains (see Figure 8.4).[4]

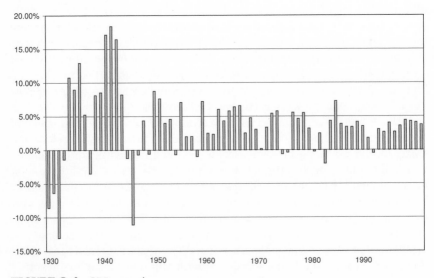

**FIGURE 8.4**  GDP growth

What is absolutely incredible is that the fundamental base for a major market reversal was there for all to see. Alan Greenspan warned us about it during the mid-1990s, when the equity market first began to accelerate higher, in his famous "irrational exuberance" speech. Fed Governor Lawrence Meyer continuously warned that the employment rate was too low and that something had to give. He feared that the economy was growing at a rate that was unsustainable. Although his forecast for higher inflation was incorrect, the bubble did burst via a collapse in stock market prices and decreased stability in the world social order.

As I write this chapter, the world remains on the edge amidst the confrontation in the tinder box that is the Middle East. Years ago I forecast that oil would rise past $40 per barrel—the jump following the first Gulf War was only the first leg of either a three-wave or five-wave advance (see Figure 8.5). When I first forecast that, oil was in the doldrums and was in the midst of a 20-month period during which it barely peeked above $20 per barrel. When I mentioned my expectations in the late 1990s to another technician who ran a hedge fund, he exclaimed that would be a disaster to the economy and was only likely to occur if there was war. Remember, this forecast was made long before the September 11, 2001 attacks and before the United States determined that Saddam Hussein had to be removed from power in Iraq. Front month oil futures exactly touched $40 per barrel just before the coalition's attack on Iraq began.

**FIGURE 8.5** Light crude oil futures, monthly

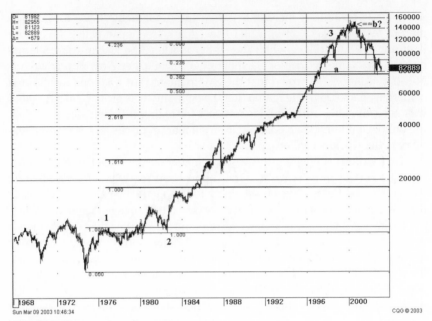

**FIGURE 8.6**  S&P 500, monthly

Elliott Wave does not provide any guarantees. Your wave counts can be wrong, but when you are incorrect, you will know fairly quickly. In the chapter I wrote for the Bloomberg Press (2000) book *New Thinking in Technical Analysis: Trading Models from the Masters*, I gave two possible levels where the S&P 500 could top. One was in the low-1600s and the other was a bit above 1550. As you can see in Figure 8.6, the S&P topped at 1552.87, less than 2 points from my lower forecast level.

The main question right now is, "Where do we go from here?" As I showed in the table at the start of this chapter, stocks are far below the highs set in 2000. By almost all measures, they are way overextended on the down side. However, brokerage strategists mostly continue to recommend buying stocks. The average weighting given to equities in asset allocations published by Wall Street firms is 65%. Although this is off the 70% ratios seen last year, it is still far above the typical 50% ratio seen around market bottoms.

Analysts keep pointing to sentiment surveys and technical measures that are at their lowest levels in 10 years or more. What they refuse to consider is that we are in a bear market. The only valid comparisons should come from the Great Depression and maybe from the bursting of the Japanese bubble in 1989. Let's hope that U.S. equities do not follow the Japanese example, since the Nikkei-225 index has still not bottomed as of March

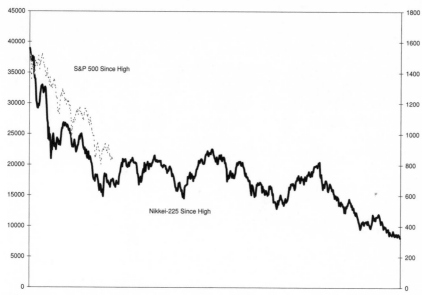

**FIGURE 8.7** S&P 500 and Nikei-225 since high

2003! Figure 8.7 compares the price action in the Nikkei-225 with that of the S&P 500 at the time that each of those indices peaked. Even the so-called bear market in the early 1970s is not a particularly good example since that was really just the last leg of a long trading range. That said, the period from the mid-1960s when the Dow Jones Industrial Average first touched 1,000 and into the mid-1970s when the venerable index bottomed may provide a more valid point of comparison. This is clearly shown in Figure 8.8.

What is actually rather interesting is that I have rarely seen any mention comparing the current period to that of the mid-1960s. Although there is little doubt that the extreme excesses seen in the technology sector were not as widespread in the 1960s, the comparisons otherwise are far less disparate. For example, the Dow rose about 25-fold in the 33+ years from the 1932 low to the high at the end of 1965. In the nearly 26 years since the 1975 low, the Dow increased by a factor of about 20. The biggest difference is that the gains for the index were far greater in the five years prior to its top in 2000 than were recorded during the first half of the 1960s. Still, equities spent about 10 years moving from a high near 1,000 to a low near 500 and took another seven years before finally permanently (I hope) breaking above 1,000 in the early 1980s.

However, based on Elliott Wave analysis, you really ought not expect the same degree of overbought at the end of 1965 when compared with the

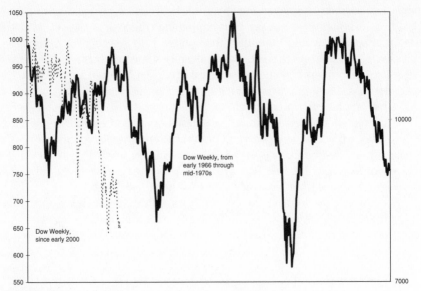

**FIGURE 8.8**   The Dow now and from the mid-1960s

degree of overbought evidenced in 2000. The rally that ended in 1965 represented the final thrust of a first wave off the 1932 lows, whereas the high of 2000 was the end of wave 3. What is a little bit scary is that wave 3 is actually shorter than wave 1, which would be a sign of weakness. Since wave 3 can never be the shortest wave, I would expect wave 5 to be very attenuated in size and time, when it finally begins. Then again, even if the Dow increases by half of the rally seen from the 1975 low, we should be looking for an increase of 10-fold in something less than 25 years. Assuming even a final bottom near 4,000, that would project the Dow at 40,000 no later than about 2035, and probably somewhat before then.

Before I get to the actual wave count, I'd like to discuss some of the things we need to see to signal a bottom. As you may recall, I've noted that the Elliott Wave theory is a kissing cousin in some ways to Dow Theory. What I mean by that is each wave has a characteristic psychological make-up. At the end of any given wave or leg, market participants, as a whole, have a set of beliefs and values with regard to the stock (and other financial) markets. This is, to a large degree, driven by the underlying social and economic forces currently surrounding our daily lives.

Early 2003 was a period in which housing prices were in a bubble and had, to a large degree, softened the blow of the stock market's collapse. One cannot truly look at the stock market on its own. The bear market in progress since 2000 is not nearly over. Past bear markets have even see the bond market fall. Although I do not see that happening (the risk is that we will see deflation, which would be bullish for bonds), I do see risk for other asset classes falling sharply. This is because, despite some nervousness from some less flexible thinkers at some central banks that shall remain nameless, deflation remains a far greater risk than inflation. The early part of 2003, however, has seen official inflation data releases pop higher due to increases in energy prices. High energy prices can act as a deflationary force as most manufacturers and service providers cannot pass these energy-related cost increases along when the economy is weak. That means that either profits will decrease or losses will increase. If the trend does not reverse, these firms will need to furlough employees, further weakening the economy.

I have already pointed out that analysts, on the whole, are far too bullish with regard to the stock market. They are looking under every rock for a reason to be bullish. Any minor reversal leads to clarion calls for the bottom being reached. In general, bearish analysts are still demeaned and are not given the full respect they deserve. Many technicians look for anecdotal evidence for a bottom via the financial media. One favorite trick is to look for pictures of a roaring bull or bear on the covers of mass-market news magazines such as *Time* or *Newsweek*. Unfortunately, a picture of a bull or a bear appearing on the cover of one of these magazines does not signal an immediate reversal. The market might not turn for days, or even weeks or months, after the article was published. For that matter, this sort of analysis is now so well known that I am not sure that it is particularly valid. Although the news might be bad enough to signal a medium-term bear market rally, I suspect the real bottom will come when the news magazines don't even bother to write about the market's latest low.

Although chart patterns are paramount in my analysis, it is always helpful to tie in anecdotal evidence of a major turn with your technical viewpoint. I have noted elsewhere that one bit of evidence will be that the stock market will no longer be a topic for discussion in polite company. What few references are made to stocks will typically include derogatory remarks regarding owning equities in general. Flip statements about how wrong the late 1990s and circa 2000 books about the Dow reaching 36,000, 50,000 or higher will be common. Nobody will admit to owning or buying such books unless it is couched in their desire to study the history of the Internet bubble, or how to reverse the strategies in these books and apply them to shorting stocks instead. Of course, that will be one of the signs that it is time to get back into stocks, and take these books seriously again.

Another point is important. I have constantly seen the financial press suggest that things are not so bad because volume was not all that high as prices tumbled in 2002 and early 2003. This is patently incorrect. Bear markets typically see increasing skepticism by the investing public and so the public tends to stay out of stocks in droves. This means that if interest in stocks wanes, volume should fall as well. A large part of the liquidation in stocks is already past. The initial leg of the bear market did see very high volume from a combination of liquidation by the quick and savvy coupled with those buyers who thought that they were getting a bargain.

Stock market bottoms do not necessarily have to trace out a true capitulation. In fact, in many of the early books on technical analysis, authors warned that although V tops were common, there rarely was ever a V bottom. Instead, they implored the analyst, investor, or trader to look for rounded bottoms. Investor apathy is the real sign of a bottom in stocks. Volume should be low throughout much of the drop. In fact, increases in volatility even may be somewhat lower when the final low is achieved since there will be less of a demand for protection via the options markets. I suspect that volume will increase as we hit the final nadir, but I doubt we will be seeing a 3-billion-share day at that time. Furthermore, though a quick 10% or so rally is possible, I would not expect to see 30% to 40% gains off the lows, as we have during many of the bear market rallies witnessed since the market peaked in 2000.

Investors and analysts have become accustomed to powerful price reversals. Everybody is looking for yet another V bottom, and they shouldn't be. Even other technicians keep pointing out the recoveries from the 1997 and 1998 correction lows. There is a huge difference between those reversals and what should happen now: 1997 and 1998 were corrections within a very powerful bull market. One could argue that 1998 was a bear market, if you use the measuring requirement of a 20% drop in value, although the time from top to bottom was a bit short. More importantly, the time to recover back to the old highs was very quick as well. Many technical analysts will tell you that the bear market started in 1998, when the A/D line peaked. I'm sorry, but even though you might make that same argument from an Elliott Wave–count perspective, mass psychology says it is a bear market when prices start falling, and not merely when an internal indicator reverses, regardless of the wave counts.

Hearken back to the low following the crash of October 19, 1987. Although stocks surged in the days following that low, the S&P 500 did eke out a lower low later that year, and stocks as a worthy investment did not return to our lexicon until after the stealth bear market of 1991 and did not become part of the daily headlines until sometime after prices began to accelerate higher in November 1994. Although the crash of 1987 and the three months leading up to it were very short indeed, the recovery was more typical of a bear market end game. The bull market psyche had not fully taken hold yet, so the damage caused by the relatively minor losses—

minor when compared to the devastation seen since 2000—caused greater consternation from the investing public. Remember, the Dow Jones essentially had only recently (five years before) broken out of a more than 15-year-long trading range.

Some still will argue that we should see strong gains almost immediately after the bear market ends. They will point out the powerful gains seen off the 1932 lows. However, this was coming off a collapse of at least one degree (in Elliott terminology) greater than we are due to recover from now. Furthermore, recall that the Dow fell 90% in three years, which is far worse than the current experience. It is even worse than the annihilation seen in the Nasdaq Composite. True, many companies have fallen from $200 per share to bankruptcy, but the index as a whole is still more than double the value it would hold upon completion of a 90% decline.

By the time that stocks finally bottom, news of the lows will no longer be an event. We'll see a brief statement on the nightly news noting that the Dow Jones Industrial Average reached yet another new 10- or 15-year low. The business news networks may be out of business and the *Wall Street Journal* and *Investors Business Daily* will have far lower circulation levels than they do now. I would not be surprised to see a merger between one of these papers and the *Financial Times*.

The current place in the downtrend depends a good deal on your overall wave counts going back to the 1932 low. There is a good deal of controversy among Elliotticians as to how they should count the price action during the Great Depression. Before I get into that, I need to include more detailed information regarding wave cycle nomenclature. I did not provide you with a detailed discussion of this elsewhere in the book, because my intent was to teach you how to apply Elliott Wave Theory in a practical manner, which makes swing trading time frames far more important than worrying about things like Grand Super Cycles. However, at a minimum, you should know what each of these time frame labels stands for before I get into the discussion of the long-term chart and where we go from here (see Table 8.2).

If I wanted to make a forecast regarding the outlook going into the next century, I would need to depend on the interpretation of what point we sit in relation to Super Cycles and Grand Super Cycles. However, as long as I do not have reason to believe that the centuries-long general trend in stock market prices has shifted to down from up, I have no reason not to expect another major bull market impulse to begin within the next 10 years. Recall that I have proposed that the mark of a major trend, no matter what your wave degree, is five-wave price action. Although there are no price data to prove it, I'd reckon that stock prices would have fallen in generalized five-wave patterns throughout the Dark Ages, if equity markets existed

| TABLE 8.2 Elliott Wave Cycle Names |
| --- |
| Sub-Minuette |
| Minuette |
| Minute |
| Minor |
| Intermediate |
| Primary |
| Cycle |
| Super Cycle |
| Grand Super Cycle |

then. As of now, since price patterns are not developing in very clear structures, I have no reason to believe that the overall bias has shifted from up
to down.

As you can see from Figure 8.9, I am showing a fairly substandard third-
wave completion as the 2000 high. There is a chance that wave III is not
actually done, but the kind of fall we are currently experiencing just does

**FIGURE 8.9**   Dow Jones Industrial Average, quarterly

not fit into the characteristic of a correction within a third wave. The reason that I call wave III substandard is because it is shorter than my first wave. I could remove that difficulty by doing one of two things:

1. Ignore everything I've said so far and only use price levels rather than percentage moves. If I do that, there is no problem—wave III would be enormously larger than wave I.
2. Use one of the post-1929 triangle ideas proposed by some Elliott Wave analysts.

Choice 1 makes almost no sense to me. Although I can and do understand why some people have a problem using percentage moves for short-term charts, I cannot fathom using price levels for indices over multigenerational periods. There just is no way of accurately comparing price action between the Dow at 90 and the Dow at 11,000! To suggest that a rally from 90 to 1,000 is less than a rally from 8,000 to 11,000 shows a total lack of understanding of the business world, let alone stock market or technical analysis.

I have two problems with the second choice (using a triangle for the crash which began in October 1929). If the triangle includes the leg down from 1929 to 1932, as shown in Figure 8.10, then there is absolutely no way that this can be considered correct. The move from 1929 to 1932 was com-

**FIGURE 8.10** Dow Jones Industrial Average, monthly

pleted in five waves. Five-wave structures are impulse moves and the legs of a triangle are all in three waves. I cannot see any reasonable way of viewing the 90% fall from the 1929 peak as three waves.

Most Elliotticians consider the drop from 1929 to 1932 as wave C of the great bear market. They count the high in 1929 as part of an irregular top. This is what R.N. Elliott's initial interpretation was as well. There are some who end the triangle in the early 1940s. They really have to do some dancing to get that kind of count, because there were only three legs completed from the 1929 high (plus, again, 1929 to 1932 could not have been part of a triangle as it was completed in five waves, not three). Some have chosen to make the triangle end in 1949. If we ignore the initial market collapse, we do get the look of an ascending triangle, which is a bullish pattern. Unfortunately, that also is quite arbitrary, and since there are still only three legs, without the initial fall, the pattern fails. The triangle pattern would be five legs including 1929 to 1932, but then you really cannot draw a proper triangle—plus, for the umpteenth time, 1929 to 1932 is five waves.

I have to admit that I would like to find a way of making wave I shorter, but I cannot find a reasonable alternative. The only possible count that I can fathom, shown in Figure 8.11, would put the end of wave I in 1937. Then the high in 1966 possibly could be the first wave of wave III, with the just

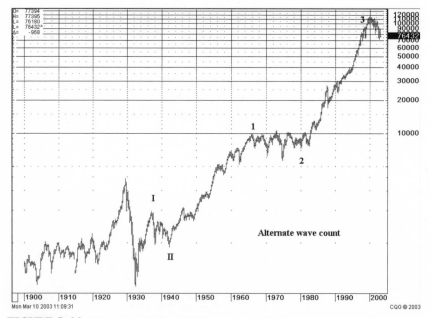

**FIGURE 8.11**   Dow Jones Industrial Average, quarterly

completed rally the third wave of wave III. There are multiple problems with this wave count:

- Wave I is too short in time.
- The current depth of the losses makes it difficult to imagine as wave 4 of larger wave III.
- In all likelihood, when the next five-wave rally does complete, we will see, at virtually every time frame, substantial momentum divergences when compared with the high in 2000 (and even earlier highs, which I will discuss with regard to the idea of an irregular top in 2000). Momentum divergences ought not be present at the end of a major third wave.
- If demographics mean anything, prices will likely move sideways for many years to come. Third waves are typically very impulsive, and even if we are in a very long term major wave cycle, it is difficult to justify a 50% or greater loss in total equity value and a 10-year or 15-year consolidation and still call this a third wave.

For this set of reasons, I will stick with the pattern shown in Figure 8.9, as far as the placement of where wave I and wave II end.[5] Before I get to the forecast however, I need to review the wave count starting with the 1975 low.

The more recent labeling is only slightly less controversial, although it certainly can have a lot to do with your expectations going forward. Some analysts believe that a full five-wave cycle from the Great Depression lows has completed. Admittedly, I can see a possible five-wave advance too, if I assume the 1932 to 1937 action was wave I, but that does not fit very well into the kind of time and price pattern I would expect to see at this degree. For that reason, I have labeled the end of wave I as stocks first broke 1,000 in 1966. Wave II then was a relatively short almost nine-year period that encompassed a wide trading band during which the Dow fell nearly 50% on two separate occasions. Wave III higher began, not in 1982, when many people refer to the start of the Great Bull Market, but rather at the low in 1974. From there, stocks rallied fairly sharply into 1976, gaining more than 80%. A protracted second wave took us to what most people consider to be the start of the bull market, and was actually the beginning of wave 3 of the bull in August 1982. The actual wave labels are shown in Figure 8.12, while the sizes of each leg are displayed in Table 8.3.

The crash of 1987 ends up being a second wave within a larger third-wave rally. This is my biggest concern with my wave count since the markets really were greatly damaged by that event. However, although market psyche was hurt, prices completely recovered from that event in only 26 months. The third wave of wave III terminated at a nearly perfect Fibonacci extension of wave 1 at the top made as the Russian debt crisis unfolded dur-

**TABLE 8.3**   The Size of Each Leg

| Wave Name | Start | End | Best Gain or Largest Loss During Wave |
|-----------|-------|-----|----------------------------------------|
| Wave 1 | Dec. 1974 | Dec. 1976 | +80% |
| Wave 2 | Dec. 1974 | Aug. 1982 | −29% |
| Wave 3 | Aug. 1982 | July 1998 | +1,117% |
| Wave 4 | July 1998 | Sept. 1998 | −21% |
| Wave 5 | Sept. 1998 | Aug. 1999 | +54% |

ing the summer of 1998. Many technical analysts suggest that the bear market began slightly before then, calling it a stealth bear market, because the A/D line topped a few months before the summer high, in April 1998.

The sharp fall caused by the Russian debt crisis, which then helped precipitate LTCM's collapse, is then wave 4 of wave III. Although the amount of time that wave 4 took to transpire was relatively short, the distance traveled—more than 20%—was not. You need to consider both time and price when developing your wave counts. A very deep correction, one more

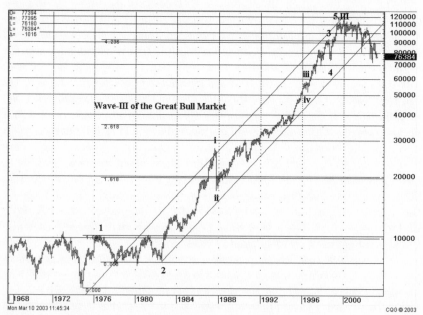

**FIGURE 8.12**   Dow Jones Industrial Average, monthly

extensive than you typically would expect, can replace a more meandering consolidation. Likewise, especially in fourth waves, I have found very extended (in time) but very shallow trading ranges replace the need for an equal-time and 38.2% fourth-wave correction. In this case, the drop in 1998 was the former—a quick, powerful, and damaging fourth-wave correction (see Figure 8.12).

Wave 5, of course, is our most recent history. It includes the great Internet bubble. The fifth wave for the Dow actually ends prior to the 2000 high, but near the channel line touch from the start of wave 3. (Note that this channel is not drawn based on Elliott Wave–based rules since the second touch in 1994 is not the bottom of wave 4, but rather represents the end of the wave iv subwave of wave 3.)

Part of me would like to end the stock market discussion here. I've explained in detail how I see the patterns leading up the current bear market, as well as describing all of the problems the global economy currently faces. I have to admit that I do see, from the latter perspective, some risk that the most bearish analysts—those that believe we are in a Super Cycle fourth-wave decline, rather than a Cycle-level fourth-wave bear market— may be correct. If American influence completely disappears now, and if terrorists gain ascendancy, the Super Cycle counts would be correct. Usually, however, history provides us with a period where the old Super Power remains ostensibly in charge, although during that time, it steadily loses its grip. I suspect that is where we are heading right now. The United States will ultimately hang on for another 10 or 20 years before there is a true paradigm shift in the world. It is too soon, and the excesses should be greatest at the end of the third wave.

The price action since the market topped in 2000, be it the orthodox top or the actual price high, has been hellacious. The Nasdaq Composite has fallen nearly 80%, as have several European stock markets. The Dow has not quite kept up, losing a mere 35% from its peak, while the broader-based S&P 500 has lost as much as 48%.

I see a high probability that at least the current leg of the bear market was nearing an end as I wrote this chapter during early 2003. Recall that I show prices as having made an irregular top. That means that the bear market should develop in a five-wave pattern lower. Some analysts have called for a very deep drop—on the order of 90%. That argument does make sense, as difficult as it is to believe, if you believe we are in a similar cycle position to where we were in 1928 to 1929. However, even if we are in that same spot, a correction of a Super Cycle phase, the wave count, according to those analyses, places us currently in a fourth-wave drop. The 1928 to 1932 bear market was a second-wave move. Using the tendency of alternation, I would expect a shallower fall, so there is no reason why this bear might not be reaching its nadir.

With that said, I am incredibly nervous from a social and a long-term valuation perspective. There does appear to be an enormous shift in how people look at the stock market. Turnover is falling, as I would expect at a major turn. Asset allocation rules are going to start changing at some point soon as well (although Wall Street analysts continue to foolishly hold to a nearly 70% weighting in the stock market). The possibility of major changes in the geopolitical forces caused by the United States and the United Kingdom launching a war against Iraq, without United Nations approval, leaves the world at its greatest danger point since the days of the Cold War.

Completely separate from that fact, the mere notion that anybody could possibly believe that the stock market is cheap right now is simply laughable. Although measuring P/E ratios during a downturn in the economy is fraught with difficulty, as the ratio may expand as corporate earnings are more volatile than stock prices are (meaning that the earnings will fall more than price will), the fact that P/E ratios sit at extreme levels, even on a forward 12-month basis, leaves me concerned that this bear market has not run its course as yet. As Figure 8.13 shows, five waves lower from the highs are nearly completed, there is definitely a chance that the next low in the stock market (the Nasdaq Composite already might have seen its worst level), that wave V of the Super Cycle Great Bull Market, may soon be getting under way.

**FIGURE 8.13**  S&P 500, weekly

Stocks are likely now in the endgame of this five-wave fall. Note that the wave counts are a bit difficult to discern. This further favors the idea that, although the losses have been ugly, they are corrective in nature. While the present misvaluations leave me concerned that the next move up will merely be an X wave and that we could see a lower low in the years ahead, I expect that the S&P 500 ought to bottom during middle or late 2003 near the wave 5 equals 1.618 times wave 1 Fibonacci extension target of 737.07. This is the best case scenario.

Note, by the way, how close wave v of wave 3 was to the 2.618 extension target of the first wave of wave 3. I suspect things might have taken a much different shape if it had not been for the terrorist attacks of September 11, 2001, but those led to an extended third wave and then a very powerful wave iv higher. Wave iii ought to have terminated at a somewhat higher price, but the attacks led to a more powerful collapse, and then a globally concerted action to keep the financial markets working relatively smoothly, flooding the banking system with liquidity and permitting a huge rally to take place.

Since that time, the stock market has continued lower anyway. The U.S. and global economies remain moribund, as we continue to work off the overspending on technology in 1999 and 2000, as well as the hugely overextended stock market valuations of the bubble. My fear regarding the economy, overall, is not just from the still high stock market valuations, and the continued risk of terror attacks, but also from a housing sector that is set to burst as well. However, the coming risk of deflation may keep interest rates low enough such that residential home prices may not collapse. By collapse, I mean a fall of more than 50%. I fully expect home prices to tumble 25% to 50% in many areas over the next few years. With stocks so low, that will put a real damper on the U.S. economy. Alan Greenspan has warned us of the risks in a speech during which he discussed how much money has been taken out in refinancings of home mortgages. Debt loads are incredibly high right now, and paying any interest, even low interest rates, will be onerous if deflation finally takes hold.

It is for this reason that I expect the current bear market will continue for several more years. An X wave, which could retrace half or more of the losses thus far, should make much of the latter part of 2003 and 2004 bullish. Even a 50% retracement would mean a nearly 50% rally in the S&P 500 from my forecast lows, and it would permit the Nasdaq to more than double.

Unfortunately, when the next three-wave decline begins, we could ultimately see a 500 handle on the S&P 500, below 800 on the Nasdaq Composite and sub-6,000 on the Dow Jones Industrial Average. I would expect a final bottom to occur in the 2007 to 2010 time frame. The demographic barren period forecast by many probably will not develop as so much money will have been taken out of stocks already.

It is worth emphasizing that we must be on the lookout for an end to the bear market during 2003. Once a new low is achieved, a completed A-B-C off the highs will have been traced out. The damage caused by the bubble, coupled with the effects of war, could permit a final bottom earlier than my preferred forecast.

Once we do bottom, I see no reason why wave V of this Super Cycle would not fail to see stock prices increase by at least fivefold, and more likely tenfold or more. The timing will probably be about 34 years from now with the Dow ending in the 50,000–100,000 range, and the S&P at 5,000 or more. So, you see, those Dow 36,000 books are probably setting their sights way too low. Of course, they are also about 40 years too early as well!

## WHENCE THE DOLLAR

Forecasting the U.S. dollar (USD) requires me to invoke the ideas I developed in Chapter 4. I have always had a hard time justifying the 5-3-5-3-5 pattern requirement in the foreign currency markets. The usual assumption is that we should expect five-wave patterns in the bullish direction of the currency with the larger economy. While that has meant, at least since foreign exchange rates from the major free nations started floating again in 1972, that the USD always should be favored with a five-wave count in its bullish direction, I find that methodology to be arbitrary. In general, my assumption would be that most major cycles in the currency markets develop in five waves. Trends, which may last from weeks, to months, and even to several years, reasonably can be expected to display five-wave patterns, *if there is a good underlying technical and/or fundamental reason to expect such price action.* However, five-wave long-term waves are most likely the exception rather than the rule.

I am going to provide forecasts for the dollar based on an index, rather than based on the dollar versus the yen, the Euro, or some other currency pair. Looking at currency pairs is not all there is to analyzing the direction of the U.S. dollar. Although the dollar's values versus the yen and the euro are probably the most widely quoted from a speculative basis, neither Japan, nor Europe, come close to Canada when measured by bilateral trade flows with the United States. Given that many economists believe that the value of a currency pair should be closely related to trade flows, ignoring USDCAD is probably not a good idea. However, rather than providing a USDCAD forecast, I am going to instead look at a U.S. dollar index instead, to give you a feel for the general direction of the dollar.

The first place many analysts look to when providing a USD forecast is the dollar exchange rate index (DX) published by New York Board of Trade (NYBOT). I see technical analysts write about this all the time. This is with-

**TABLE 8.4** U.S. Dollar Index Weighting Scheme (DX)

| Currency | Weight (in percent) |
|---|---|
| Euro | 57.6 |
| Japanese yen | 13.6 |
| U.K. pound | 11.9 |
| Canadian dollar | 9.1 |
| Swedish krona | 4.2 |
| Swiss franc | 3.6 |

out a doubt one of the biggest reasons why technicians really do need to understand economics before they start spouting wisdom regarding the direction of exchange rates. Although being able to forecast the direction of DX is interesting, the investing public might actually believe that DX has some sort of financial importance. It doesn't. The index's makeup (see Table 8.4) has no basis in bilateral trade flows whatsoever and therefore has little correlation to that currency methodology valuation.

Instead of using the NYBOT's DX index, I will use the trade weighted U.S. dollar index published by the Federal Reserve on a daily basis since January 1973. This index is revised periodically and reflects the relative importance of international bilateral trade flows between the United States and its trading partners (see Table 8.5).

**TABLE 8.5** Currency Weights in Federal Reserve U.S. Dollar Trade Weighted Index (as of January 2003)

| Currency | Weight (in percent) |
|---|---|
| Euro | 17.4 |
| Canadian dollar | 17.0 |
| Japanese yen | 12.1 |
| Mexican peso | 10.6 |
| Chinese yuan | 9.0 |
| U.K. pound | 4.4 |
| South Korean won | 3.9 |
| Taiwan dollar | 3.3 |
| Other | 20.3 |

I should note that there is an argument for using DX, mostly from the market psychology perspective. If you believe a currency's value is a poll that ratifies the importance or value of a nation's economy, then given that DX is weighted more along the lines of the sizes of the relevant economies, this index can be seen as having some relevance as to how the world views the American economy. For that reason, I will show a chart with a wave count that implies that a U.S. dollar rally is due to start very soon, also supporting the idea of an approaching bottom in U.S. stocks.

As you can see from the perspective of Figures 8.14 and 8.15, there is little reason to believe that my Chapter 4 proposition regarding three-wave price movements is incorrect. The currency markets are one of the places where I forecast that three-wave price action, for longer-term time frames, should hold sway. And, as you can see, once we get beyond a period of a few years, the dollar, in price actions vis-à-vis its major trading partners, has tended to move in broad three-wave cycles. Even if I wanted to come up with a very long term chart depicting the value of the U.S. dollar, I would not be able to. The misguided Bretton Woods agreement kept exchange rates fixed for much of the post–World War II period. There were periodic revaluations and devaluations as economic realities were forced upon governments, but it was not until the pressures became too great, with changes in terms of trade across the globe, that the fixed-exchange-rate regime

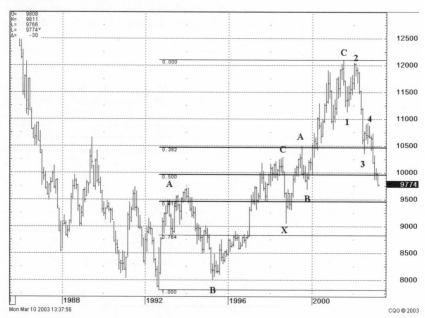

**FIGURE 8.14** NYBOT U.S. Dollar Index, monthly

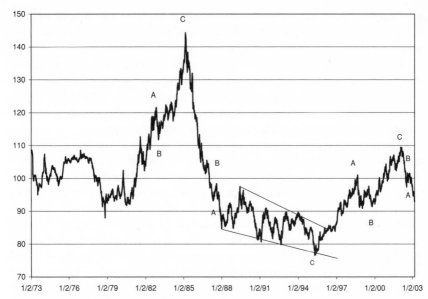

**FIGURE 8.15** U.S. Federal Reserve trade weighted index

finally burst apart in the early 1970s. The Fed's trade weighted index actually begins a bit later than that, starting in January 1973. Therefore, it is pointless to attempt to label the dollar's counts prior to that time. Given the major turn, after an apparent drop due to the market's repricing an artificially overpriced dollar after fixed exchange rates fell, my wave counts start with the major low set in early 1978.

We see a fairly clear zigzag higher from the 1978 low to the 1985 high. Both internal legs have decent five-wave structures. Remember, I said the larger wave counts should subdivide into three-wave patterns. There is no restriction against shorter-term five-wave price motion. I fully expect that to be the case, since I still subscribe to the definition that impulse moves must develop in five waves.

The dollar collapsed after 1985. However, the five-wave reaction to the decision to push the dollar down actually ended in the middle of 1987. The ensuing minor rally was wave B with wave C developing as a terminal triangle, which ended in 1995. Another A-B-C zigzag followed to the dollar's peak in early 2002. As I write this in early 2003, the dollar appears set to complete a fairly small wave C off that top. The target range is from the just-achieved low at 92.88, which is just a bit beneath 50% of the way back to the 1995 low, on down to where C equals A near 90.55. Note also that a 62% retracement back to the 1995 low would target 89.12. Therefore, in all likelihood, the dollar is not more than 4% from its low, and given the shorter-term patterns and an expected turn higher in the U.S. stock market soon as well, we should see a low closer to the C equals A target than the 62% retracement.

It is worth reminding you that all the calls for a weaker or stronger dollar due to the price action in the stock market ought to fall on your own deaf ears. The dollar continued to move higher long after U.S. equities peaked in 2000, not turning tail until February 2002. The dollar will likely continue to fall for a month or two after stocks turn as well.

I have never understood the belief that the dollar and the stock market, or even the much larger bond market, necessarily reflect each other. Although it is true that there is a relationship, the value of the dollar is complex and includes trade flows, capital flows (plants and equipment), and financial and service flows, which may include the stock market and other investments. Shares are just one part of that equation. Furthermore, although U.S. stocks are falling, so are other stock markets. As I noted earlier in the chapter, U.S. equities as measured by the Dow Jones Industrial Average have fallen less than almost any other major stock market index. There is no reason, based on that information, to believe that the weak U.S. stock market should harm the dollar in any way, shape, or form.

Although the dollar is nearing a short-term low, I am not yet prepared to declare the dollar's bear market completed. First of all, if I am wrong, and the dollar accelerates lower, especially if it falls beneath its 62% retracement at 89.12, I would assume that the index was actually only in wave 3 of wave A. That would imply substantially lower levels, possibly beneath the 1995 nadir, later this decade. Given my expectation of a state of flux in the world for many years to come, I would not be surprised if the dollar reflects this by range trading for another five to eight years. We could then form a triangle. Given that I still see a fifth wave higher for stocks and do not expect the United States to fall apart, I would not be at all surprised if the next major U.S. dollar move and breakout will be to the upside. Note also that there is a decent chance that the 1995 low in USDJPY was a fifth-wave bottom, meaning that the current U.S. dollar weakness is merely corrective as well (see Figure 8.16).

## JAPANESE BEAR MARKET ENDS

There is reason to be concerned that the U.S. dollar will run into some troubles against the yen. The Nikkei-225 Index is nearing the end of what has been a bit more than a 13 (Fibonacci)-year bear market. Prices are already beyond the 144 Fibonacci month count, but the last major high,

**FIGURE 8.16** Nikkei-225 Index, monthly

set in April 2000, was in its thirty-fifth month as of February 2003. Wave a of wave B took 35 months to complete, and the initial drop was 32 months. All of wave B was 92, and 38.2% of that is also 35 months. Given that set of timing concordance with the fact that there are several price targets within 10% of recent trading levels of around 8,000, I am reasonably confident that the bear market in Japan is nearly over. Key price targets include:

- 7,793, where wave v of wave 5 is 1.618 times the first wave of wave 5
- 7,591, where wave C equals wave A
- 7,437, long-term channel support, which falls about 37 to 38 points per month.

Once the Nikkei's bear market ends, I would expect range trading to develop. Given the fact that other stock markets may very well remain in a sideways to lower pattern for another several years, I doubt that the Nikkei will be able to explode higher. Also, remember what I've said in the past about bear markets: V bottoms are the exception and not the rule. I would not be at all surprised to see a very quick rally toward the November 2002 high, which was near 9,300. We might even attract some bulls and push a bit above there. However, most likely, prices will slip after that and move sideways for many months. I doubt that the Nikkei permanently surfaces again above its 2002 wave-4 of wave-C high for at least another two years, and maybe longer than that. However, much as I expect that the Dow will ultimately push above 50,000 and possibly past 100,000, the Nikkei-225 could reach those levels in many of our lifetimes!

# Notes

## Chapter 1: Surfing Basics

1. From *The Major Works of R.N. Elliott* edited by Robert R. Prechter, Jr., New Classics Library, Gainesville, GA, 1980, 1990.

2. The Market Technicians Association (MTA) is a society of professional market technical analysts bound by a constitution that governs ethics and basic knowledge requirements for membership. The author is a member of the MTA.

3. For a good description of the different chart types, please see *Technical Analysis of the Financial Markets*, John J. Murphy.

4. A triangle is also a correction, and is a nonimpulsive five-wave pattern.

5. Fractals come from the mathematical science of chaos theory. For an excellent and easy-to-read discussion of chaos theory, see *Chaos: Making a New Science* by James Gleick, Penguin USA, New York, NY, 1988.

6. Dalbar, Inc., Boston, MA. "Quantitative Analysis of Investor Behavior," June 2001.

7. By volatility, we are referring to implied volatility from options pricing formulas. Implied volatility, especially in the equity market, tends to increase as prices fall and decrease as prices rise.

8. "A Multifractal Walk Down Wall Street," *Scientific American*, February 1999.

9. For information on this controversy, please visit http://www.elliottwave.com/response.htm.

10. Sigma refers to the standard deviation of price changes. If prices were random and followed a standard normal distribution, the probability of a change in price greater than six standard deviations from the norm would be less than 0.3%. In the real world, this is patently incorrect.

11. *Elliott Wave Principle: Key to Stock Market Profits*, A.J. Frost and Robert R. Prechter Jr., New Classics Library, Gainesville, GA, 1978.

12. A tick chart shows every price change that occurs for an instrument. Some software allows the user to create a bar or candlestick by accumulating a certain number of ticks. My comments regarding tick charts do not apply to that application.

## Chapter 2: Advanced Concepts

1. See Chapter 3, "The Tendency of Alternation," for a detailed discussion of alternation.

2. Welles Wilder's smoothed Average Directional Index.

## Chapter 3: Tsunami or Wavelet—Measurement Techniques

1. Fibonacci, *Scritti di Leonardo Pisano*, Baldassarre Boncompagni, Tipografia delle Scienze Mathematica e Fisiche, Rome, Italy, 1857–1862.

2. An irregular fourth wave typically would imply strength in the trend, while failure to exceed the top of wave b of wave 4 is certainly a sign of weakness.

3. The law of large numbers essentially states that as the number of chances for even a highly improbable event increases, the probability of that event occurring approaches 100%. Those who do not believe in market timing would suggest that the "observation" of Fibonacci ratios and targets working is merely an artifact of the law of large numbers. That is, given how many opportunities there are for individual securities to display behaviors consistent with the Fibonacci time series, it would be extremely likely to be able to find many examples where the series worked. However, the law would also imply that applying Fibonacci numbers should not be more profitable than random trading.

## Chapter 4: Interlude—Does Elliott Work Outside of the Stock Market?

1. Some Elliot Wave–based analysts, as of late 2002, were forecasting that the bear market active at the time this book was written could last many more years and that the Dow Jones Industrials might bottom near or even below 1,000. Although the author agrees that stock prices are likely to make substantially lower lows in the coming years, his expectations are for the Dow to bottom closer to 5,000 than 1,000.

2. Purchasing power parity (PPP) suggests that in the long run, relative changes in gross price levels in different currency regimes must be accounted for by nearly equal and opposite changes in the exchange rate between the two currencies.

3. *Forecasting Financial Markets: Technical Analysis and the Dynamics of Price*, by Tony Plummer, John Wiley and Sons, New York, NY, 1991.

## Chapter 5: Building an Elliott Wave Trading Plan

1. CANSLIM stands for an investing philosophy and system developed by William O'Neil of *Investors Business Daily*. The methodology combines fundamental and technical research to help select stocks of companies that should provide investors with superior returns.

## Chapter 6: Tying It All Together

1. The term *front month* is derived from the position the people who are trading the most important in a series of a given futures contract physically hold in the pit. Front month means they are at the front of the pit. Sometimes, since the pits are tiered, the term *top step* also is used. The exchanges determine how a contract gets the front month moniker. Some use a specified date to roll from one calendar contract to the next, others use the contract with highest volume over a period of days, and others determine front month based on open interest levels. Interestingly, the term likely will become an anachronism as electronic trading overtakes and likely eventually replaces the pits.

2. Note that most futures markets now have extended trading sessions. For example, the 10-year Treasury note futures, besides their 8:20 A.M.–3:00 P.M. EST day session, are available for electronic trading from 9:00 P.M.–6:00 A.M. the next day EST. At the time this book was written, volume was thin during the nonpit trading hours. Therefore I have chosen not to use the data from the electronic-only periods in my analysis. However, if price activity increases substantially over the years, you will be better served by including all available trading sessions. For example, when analyzing the foreign exchange markets, you should use 24-hour data and not just the New York–based session.

## Chapter 8: Future Waves

1. One of LTCM's most egregious errors was the decision to hedge long positions in emerging market debt with short positions in U.S. Treasury obligations. The LTCM models showed that there was a positive correlation between these markets. Unfortunately, none of the modelers ever even bothered to take a look at what happened just one year earlier, when some of the Asian economies spiraled out of control. During that period of time, emerging market debt and U.S. Treasuries moved in the opposite direction. This is exactly what happened in 1998. In the end, LTCM's "hedges" actually compounded their problems. And, much as happened to Orange County earlier in the decade, everybody knew their position and had no intention of letting them get out of it. The U.S. Federal Reserve Bank had to come in and do some serious arm twisting to ensure the financial markets kept functioning properly.

2. In partial defense of the media, anchors and reporters often received threats when bearish forecasts were made on the network. Investors never want to see their money evaporate simply because some "talking head" announces that the company they've invested in was not worth what the market said it was worth. The networks were acutely aware of how closely their ratings were correlated to the direction of the stock market and I assume, rightfully had no desire to precipitate concern among their viewers before they absolutely had to.

3. Sadly, that may very well been part of what was going on. The lawsuit by the New York attorney general alleges that while Wall Street analysts were foisting

new issues and revising ever higher their price targets on some Internet issues, they were privately expressing the exact opposite opinions.

4. There is an argument that would partially invalidate the weaker GDP growth discussion. However, I believe the overall analysis stands without having a GDP leg to stand on. Simply put, GDP growth is now on a much larger base than it was as America was transforming from a second-tier nation in the first third of the 1900s to where it is now as the world's most powerful nation. There is no reason to believe that GDP growth could possibly match prior gains when the nation was in an exponential growth spurt, regardless of the stock market's wave counts. It is entirely possible that the social waves and stock market waves may be offset in time.

5. Elsewhere in the book, I have shown long-term charts using the S&P 500. Standard and Poors was kind enough to provide theoretical values for this broader stock market index prior to the index's actual birth. I would actually need to proffer a different wave count if I was to use this data because the rally from 1932 to 1937, though at first glance appears to be five waves, includes a rather substantial overlap. However, because that time period is merely theoretical and was constructed after the fact, the data are meaningless. S&P has constantly changed the components of the index, and we therefore have no way of knowing what the actual price action would have been if the index existed at that time.

# Index